The Common-Sense Mortgage

The Common-Sense Mortgage

How to Cut the Cost of Home Ownership by $100,000 or More

1995 Edition

Peter G. Miller

HarperPerennial

A Division of HarperCollinsPublishers

To Caroline

HarperCollins books may be purchased for educational, business, or sales promotional use. For information, please write: Special Markets Department, HarperCollins Publishers, Inc., 10 East 53rd Street, New York, NY 10022.

FIRST EDITION

ISSN 1050-9429
ISBN 0-06-273332-X

95 96 97 98 99 ❖/RRD 10 9 8 7 6 5 4 3 2 1

Contents

Acknowledgments

Major portions of this book were first printed in *The Washington Post* as part of a weekly column on real estate finance. The sections on timesharing, reverse loans, equity-sharing, and GEM mortgages first appeared in *Goodlife* magazine. The sections on Computers and the Searching Process and the material on hidden refinancing costs were originally published by *Fact, The Money Management Magazine*. Portions of the material concerning computer services have been rewritten and updated for this edition. Some portions of the book originally appeared in slightly different form in *The Washington Weekly*.

This book would not have been possible without the cooperation and assistance of many individuals and organizations. The author wishes to thank Albert B. Crenshaw of *The Washington Post;* Bill Winn and Gene-Gabriel Moore of *Goodlife* magazine; Daniel M. Kehrer and Joseph Lisanti of *Fact, The Money Management Magazine;* and Edward R. DesRoches, editor and co-publisher of *The Real Estate Professional.*

Also, Katherine B. Ulmann and the United States League of Savings Institutions; Bonnie O'Dell, Kevin Hawkins, and Eugene R. Eisman and the Federal National Mortgage Association (Fannie Mae); John J. Coonts, director, FHA Single Family Development Division, HUD; John Flynn and Angelina M. Ornelas, HUD; Victor S. Parra of the National Timesharing Council; Jerry Karbon and the Credit Union

National Association; Phyllis R. Pleasants of the Mortgage Insurance Companies of America; Hilda Pena, Erica Greenberg, and Gerald Ferrance; and the Veterans Administration.

And James Sherman, Talman Home Federal Savings & Loan (Chicago); James J. Hall, James J. Hall, Inc., Realtors (Silver Spring, Maryland); Douglas M. Bregman, Esq. (Bethesda, Maryland); Leon Pomerance, Esq. (Marrietta, Georgia); John Hemschoot, Director of Home Mortgage Standards with the Federal Home Loan Mortgage Corporation (Freddie Mac); Steven A. Skalet, Esq. (Washington, D.C.); and Charles R. Wolfe (Gaithersburg, Maryland).

Over the years this book has greatly benefited from the inclusion of materials first published in **The Real Estate Professional** (Suite 4, 1492 Highland Avenue, Needham, MA 02192, Phone: 617-444-4688). In this edition as well, material first produced by the author as part of his regular column in **The Real Estate Professional** has been included in this text.

Portions of this book originally appeared in a weekly column written by the author and syndicated nationwide by the Crain News Service (740 Rush Street, Chicago, IL 60611).

Portions of the material concerning MCC financing were originally developed by the author and electronically posted on America Online.

The author would also like to thank Warren Dunn and the Mortgage Bankers Association of America and Martin Keithline and the Montgomery County (Maryland) Board of Realtors, who graciously provided amortization statements and other valued information used in the first and second editions of this guide. In this edition, amortization statements have been recalculated by the author with the use of a business calculator, commonly available spreadsheet software and a personal computer.

Introduction

A strange thing has happened for more than a dozen years: since the prime rate hit 20.5 percent in 1981, interest rates have gradually fallen in a more or less steady pattern.

If you want to buy a home, keep a home, or refinance a home, lower rates mean smaller monthly payments and a greater ability to borrow. No less important, lower interest costs mean fewer dollars devoted to housing and more money for other choices such as savings, investments, and purchases.

Will the era of low rates continue? No one can be certain, but one point should be mentioned: Even if you cannot buy or refinance at the absolute bottom of the market, rates at this time are better than they have been in years. It makes sense to finance and refinance at this time if only as a hedge against rising interest levels. And if it should happen that rates continue to plummet, then it may also make sense to refinance a second time or even a third time if interest costs fall sufficiently.

In the late 1970s, when writing a weekly column for *The Washington Post*, the idea of a better deal for borrowers was a constant theme. There seemed to be many strategies that would lower loan costs and cut interest rates, yet people were surprised that such ploys were legal, ethical, moral, and money-saving.

Those columns were the basis for *The Common-Sense Mortgage* and over the many years that this guide has been published and updated, four themes have remained constant.

- Better deals for borrowers are still a good idea.
- There are many strategies that can reduce loan costs and cut interest rates.
- Such strategies continue to be legal, ethical, moral, and money-saving.
- People still find it hard to believe that their home financing and refinancing choices can produce huge savings.

Each year this book generates vast numbers of articles and interviews and sometimes the question is asked: Can people really save $100,000 through careful mortgage planning?

The answer will be obvious from the pages which follow. Enormous savings are possible, and for many people such economies can exceed $100,000.

It's only speculation, but imagine that everyone who uses this book is able to cut their home interest expense by just $10,000, then for every 100,000 readers loan expenses are reduced by $1 billion. Such figures may well explain why this book is not entirely popular in all circles.

The Common-Sense Mortgage is now in its ninth incarnation, and the principles which have guided each version remain valid today.

The best way to finance real estate is to examine the myriad choices available in today's marketplace and select the financing alternative which leaves the most money in your pocket.

But to examine alternative mortgage formats you have to know how each loan works, what it really costs, and how to evaluate financing options. It's not always easy to wade through conflicting claims, but this guide will make the process easier.

This is a book about money, real estate and choices. The choices you make when financing a home can save tens of thousands of dollars, and often a lot more. Designed to serve as a basic reference, consumer aid and classroom text, this guide stresses the idea that with so many loan choices now available, borrowers can customize home financing options to meet individual needs and save substantial sums of money in the process.

Peter G. Miller

The Common-Sense Mortgage

1
The Case for the Common-Sense Mortgage

Few of us are so rich that we can needlessly give away tens of thousands of dollars and yet it happens every day. We pay too much for home mortgages and the money we waste can easily send our kids to college, underwrite retirements or simply make home ownership more affordable to millions of people.

While much attention, debate and haggling surround real estate selling prices, financing is rarely given equal time or study and the result is that enormous sums of money—often amounts as great or greater than the original purchase price of a property—are lost to borrowers.

But why lose the money-making and money-saving advantages that sound mortgage planning can create? Reducing home interest costs is not an activity reserved for the rich or real estate pros. There is nothing illegal, immoral, unfair or abusive about cutting mortgage expenses. You don't have to be a financial whiz to succeed; there are no miracles involved, nothing difficult to understand and no tax rules to violate. Getting a good mortgage deal does not presume that you find a foolish lender or an impractical seller.

What you need is time to study your financial position, honesty to realistically evaluate where you are economically and where you're going, probing questions to find the best possible deals and professional assistance from brokers, lawyers and tax advisors. You'll have to work with lenders to arrange mutually attractive deals and you'll have to forget the idea that mortgage financing is a once-in-a-lifetime event:

it isn't. You can finance and refinance at any time and the choices you make can put thousands of dollars in your pocket.

Whether you earn $20,000 or $200,000 a year you may think that you can't possibly spend an extra $50,000 on home financing without noticing. Yet if you've managed to waste "only" $50,000 you're probably doing better than most friends or neighbors. Here's where the money goes.

Suppose Mr. Matthews buys a home for $180,000. He puts down $30,000 in cash and gets a 30-year, fixed-rate mortgage for $150,000 at a time when interest rates are at 8.5 percent—a "conventional" loan at then-current market rates and terms. Monthly payments for principal and interest total $1,153.37.

At the end of 30 years Matthews has made 360 mortgage payments and spent a total of $415,213. Of the money paid to the lender, $150,000 was principal and $265,213 was interest—an amount substantially greater than the property's acquisition price.

But a 30-year loan is not the only way to organize a mortgage. Within the bounds of an 8.5 percent interest rate, Matthews—or you or I—can easily cut mortgage interest costs by $50,000, $75,000 and— if we have the discipline—$100,000 or more.

Imagine that Matthews decides to increase his mortgage payment by $5 a day—not an unreasonable expense in the context of a $180,000 home. Let's look at what happens:

- Monthly mortgage payments rise from $1,153.37 to $1,303.37—a difference of $150 ($5 x 30).
- Because principal payments have been increased, the length of the loan is shortened from 360 months to 239.2 months. In other words, the loan term is now a little less than 20 years rather than 30 years.
- Interest costs go from $265,213 to $161,766—a savings of more than $100,000 in excess interest.

Ask yourself: If you were Matthews, would you set aside $35 a week— hardly the cost of a meal for two at many restaurants—to cut your mortgage bill by $100,000? Is it worth spending $150 a month to knock off 10 years of mortgage payments?

How Mr. Matthews Could Save $100,000 with a $150,000 Mortgage		
Loan size	$150,000	$150,000
Interest rate	8.5 percent	8.5 percent
Monthly payment	$1,153.37	$1,303.37
Extra monthly cost	None	$150
Number of payments	360	239.2
Potential interest cost	$265,213	$161,766
Potential cash saving	None	$103,447

LOWER COSTS WITH ARMs

Our example with Mr. Matthews shows that by increasing monthly payments, the length of a *fixed-rate* loan will decline dramatically and significant interest savings result. But what happens with an adjustable rate mortgage (ARM), financing where interest rates and monthly payments can change?

Depending on the loan agreement's precise terms and conditions, borrowers with ARMs will still be able to reduce interest costs. The manner in which ARM costs are slashed, however, is radically different than the approach used with fixed-rate financing.

With fixed-rate mortgages, we saw that additional monthly payments reduced the loan's term. In the example with Mr. Matthews, the loan term went from 360 months to 239 months. If a borrower with adjustable-rate financing also makes prepayments, the loan term will be reduced but, more importantly, the major advantage will be declining monthly payments.

Suppose Mr. Sharpe, like Matthews, borrows $150,000. But instead of fixed-rate financing, Sharpe finds a 30-year, adjustable-rate loan with these terms:

- The interest rate is established yearly.
- The interest rate is based on movements of the 1-year treasury bill index.
- The maximum interest rate increase or decrease is 2 percent each year. The maximum lifetime increase is 6 percent.
- The initial interest rate is set at 5.5 percent, the so-called "teaser" rate. In practice, *start* rates for ARMs tend to be 3 percent to 3.5

		Original Loan Amount $150,000		
Year	Monthly Payment	Interest Rate	Yearly Interest	Year-End Balance
1	1,001.68	5.50	8,153.49	146,133.33
2	1,170.59	7.50	10,851.64	142,937.89
3	1,316.80	9.00	12,740.17	139,876.46
4	1,375.55	9.75	13,506.23	136,876.09
5	1,193.81	8.00	10,823.52	133,373.89
6	1,071.50	6.75	8,881.20	129,397.09
7	1,018.48	6.25	7,966.80	125,142.14
8	1,122.79	7.75	9,561.50	121,230.15
9	1,056.13	9.00	10,836.15	119,392.74
10	1,285.16	10.00	11,775.13	115,745.95
11	1,136.23	8.25	9,390.95	111,502.15
12	1,035.54	7.00	7,653.96	106,729.63
13	929.46	5.50	5,734.89	101,311.00
14	874.76	4.75	4,686.86	95,500.74
15	824.23	5.50	5,133.81	90,743.79
16	855.83	4.75	4,178.86	84,652.69
17	895.99	6.00	4,920.53	78,821.34
18	891.36	6.30	4,797.34	72,922.36
19	899.92	7.00	4,918.27	67,041.59
20	870.93	6.75	4,338.49	60,928.93
21	865.31	7.25	4,215.04	54,760.25
22	832.08	6.90	3,578.37	48,353.65
23	785.44	6.00	2,718.78	41,647.16
24	750.45	5.60	2,158.27	34,800.03
25	728.38	6.10	1,934.61	27,994.08
26	704.32	7.00	1,747.19	21,289.42
27	653.90	6.40	1,168.98	14,611.52
28	602.83	7.25	849.97	8,227.53
29	514.65	6.00	334.76	2,386.49
30	354.03	4.75	22.14	0.00

Note: In Year 29, payments are made for only six full months and one partial month.

percent lower than interest levels for fixed-rate financing *when rates are going down*, perhaps 2 to 2.5 percent when fixed rates are rising or relatively high.

- Under the ARM agreement, Mr. Sharpe is allowed to make pre-payments in whole or in part without penalty.

Along with our mythical Mr. Sharpe, we also need to create a mythical world, one where interest rates rise and fall. We have no ability to predict the future, but in our example we will say that interest rates for Mr. Sharpe's loan are sometimes up, sometimes down, but always in flux.

In the first year Sharpe has a 5.5 percent loan and pays a total of $1,001.68 each month—$851.68 for principal and interest required by the lender, plus an extra payment of $150.

In the second year, the loan must be recalculated. The interest rate in our example rises to 6 percent, but since a year has passed we must now compute our payments for the loan's remaining term, 348 months (360 less 12).

Our new monthly costs are based not only on the interest rate and loan term, but also on the remaining debt. As he enters the second year, Mr. Sharpe owes the lender $146,133.33. At 7.5 percent over 348 months, the monthly payment will be $1,020.59. Add $150 as a voluntary payment and Sharpe's total monthly bill is now $1,179.59.

Sharpe's payments rise even though his loan balance has been reduced by nearly $5,000—in large measure because the teaser rate has risen a full 2 percent.

While Matthews is able to reduce the term of his loan from 360 months to 239 months—about 20 years—Sharpe obtains different results. His ARM loan term is only shortened by five full months.

The catch is that while Sharpe has a longer loan, his monthly payments fall. Matthews pays one amount—$1,303.37 per month—during the loan's entire course. Sharpe starts out at $1,001.68, sees his monthly costs go up at first, and then watches as his monthly costs decline over time.

Matthews cut his potential interest bill by more than $100,000 in our example, and Sharpe saw his interest cost fall from the $265,213 he might have paid with conventional financing to $183,444. Sharpe saved $81,769 when compared with the potential cost of a plain 30-year mortgage.

We can see that both Sharpe and Matthews saved enormous sums of money when compared to fixed-rate borrowers. Matthews achieved the largest interest savings, but Sharpe had interest savings plus substantially lower monthly costs over time. Depending on a borrower's goals, either result can be attractive.

In every community you can find loan plans that slash home ownership expenses. Growing Equity Mortgages (so-called "GEM" financing), wraparound loans, bond-backed mortgages and buy-downs are just some of the approaches savvy borrowers use to cut interest costs. Just as importantly, you don't need a new loan to drop interest expenses. Borrowers refinance and restructure old mortgages daily and save thousands of dollars when they do.

In many cases, lenders will help you develop money-saving strategies—while you pay less interest overall they have less risk, get their money back quicker and preserve or enlarge their buying power in the face of inflation. The interest you're not paying is more than made up by the lender's ability to issue additional loans that generate not only interest but high-profit fees and charges as well.

THE COMMON-SENSE MORTGAGE DEFINED

There is nothing sacred about being in debt for 30 years, especially since conventional mortgages—30-year, fixed-rate loans with 20 percent down—are not always the best deals for most borrowers. What borrowers must look for today is the common-sense mortgage.

What is the common-sense mortgage? Since everyone's income and needs differ it follows that no single mortgage format works well for all borrowers. Not only are needs different; needs change. The conditions that made one loan ideal several years ago may no longer exist. A new job, more or less income, the repayment of other debts, an inheritance, retirement or a killing on the stock market may each influence mortgage thinking.

Rather than being a particular type of loan with so much down or a certain interest rate, the common-sense mortgage is a viewpoint, an idea, a way of looking at real estate debt. In very basic terms the common-sense mortgage can be defined as the best available financing for each borrower at any given time. Going further, the search for the common-sense mortgage is guided by nine basic principles.

First, borrowed money represents *actual debt* that must be repaid, preferably at discount or with cheaper dollars over time. Interest is a *potential cost* that can be controlled, reduced or eliminated through sound financial planning.

Second, mortgage rates and terms are not set in stone. Selecting a mortgage should not be viewed as a static, one-time event which ends once property is bought. Borrowers must instead search continually for profitable opportunities to acquire, refinance, curtail or restructure loans. New mortgage opportunities that lower interest costs, cut tax bills, preserve buying power and raise additional capital can be available at any time, opportunities about which borrowers will want to be aware in light of changing needs, resources and goals.

Third, when buying or refinancing property, look for loans that offer the lowest possible interest cost. Note that "the lowest possible interest cost" does not necessarily mean the lowest interest rate, say 7 percent as opposed to 8 percent. Structure counts. For instance, both a 30-year conventional mortgage and a GEM loan may each have a 7 percent interest rate, but the absolute interest cost of the conventional loan is likely to be thousands of dollars higher than a GEM mortgage. How a loan is paid off can be more important than interest rates alone and the money you save can be spent or invested elsewhere.

Fourth, a mortgage must be seen as an alternative investment choice. Does it make sense to rapidly pay down your mortgage or is your money better spent on retirement plans, stock, mutual funds or other investments? What about after-tax results and the effect of inflation?

Fifth, reducing mortgage costs should not be seen as an exclusive financial option. There is no reason why an individual cannot have investments, a savings account, insurance and the best possible mortgage financing.

Sixth, saving interest and making interest are really two sides of the same coin. One thousand dollars invested today at 10 percent interest will be worth $6,727 in 20 years because of compounding. Conversely, small mortgage reductions today produce big savings over time because there is less principal on which to pay interest and less interest to compound. Also, "savings" and "interest" are treated differently for tax purposes. Earned interest is generally taxable while savings are tax-free.

Seventh, leverage is an important financial tool that can be made even more valuable by cutting potential interest costs.

Eighth, personal decisions are not always economically rational. If it makes you feel good to pay off the mortgage, at least consider that feeling even if higher returns are available elsewhere.

Ninth, you and I can make financial choices that are both different yet equally valid. Our economic decisions will be based on individual needs, incomes, assets, ages and perceptions and no single strategy is always "correct." The important point is to have a strategy, to consider alternatives and to actively take those steps which produce the best financial results.

INFLATION AND THE COMMON-SENSE MORTGAGE

Over time most people who have held real estate have seen values rise, at least in cash terms. Whether such increases in value are "real" is sometimes difficult to demonstrate.

Suppose Mr. Sullivan bought a home for $125,000 in 1980 and sold it for $198,250 ten years later. There is the appearance of a profit, at least in cash terms, but what can Sullivan buy with his extra dollars?

If Sullivan moves into a house of equal size in an equivalent neighborhood it will probably cost him $198,250 to buy the new property. Why? Because the cost-of-living index between 1980 and 1990 rose from 100 to 158.6, according to the Bureau of Labor Statistics. Only if Sullivan's house sold for more than $198,250 will he gain additional buying power.

(In fact, home prices commonly went up faster than the rate of inflation in many areas between 1980 and 1990 so most property owners earned additional buying power relative to the cost of living. Those who bought in California, Hawaii and such metropolitan areas as Boston, New York, and the Washington, DC area did especially well if they held for the 10-year period.)

What really happened here is not so much that the value of Sullivan's home rose but rather the buying power of cash declined as a result of inflation. Thus while Sullivan had more dollars, each dollar bought less than it did ten years earlier.

While Sullivan came out even in terms of inflation not everyone was so lucky. Sullivan financed his house with a fixed-rate mortgage at 9.5 percent interest.

The folks who so generously loaned Mr. Sullivan money did not do so well. They gave Mr. Sullivan a 30-year mortgage that was financed with short-term borrowing. Unfortunately short-term rates reached historic levels during the decade. In 1980 and 1981 the prime rate topped 20 percent so while Mr. Sullivan paid 9.5 percent, his lender paid much more.

The result was that Sullivan's lender, not Sullivan, lost buying money. Multiply Mr. Sullivan's experience and that of his lender by millions of real-life examples and you can quickly see how lender buying power worth billions and billions of dollars vanished when interest rates and inflation were high in the 1980s.

In this decade the story is different. Inflation is low, interest rates have tumbled, and savvy borrowers are still doing well.

Those with ARMs have watched as rates have steadily drifted lower while fixed-rate borrowers have refinanced once and sometimes two or three times. As to lenders, falling rates and reduced inflation have created a huge windfall, one that may well have saved the mortgage lending and commercial banking industries from huge losses not unlike those that decimated the S&L industry.

The bottom line:

- Faster loan pay-offs mean lenders have less exposure to inflation and thus less risk. Less risk, in turn, permits bigger loans and lower interest rates to borrowers at every income level.
- A large proportion of lender revenues are derived from the fees and charges which result from generating new loans, and from loan "servicing"—collecting payments and performing other

chores for mortgage investors. Because of these new profit centers, lenders often have an incentive to favor mortgages with quicker pay-offs.

- Fixed-rate, conventional financing commands premium interest rates and steep up-front charges. Alternative forms of financing are packaged with incentives for borrowers such as low initial interest rates and more liberal qualification standards when compared with conventional, 30-year mortgages.

- The recession, weak economic growth, and mild inflation that are hallmarks of the 1990s have created a new alternative for long-term homeowners: refinancing at rates unseen since the 1960s and 1970s.

- New loan variations allow borrowers to fine-tune lending needs. Opportunities to cut home ownership costs abound, but to be successful borrowers must shop carefully in a marketplace deluged with choices.

TAXES, ECONOMICS AND THE
COMMON-SENSE MORTGAGE

It is clear that widespread real estate ownership would be virtually impossible without the present tax advantages property owners enjoy. Tax deductions are crucial to homeowners because they reduce effective interest rates. If, for instance, you pay 10 percent interest but are in the 28 percent tax bracket, your true financing cost is 7.2 percent. As tax brackets rise, effective financing costs drop, so the true expense of being in debt falls less heavily on the rich. (See table, p. 11.)

Combining tax and inflation factors produces an interesting view of true mortgage costs. If Mr. Green's mortgage interest rate is 10 percent and he's in the 28 percent tax bracket, his out-of-pocket mortgage cost is 7.2 percent. That is, if Green spent $6,000 on mortgage interest last year his real cost was only $4,320. The other $1,680 will not otherwise be available to Green because it must be spent on taxes.

But if the inflation rate was 10 percent there was no "real" economic

Tax Effects on Interest		
Interest Rate (%)	Tax Bracket (%)	Effective Rate of Interest° (%)
6	15	5.10
6	28	4.32
6	31	4.14
6	36	3.84
7	15	5.95
7	28	5.04
7	31	4.83
7	36	4.48
8	15	6.80
8	28	5.76
8	31	5.52
8	36	5.12
9	15	7.65
9	28	6.48
9	31	6.21
9	36	5.76
10	15	8.50
10	28	7.20
10	28	6.90
10	36	6.40

°Not corrected for inflation

cost for Green's loan because the rate of inflation (10 percent) was greater than his effective, after-tax interest rate (7.2 percent). In this case, Green's buying power actually increased because the after-tax cost of borrowing money was less than the rate of inflation. (See table above.)

Does not this illustration suggest that it's always best to have the largest possible mortgage, particularly if you're in a high tax bracket? How can someone maximize his or her financial position with a mortgage that is quickly paid off or with one that features reduced interest expenses?

THE COMMON-SENSE MORTGAGE
AND FINANCIAL PLANNING

To answer the questions above a mortgage must be viewed as only one of several financial necessities which should be part of a sound personal financial program. A good personal finance strategy will include not only home ownership but also:

- Life and health insurance, particularly to protect against catastrophic medical costs.
- The equivalent of three to six months' income in a savings account or money market fund.
- A retirement plan.

Once your basic financial foundations are in place—homeownership, adequate insurance, cash on hand and a good retirement program—you can begin to devise an investment strategy. Just where should you put extra dollars? Does it ever make sense to pay down your mortgage early? If you are now paying 8.5 percent interest or whatever figure for real estate financing, where else can you get an equal or better rate of return with as little risk?

Suppose—to create an example—we live at a time when mortgages are at 10 percent, you have an extra $1,000, and your income places you in the 28 percent federal tax bracket. Where can you put your money?

By investing $1,000 in a home loan, the size of your mortgage will be reduced and thus interest costs will be cut. The interest you don't pay—$100 per year in this case—is not "income," however. It's considered a "saving" and is therefore untaxed. In effect, by investing in a mortgage you will earn 13.8889 percent in this example. (13.8889 percent less 28 percent equals 10 percent.)

If you're in the 28 percent bracket, excluding social security, state and local income taxes, $1,000 placed in a savings account that paid 10 percent interest will yield only $72 after taxes. To earn $100 after federal income taxes from such an account you will have to deposit $1,390.

The True Cost of Mr. Green's Mortgage	
Interest rate	10 percent
Tax bracket	28 percent
Effective interest rate	7.2 percent
Inflation rate	10 percent
Interest rate corrected for inflation	−2.8 percent

A savings account is an investment of sorts, but there is a difference between a savings account and mortgage prepayments. With the savings account, a $1,000 deposit produces immediate cash returns. The mortgage reduction creates an economic benefit that is only realized when the property is sold, refinanced or paid off. Borrowers who need an immediate cash benefit from the placement of their $1,000 may not be able to make the long-term commitment represented by a reduced mortgage balance even when it is economically attractive.

You can also take your $1,000 and deposit that money in an IRA or Keogh Plan producing a 10 percent annual return. These retirement programs are structured so that *if you qualify* the amount you deposit each year is deductible and the income or appreciation is untaxed until withdrawn. Putting $1,000 in an approved retirement program will lower current income taxes by $280 and produce interest worth $100 before deferred taxes. To earn as much after federal taxes from a 10 percent savings account you will have to deposit $5,280.

IRA and Keogh plans are blessed with extensive tax preferences and so they are likely to produce better after-tax returns than most investments. But contributions to such plans are limited (and sometimes not allowed). While income and appreciation are untaxed until withdrawal, taxation is surely possible. Worse, early withdrawals can be subject to a 10 percent penalty. Speak to a qualified tax advisor for complete details and the latest information.

Another "investment" choice might be to pay off credit card debt. Since the cost of consumer credit generally ranges from 18 to 21 percent, reducing credit card bills by $1,000 will produce returns of $180 to $210—money which is again a "saving" and not taxable income.

In the past, some borrowers have used real estate tax shelters to reduce taxes by ratios of one to two, one to three and sometimes more; that is, for each dollar invested tax bills dropped by two dollars, three dollars or whatever. In addition, the best tax shelters produced cash profits plus appreciation. Investing $1,000 in a shelter will produce far higher returns than a simple mortgage reduction.

The difficulty with tax shelters today is that the legendary deals of yesterday are gone. Tax changes over the years have eliminated much of the favorable treatment partnerships once enjoyed, go-go economics are largely dead, and the public has been soured by big-time partnership busts on Wall Street.

The view here is that *relative to alternative investment choices,* selected properties and situations represent excellent investment opportunities—especially for investors with gross adjusted incomes of $100,000 or less. Unlike the tax-driven deals of the past, real estate investments today must be based on economic fundamentals. Strange deals that feature little income and lots of fees should be avoided. Deals must make economic sense—properties that produce a stream of income and offer the possibility of future appreciation above the rate of inflation.

In terms of residential real estate, interest on as much as $1 million in acquisition financing for first and second homes is usually deductible. Interest on home equity loan balances of $100,000 or less is also deductible in the usual case.

But not everyone benefits equally from tax costs. As a logical matter, as your bracket rises, tax-deductible debt becomes increasingly interesting. Here's what it means:

- If you're poor, your tax liabilities are limited or non-existent. In essence, the mortgage interest rate you pay is likely to be your real cost of financing before inflation. In most instances you'll do better paying off credit card bills and auto loans before putting additional dollars into a mortgage.
- If you're in the middle income brackets, you appear to have a larger number of financial options than the poor. But these options are limited by the fact that home mortgage payments are likely to represent your largest monthly expense, a huge cost that

influences job flexibility (Can you pay the mortgage if you quit?), family roles (Must both husband and wife work?) and life-style choices (Are you able to save money for the kids, retirement or a better vacation?). At best, tax benefits make mortgage payments more bearable.

• If you're wealthy—if you have a taxable income of $250,000 or more—then your top rate is 39.6 percent—not counting state and local taxes or a 2.9 percent Medicare payroll tax. In effect, by raising tax rates, Uncle Sam is subsidizing more of your mortgage than at any time in recent years.

For the wealthy—the folks who have the greatest number of economic choices—the issue of rapidly repaying a mortgage must be seen in the light of alternative investments. Should you accelerate mortgage payments or place your money elsewhere? Where can you get the highest rate of return after taxes and inflation? Should you pay off a home mortgage merely as a matter of personal preference?

When considering loan repayments, the wealthy must also contend with the "alternative minimum tax," or ATM.

Under the ATM, individuals calculate their taxable income and then *add back* many deductions they might normally take. For example, personal exemptions and certain medical expenses must be added back. Accelerated depreciation must be recalculated using straight line schedules. The government suggests that "learning about the law or the form" will take 16 minutes, but many believe it is quicker, and easier, to memorize *Macbeth*.

Once ATM income is calculated, taxpayers then subtract $20,000 to $40,000 for allowable deductions (depending on your filing status) and multiply the balance by 26 percent (28 percent on taxable income over $175,000). The result is the ATM tax. If the ATM tax is lower than your regular tax, no extra payment is due. If the ATM amount is larger than your regular tax, you'll need to write a check. (Under the 1993 budget deal, the ATM tax rate was raised from a flat 24 percent to a two-tier system so that the more you make, the higher the ATM.)

In the process of adding back and recalculating, *home mortgage interest remains generally deductible under the ATM*. Given this fact, it may make sense for those in the upper income brackets to have the largest allowable home mortgages, to move personal debts and perhaps even investment debts under the home mortgage banner, and to devise an aggressive mortgage prepayment program.

The bottom line for all borrowers:

First, both taxes and interest are expenses.

Second, tax policies reward certain types of behavior. As tax rules and rates change, borrowers need to see how shifting tax requirements may affect their interests. For instance, lower rates add little to the value of mortgage interest write-offs while higher rates make mortgage interest less burdensome.

But how do tax rules influence your specific mortgage choices? When looking at tax rates one must be extremely careful because general rules which seem so clear and absolute are commonly accompanied by pages of exclusions, exceptions, limitations, and caveats.

If the tax codes were ever truly simplified, if the rules and regulations could be reduced to a single 3 × 5 card, then thousands of tax attorneys, CPAs, and enrolled agents would be forced to find new and, perhaps, socially redeeming modes of employment. However, since the moment of glory marking the arrival of simplified tax laws has yet to occur, always consult a tax professional for the latest information, rulings, and requirements.

Third, it's *always* cheaper to pay taxes rather than excess interest. If you're in the 28 percent tax bracket, it's far better to pay $28 in taxes than $100 in excess interest. Spending $100 on unnecessary interest creates, in this case, a $28 tax deduction. Not spending $100 in additional interest creates a $28 tax debt—but leaves $72 in your pocket.

If excess interest costs made sense, then we would have borrowers demanding 9 percent interest in a 7 percent market for loans of equal size. Yet, while borrowers constantly seek low interest *rates,* many wind up with high financing *costs.* How? Because excess interest can be created by loan *structure*—the way money is repaid—as well as high interest rates.

In example after example you can plainly see that two loans of equal size create different interest costs. If given a choice between such financing alternatives, why pick the mortgage with the higher cost? In some cases borrowers with limited finances have no option—the only loan they can afford is a stretched-out mortgage with high overall interest expenses. But many of us *do* have choices, particularly those who know that alternatives exist and that by selecting the best possible mortgage option we can save substantial amounts of money, *our* money if we don't needlessly give it away.

The point about real estate financing is that it is one of several valid investment choices, so why not buy property with a mortgage that represents the best possible arrangement in terms of interest, monthly payments, debt reduction, inflation, taxes restructure when it is to your advantage?

Why not hold your mortgage to the same criteria that you would use to evaluate stocks, bonds or any other investment? Surely you would check the stock tables every day, wait for dividends and splits, look for opportunities to buy, sell or trade, compare your stock with other issues and generally take an active interest in "your" company. Why be less concerned about you own mortgage?

DO LOW RATES CHANGE PREPAYMENT STRATEGIES?

With interest rates now substantially lower than at any point in the 1980s, the time has come to re-think a basic concept: does it make sense to prepay your mortgage?

Some financial planners have pointed out, correctly, that as rates fall the absolute value of prepayment programs decline. In other words, prepaying an $85,000 loan by an extra $75 a month reduces potential loan costs by $60,060 if the interest rate is 9 percent. Lower the rate to 7 percent, prepay the same $75 a month, and the possible savings are reduced to $39,743.

Since potential benefits from a prepayment program shrink with lower rates, it logically follows that such programs are now less valuable. Except, of course, if you look at the wider world.

Let's say we have 7 percent financing. We know that prepaying will not yield as much as a loan with a 9 percent rate, but a loan with a higher interest cost is irrelevant for our purposes. Why? Because a 9 percent mortgage cannot exist at the same time as 7 percent financing, therefore the correct comparison is this: is it better to put money into a 7 percent mortgage or invest elsewhere? If we invest it elsewhere, just where is elsewhere?

When we repay a 7 percent mortgage the interest we don't pay is a "savings." A saving is not taxable, so our true rate of return is more than 7 percent. If, for example, we live in a state with a 5 percent income tax and we are also in the 28 percent federal bracket, then prepaying a 7 percent loan produces an effective, before tax, yield of 10.45 percent (10.45 percent less 33 percent equals 7 percent).

So, if we are at a time when "investing" in a mortgage can yield 10.45 percent before taxes, where else can we put our money? Money market funds, savings accounts, Ginnie Mae's, corporate bonds and similar instruments are surely paying less than 10.45 percent when mortgage rates are at 7 percent.

Not to be overlooked is the stock market. The stock market offers both unlimited potential and unlimited risk, while "investing" in a mortgage is a low risk financial choice with known results. Not perfect protection against risk, but as good as anyone can get.

So should people prepay mortgages even when rates are lower? After paying down credit cards, auto debt, and other consumer obligations, and after setting aside money for liquidity, the answer for most borrowers is clearly yes. Saving $40,000 may not be as good as saving $60,000, but it's likely to be a lot better alternative then available investments of equal risk.

CAN THIS BE TRUE?

Every so often the idea of lower mortgage costs is challenged in a way that, upon careful examination, makes little sense.

One interesting example is the case of a 30-year, $100,000 loan with an interest rate of 10.5 percent. After 10 years we refinance at 9 percent and costs for principal and interest drop from $915 a month to $737.

So far refinancing looks like a winner, until this point is raised: the old loan had 20 years to go and total interest costs to pay off the debt would amount to $127,915.38. The new loan will have a 30-year term and a starting balance of $91,622.22. The total interest cost for the second loan will be $173,774.50.

Since $174,000 is a lot more than $128,000, it's clear that staying with the old loan is a better strategy since we would save interest worth roughly $46,000. Also, we would save on transfer costs, closing expenses, and taxes.

There is only one flaw in this example, but it's a gem. Remember the monthly mortgage payments? They dropped from $915 a to $737, a difference of $178 per month.

That $178 a month must be worth something, especially since it will not be paid over the remaining term of the old loan—20 years in this example. And, as it turns out, $178 multiplied by 240 months represents a savings of $42,720.

Even when we figure monthly savings, **not** refinancing still looks good. We need something more to justify refinancing, and that something is the time value of money.

Refinancing saves $178 a month in this example. That money can be used to buy clothes or to eat out more frequently. The money can also be invested in an interest-bearing account.

Pick a conservative rate of return, say 5 percent annually, and $178 invested each month will total $73,163.99 after 20 years.

But 5 percent is not a hot rate of return, so where else can we put our monthly savings and get better results with little risk?

Let's take the $178 a month and simply add it to the $737 we pay on the new, 9-percent loan. In other words, the monthly payments will remain the same as with the old loan but the interest rate is 1.5 percent lower. Invest our monthly savings in the shiny, new 9 percent mortgage and it will be paid off in 15.52 years. The total interest bill in this scenario is just $78,702.37.

When compared with the $127,915 it would have taken to stick with the old loan, the new arrangement cuts total mortgage costs by $49,213 ($127,915 less $78,702).

True, there will be some up-front costs for closing expenses and lender fees. But some other things are true as well:

- If we make "voluntary" prepayments on a loan and we have a rough month, voluntary prepayments are not required.
- We can take our savings, $178 a month in this example, and "invest" in such items as high-cost credit card debt or auto loans.
- We can take our savings and invest in the future by placing our monthly savings in tax-deferred retirement accounts.

Most importantly, the $178 a month is ours. Rather than pay it to lenders, we can do what we want with it.

LEVERAGE AND THE COMMON-SENSE MORTGAGE

It is commonly argued that borrowers should put down as little cash as possible when buying real estate. Use "other people's money" (OPM) and you'll have leverage and a better chance at big returns. If you can buy property with 10 percent down that's fine. If you can buy with 5 percent down that's better. Some argue that no money down is best of all.

There is no conflict between the idea of a common-sense mortgage and maximizing leverage. Whether you put down 5 percent, 10 percent or 20 percent you are still financing the bulk of the property so why not borrow money under the best possible terms and conditions?

A problem arises, however, when the idea of maximum debt is thought to be synonymous with maximum interest. There is no benefit in terms of leverage with steep interest costs. Putting down 5 percent to buy property and having a $100,000 interest bill is likely to be a much better deal than putting down 5 percent and paying interest costs of $200,000. Although the leverage factor is the same, the property's ultimate cost is not.

INVESTMENT REAL ESTATE AND
THE COMMON-SENSE MORTGAGE

There are significant distinctions between real estate purchased for personal purposes and property bought for investment. Two identical townhouses in a single subdivision may be physically alike but if one is residential property and the other investment real estate, the financing of each will be influenced by different factors.

First, owners of pure residential property—real estate used for no purpose other than personal housing—may not claim deductions for depreciation, maintenance, utilities, repairs, improvements or condo and co-op fees. Investors can claim deductions for such expenses.

Second, residential owners may move from one personal property to another of equal or greater value and defer all taxes from the sale of the first house. Investors face taxes whenever they sell at a profit.

Third, personal property owners over the age of 55 may claim a one-time profit exclusion of up to $125,000 when they sell their homes. There is no similar exemption for investors.

Home ownership and investment choices are guided by different philosophies, motivations, economics, tax policies and goals. These factors mean that strategies which work well for personal real estate deals may be inappropriate or even harmful when making investment decisions and borrowers must adjust their planning to suit the type of real estate being financed.

HOW TO PROFIT FROM THIS BOOK

This book has been written to help you both make money and save money. It is designed to serve as a basic reference guide and as a tool to help you choose the best loan at any given time.

This book is a starting point in the search for the best available deal, a guide to the deals that make sense for you, and a reference during the borrowing process. It provides information, raises ideas, and poses questions. It creates the opportunity to be a better consumer, and it encourages you to aggressively assert your interests in the marketplace.

But although this book is a starting place, it is not a substitute for other actions and activities.

To get the best deal you must ask questions, speak to mortgage loan officers, talk with real estate brokers, consult with attorneys and tax advisors and always consider alternative approaches. You'll need paper and pencil, a calculator that can figure interest rates and monthly loan payments and a willingness to study, listen and explore.

If it seems as though finding the best financing is a lot of work, you're right. But it is also true that a properly structured mortgage can easily save the equivalent of several years' income, a fact few of us can ignore.

2
How the Lending System Works

Real estate financing is more than a matter of interest rates and loan terms. To prosper in the mortgage lending system borrowers must first understand its language, how it works, who the players are, why they act the way they do and what they expect from you. Let's get started by looking at basic words and concepts.

THE LANGUAGE OF REAL ESTATE FINANCE

Every trade has its tools, each discipline its special words and so it is not surprising that real estate financing has a unique vocabulary.

The most frequent words you will encounter are *mortgage* and *trust* or *deed of trust*. Simply stated, mortgages and trusts are both promises to repay a loan secured by real estate. The actual loan terms—its length, interest rate, size, etc.—are found in a separate document, the *note*. For the general purposes of this book, the terms *mortgage* and *trust* are used interchangeably.

On a more technical basis, however, mortgages and trusts are different. A mortgage represents a direct arrangement between lender and borrower. A deed of trust is a triangular affair in which there is a borrower, a lender and trustees selected by the lender. If a borrower fails to make adequate or timely payment, the trustees have the right to foreclose on the property. In many jurisdictions, foreclosure is faster with a deed of trust than with a mortgage.

From the borrower's viewpoint, real estate loans have a potential problem. What happens if the loan ends and the lender is on a two-year trip to Nepal or was hit by a bus and is now comatose in a hospital? You cannot sell or refinance the property as long as your debt to the lender is outstanding. Who can sign all the papers needed to show your debt has been paid? With a deed of trust the trustees must promptly sign all requisite documents upon payment of the debt and therefore a borrower is not dependent on the lender's availability.

There are many words and phrases commonly used in real estate finance, expressions with which borrowers should be familiar. Here is a selected list of important terms that can help you better understand how the mortgage system works.

Amortization.   As payments are made to a lender each month, the mortgage debt, or *principal*, declines in most cases. This process is called *amortization*. Also, see SELF-AMORTIZATION, and NEGATIVE AMORTIZATION.

Amortization Schedule.   A table that shows how each monthly payment is divided into principal and interest during the loan term and the remaining principal balance after every mortgage payment. For a level-payment, 30-year, $85,000 loan at 10 percent interest, monthly payments will total $745.94 and an amortization schedule will look like this:

Payment	Interest	Principal	Balance
1	$708.33	$37.60	$84,962.40
2	$708.02	$37.91	$84,924.49
3	$707.70	$38.23	$84,886.26
4	$707.39	$38.55	$84,847.71
Etc.			

Annual Percentage Rate (APR).   The true rate of interest for a loan over its projected life, say 30 years; may be different than the initial interest rate or the nominal interest rate before compounding.

Balloon Payment.   It sometimes happens that loan payments are not sufficient to pay off a debt and the result is that when the loan term ends a large, or *balloon,* payment remains. This can be the case when monthly payments are not large enough to cover the combined value of principal and interest or when monthly payments do cover principal and interest but there are not enough of them to repay the debt in full. Because unpaid balloon payments can lead to foreclosure, such financing is not normally recommended for homebuyers.

In the case of an interest-only loan, the balloon payment at the end of the loan term will be equal to the original amount borrowed. Second trusts often feature balloon payments because they tend to be short-term obligations, usually two to ten years in length.

Blanket Mortgage.   A single mortgage secured by several properties.

Bridge Loan. Financing placed on one home and used to purchase a second home. The first home is typically for sale. As soon as it sells and settles, the bridge loan is repaid in full. Many bridge loans are interest-only loans, or require no monthly payments. Many bridge loans last a few days, weeks, or months.

Closing.   See SETTLEMENT.

Conventional Mortgage. A loan with a value less than or equal to a specific amount established each year by major secondary lenders. As of mid-1994, financing worth less than $203,150 was regarded as "conventional" financing. Loans for more than $203,150 are regarded as "jumbo" mortgages where rates and terms are likely to be somewhat stiffer. *Important note: At the time you read this book the value of conventional financing may have been raised. Check with lenders and real estate brokers for the current definition of "conventional" financing.*

Community Reinvestment Act.   Federal legislation which encourages lenders to provide mortgages and other services in areas historically underserved by financial organizations such as banks, savings and loan associations, etc. CRA regulations do not require lenders to make imprudent loans or to lower lending standards, rather CRA urges lenders to assist marginal borrowers by acting in a flexible manner, by creating community programs, and by locating offices in underserved communities.

Cram Down.   A less-than-charming expression which means that someone cannot pay all that is due in a bankruptcy, so creditors must accept whatever is available. As in: "Take this offer or the bankruptcy court will cram it down your throat."

Curtailment.   A payment that shortens or ends a mortgage. For example, if you have a $15,000 balance on your mortgage and pay off the entire debt the loan has been curtailed.

Deferred Interest.   See NEGATIVE AMORTIZATION.

Entitlement.   A right due to an individual. Used with VA mortgages. For instance, a $15,000 *entitlement* will mean that a vet can borrow that sum from a lender and the VA will guarantee its repayment. Since lenders usually want a 1:4 ratio between the value of an entitlement and the loan amount, having a $15,000 guarantee will allow a borrower to get a $60,000 loan—$15,000 backed by the VA and $45,000 secured by the borrower and the property's market value.

Equity.   The cash value of property, less marketing expenses, after all liens have been paid off.

Escrow.   When money is held by one party for another it is usually placed in an *escrow,* or trust, account. For example, if you give a real estate broker a $10,000 deposit to purchase a house and those funds are placed in an escrow account, the broker does not have the right to use that money (*commingle*) for his own purposes.

Installment Sale.   A transaction in which the buyer pays the seller in whole or in part after title has been transferred. For example, Wilson buys a house from Davis and pays $100,000 for the property. Davis receives $20,000 at settlement and $20,000 a year plus interest for the next four years. The advantage to Davis is that his profit is spread over several years and thus he may enjoy a reduced tax rate.

Junior Lien.   Much like shoppers in a supermarket, lenders line up to be paid when a property is foreclosed. The order of repayment is established by the loan documents recorded in local government offices. The lender with the first claim has the first mortgage or first trust, the lender with the second claim holds the second mortgage or second trust, etc. If a loan is not a first trust or mortgage it is a *junior lien*.

Leverage.   A general investment concept meaning that you have been able to borrow funds and thereby use other people's money (**OPM**). If you buy a home for $100,000, put down $20,000 at settlement and get an $80,000 mortgage for the balance, your *leverage* is 1 to 4. If you put down only $10,000 your leverage is 1 to 9, a better deal as long as the $10,000 you didn't put into the property can earn an equal or better return elsewhere.

Liens.   A *lien* is a claim against property. Not only are mortgages and trusts liens, but overdue property taxes, unpaid repair bills, condo fees and even water and sewage charges can all be liens. A major purpose of a title search is to be certain that all liens are known as of the day of settlement.

Locking In.   Mortgage rates are often widely advertised but the rate you see may not be the rate you get. Borrowers must ask when a rate is "locked in," that is, guaranteed by the lender. Rates may be locked in at the time a loan application is made, several weeks later when the loan is approved or at the time of settlement. If a loan is not locked in at the time of application, then a borrower may pay higher rates if interest levels rise. Some lenders not only lock in rates at the time of application, they also guarantee that the quoted rate is the highest a borrower will pay. With such deals, if interest rates fall between the time of application and settlement, borrowers pay the lowest rate.

Negative Amortization.   A loan in which monthly payments are too small to pay for either principal or interest reductions. The result is

Payment	Interest	Principal	Balance
1	$700	0	$85,008.33
2	$700	0	$85,016.73
3	$700	0	$85,025.20
Etc.			

that the principal balance grows by both the amount of unpaid interest and the interest on the unpaid interest. *Negative amortization* will produce a balloon payment when the loan ends in most cases. However, with some formats, such as graduated payment mortgages, there can be negative amortization in the loan's first years, but higher payments later in the loan term eliminate the possibility of a balloon payment. For example: With a 30-year, $85,000 loan at 10 percent interest a self-amortizing loan will require monthly payments of $745.94. If the payments were only $700, negative amortization will develop.

Other People's Money (OPM).   Money that you borrow from other people or lenders. To get the maximum amount of leverage you want to borrow the largest possible amount of money and have it work for you.

Package Mortgage.   A single mortgage used to acquire not only a house but personal goods as well, such as a microwave oven.

Points.   A *point,* or a *loan discount fee,* is an amount equal to 1 percent of the mortgage. This sum is paid or credited to a lender at settlement. The purpose of points is to raise the lender's yield. (For more information about points, see YIELD AND POINTS.)

Principal, Interest, Taxes and Insurance (PITI).   The four basic costs of home ownership that most concern lenders. For example, a lender might say that only 28 percent of your gross income can be devoted to PITI if you are to qualify for financing.

Refinance.   A situation in which new financing is placed on a property. The addition of a second trust is a "partial" refinancing. Replacing one loan with another is a "total" refinancing.

Restructure.   A loan that remains in place but with new terms. If you increase your monthly payments by $25 you have *restructured* your loan. By making the additional payments you will reduce the principal debt at a faster rate than originally planned, so you will pay less interest and have fewer payments. For example, if you have an $85,000 loan at 10 percent interest it will take 30 years to repay the loan with monthly payments of $745.94. If the monthly payment is raised $25 to $770.94, the loan can be repaid in a little more than 25 years.

Self-Amortization.   When monthly payments for principal and interest allow a loan to be repaid over its term without any balloon payment, *self-amortization* has occurred. See AMORTIZATION SCHEDULE for illustration.

Settlement.   *Settlement,* or *closing,* is nothing more than an accounting of who owes what to whom as a result of a real estate sale. Not only must the buyer pay the seller but the seller may have to pay off old loans, brokerage fees, etc. It is at settlement that transfer taxes, points, adjustments between buyer and seller (for such items as oil in the furnace or prepaid taxes), title insurance, and other costs are first collected from buyer and seller and then paid out or credited as required.

Take Back.   An expression used in real estate to mean that a loan has been made directly to a purchaser by the seller, as in "seller Conklin will *take back* a $30,000 second trust from buyer Hastings."

Usury.   In many jurisdictions there is a maximum rate of interest permitted for certain types of loans. If the interest rate is above the limit, this is *usury.* The usury limit varies not only between jurisdictions but according to loan types. There may, for instance, be one usury limit for first trusts and another rate for seconds.

YIELD AND POINTS

For most borrowers, the cost of mortgage financing—and the lender's income—can be measured in terms of interest. But interest is only one mortgage expense; there are others and they greatly influence the cost of financing.

Mortgage rates are described by both a nominal rate, say 10 percent, and the APR, or *annual percentage rate,* a figure generally higher than the nominal interest cost, perhaps 10.25 percent in this case. The difference between the nominal and APR figures is the result of interest compounding and possibly other factors. When comparing loans the APR figure should always be used.

In a growing number of situations, however, it is difficult to cite a specific interest cost. With adjustable rate mortgages (ARMs), for example, there may be an attractive interest rate initially but that figure is subject to change. Rate fluctuations over the life of a variable rate loan are not predictable, so determining a set APR is not possible.

There are many situations in which borrowers select one lender over another on the basis of interest rates. While it certainly pays to shop for interest rates, other expenses should not be ignored. Consider these costs:

Fees.   Many lenders charge to process loan applications and these costs vary. Ask if all or part of the fee will be refunded in the event an application is rejected.

Charges.   Most lenders require borrowers to pay for a credit report and appraisal. Some lenders, however, have additional requirements such as surveys and photos and these items are also an expense of financing.

Reserves.   Different lenders have different reserve requirements, money held by the lender to assure the payment of property taxes, condo fees or mortgage insurance premiums. Reserves can be a major cash drain at settlement, so be certain to compare lender practices in this area.

Perhaps the single lender charge that causes the most confusion is a *loan discount fee,* or *point.* A point is equal to 1 percent of a mortgage and is paid or credited to a lender at settlement.

The purpose of points is to raise the lender's yield. Suppose you get a $95,000 loan at 9 percent interest. The lender charges one point, or $950, and so at settlement you receive $94,050. The lender has loaned only $94,050 but expects you to repay the full face value of the loan, $95,000—plus interest.

In terms of interest rates, a point is usually valued at one-eighth of 1 percent over the 30-year term of a conventional mortgage. Using this figure, one might expect that if a lender is making one loan at 10 percent and another mortgage at 9 percent interest, the lower rate note will require the payment of eight points.

As a practical matter, however, loans do not last 30 years. Most loans are repaid within 12 years, not so much a result of borrowers making additional payments as the fact that people move and refinance with some frequency. For the loan above, lenders will surely ask for less than eight points, perhaps three to three and a half points.

But suppose there are two lenders in town and you have a choice: you can get a 30-year, $95,000 loan at 9 percent interest and pay two points or you can pay 9.25 percent interest and pay only one point. Which is the better deal?

The answer depends on how long you own the property. The difference between an interest rate of 9 percent and 9.25 percent is $17.15 per month ($764.39 monthly versus $781.54 for a 30-year loan). It will take almost 55 months to pay out $950 at the rate of $17.15 monthly. Moreover, paying $950 at settlement means you have lost any possible interest or investment income on that money. (See table, p. 31.)

The bottom line: If you intend to own the property much more than 55 months, pay the additional $950 charge up front. If you only intend to own the property for a short time then the higher interest rate is a bargain.

Borrowers will need to "run the numbers" and calculate the actual cost of various combinations of points and interest. In most cases, deciding whether or not to opt for a higher interest rate or more points—when such options are available—is a function of time. The longer a property is held, the cheaper the one-time cost of points.

Since points are a cost of financing it would seem that they are an expense which "should" be borne by purchasers, but this is not necessarily the case.

Points versus Interest		
	Loan 1	Loan 2
Loan amount	$95,000	$95,000
Interest rate	9.00	9.25
Monthly payment	$781.54	$764.39
Number of points	2	1
Cash value of points	$1,900	$950
Extra monthly interest cost	None	$17.15
Extra cost for points	$950	None

- With VA, FHA, and conventional loans, the question of who pays points is a matter of negotiation. If you are the buyer, you can present an offer that has the seller paying all points. If unacceptable, try splitting points. Another approach is to formulate an offer where the seller pays a set amount to you at settlement, say the first $3,000 of your closing costs or whatever figure might be appropriate.
- If you're a seller you too have a right to negotiate. From your perspective you will certainly argue that points are an expense to be borne exclusively by the purchaser. When sellers feel the cost of points is too high, they often agree to pay all or a portion of the points due if the buyer will accept a price increase. In effect, the buyer pays such costs over the term of the mortgage.

Since points are a payment for the use of money—interest—they should be tax deductible, and as this is written, points paid for the *purchase* of a new home are fully deductible in the year in which they're paid. Points paid to *refinance* a home, however, must be apportioned over the loan's life.

Suppose you have a property bought many years ago and today it's mortgage free. You want to raise money and refinance the property with an $85,000 mortgage. The mortgage has a term of 30 years and you pay two points, or $1,700, at settlement. The points in this case must be deducted over the mortgage's 30-year life at the rate of $56.67 a year.

But what if the $85,000 loan is paid off in 20 years? The remaining deduction can be taken in a single lump sum, $566.70 in this case ($56.67 × 10 years).

Although points paid to refinance property must be deducted over the loan's term, there is some question as to which loans represent "new" financing and which should be considered "refinancing."

The U.S. Court of Appeals in the Eighth Circuit, a court with jurisdiction over Arkansas, Iowa, Missouri, Minnesota, Nebraska, North Dakota, and South Dakota, has ruled in one case that points are sometimes deductible even if they are not paid at the time a property is bought.

In this situation a family had purchased a home with a short-term balloon note that was to be refinanced at a later date, when they hoped rates would be lower. Rates dropped, the homeowners refinanced, and they then deducted all points—a deduction which was unwarranted according to the government. The court ruled otherwise and said that in this particular instance the refinancing was "in connection" with the acquisition of the property and the points were therefore deductible.

Points are a sore issue and there is some possibility that the rules may be changed. Why, after all, treat points to acquire a home differently than points used to refinance a personal residence? Conversely, why change a system which reduces write-offs for refinancing and thus raises tax collections? For the latest information and advice, be sure to check with your tax adviser.

Questions to Ask:

Will your lender allow you the option of paying fewer points in exchange for a higher interest rate?

Will your lender allow you the option of paying more points in exchange for a lower rate of interest?

How long must you own the property to justify a high-interest mortgage with few points?

How long must you own the property to justify a low-interest loan with more points up front?

Can you deduct points charged when purchasing a personal residence?

Can you deduct points charged for refinancing from federal taxes?

How are points treated if the loan is used for a business purpose?

NEW POINTS RULE CUTS HOME-BUYING COSTS

The history of federal taxes has largely been associated with rising rates and falling deductions. Thus, the latest tax rule regarding the treatment of "points" is a stunner: home buyers will now be able to deduct points paid by sellers.

To see how this works let's start with a definition: a "point" equals 1 percent of a mortgage. Borrow $100,000 at 8.5 percent plus 1 point and you must pay $1,000 at closing.

The use of points produces several effects. In the example above, the home buyer borrowed $100,000 but gave back $1,000 at closing, so the lender parted with only $99,000. Even so, the borrower must pay back the full $100,000. Because the borrower is paying 8.5 percent on $100,000 but only borrowing $99,000, the real interest rate—if the loan lasts 30 years—is 8.609 percent.

In the past few years the tax treatment of points has worked like this:

- If a buyer pays points to acquire a personal residence, the points are generally deductible in the year paid.
- If a buyer pays points to refinance a personal residence, acquire a second home, or to buy or refinance investment property, such points can only be deducted over the life of the loan.
- If a seller pays points, their value is a cost of selling the property that reduces the owner's profit from the sale.

In new regulations (Revenue Procedure 94-27), the IRS takes a different approach.

- If a buyer pays points to acquire a personal residence, the points are deductible in the year paid.
- If an owner pays points to help a buyer acquire a personal residence, the owner may deduct the points as a cost of selling the property.
- If a buyer purchases a personal residence where the seller has paid points, the BUYER can deduct the points paid by the seller.
- When the buyer sells the property, the value of the points paid by the seller must be added to the buyer's profit.

- The rules regarding the payment of points to refinance, or to purchase a second home or investment property, remain unchanged.

The result of the new rule is that buyers get a tax benefit when sellers pay points. The seller deducts the cost of points when figuring the tax basis of the property, because points are a selling expense. The buyer obtains a deduction up front for the points paid by a seller, but later has less to deduct when the home is sold.

In theory, at least, the amount of revenue flowing into the Treasury should be unchanged by the new guidelines. But in practice it seems likely that taxpayers will gain a substantial benefit.

To make the new guidelines work, the buyer is taxed when the home is sold. But the reality is that few owners pay taxes when homes are sold.

The residence rollover replacement rule allows owners to defer taxes if they sell a personal residence and then buy another personal residence of equal or greater value within two years (four years for active-duty military).

The over-55 exclusion allows most owners aged 55 and older to sell property and to take a one-time deduction of up to $125,000.

In effect, the new guidelines create both an immediate write-off for buyers as well as an accounting item that increases a buyer's profit when a home is sold. However, because of the over-55 exclusion and the rollover rule, most people will never pay a tax when it comes time to sell.

Not only will the new tax rule help buyers who finance with seller-paid points in the future, it will also help many buyers who bought in the past few years.

If you bought a personal residence after December 31, 1990, and if the seller paid points, then you may be entitled to a refund.

To obtain a refund, you'll need to file an amended return with the IRS (Form 1040X). Write "seller-paid points" in the upper right-hand corner and be certain to include a copy of your closing statement (HUD Form #1).

Is it worth filing an amended return? If a seller paid a single point worth $1,000 and you're in the 28 percent tax bracket, Uncle Sam will send you a check for $280. In addition, you may also be entitled to a state refund, as well.

For details, speak with a tax attorney, CPA, or enrolled agent to see how you benefit under the new rule.

WHY LENDERS NEED APPRAISALS

What is the worth of a given property? It may seem as though a sales price, determined by informed buyers and sellers in an open market, is the best index of value. Yet this is not always the case as far as lenders are concerned. While buyers and sellers may look at a property as a home or an investment, lenders see the very same real estate in different terms. To lenders, property is security—the ultimate recourse in the event a borrower fails to repay a mortgage. In this sense, lenders must know real estate values to limit their risk.

Consider what would happen if a lender valued a real estate parcel at $100,000 and made an $80,000 mortgage based on that judgment. If the mortgage is not repaid the lender will sell the property at foreclosure, a process which in itself is costly and time-consuming. But if the property can be sold for only $60,000 or any value less than the mortgage balance and the cost of foreclosure, the lender will have a loss.

To limit such risks, lenders want a precise but conservative estimate of value before making a loan. To determine the right numbers an appraiser satisfactory to the lender will be hired to evaluate the property.

The worth of a particular property is represented by more than bricks and mortar. Here are the major factors appraisers use to determine real estate values:

Occupancy.   It is generally agreed that owner-occupants have a clear interest in maintaining property values. Tenant-occupied properties are seen as representing more risk to a lender and therefore investment loans are likely to have a higher rate of interest than residential mortgages.

Transition.   Property values which fluctuate as a result of zoning changes, growth patterns and other factors must be noted. Most instances of transition are evolutionary but in some cases there can be dramatic value fluctuations. In one situation, an appraisal was changed from $15,000 to nearly $500,000 because a property was rezoned and incorporated within a rapidly developing urban area.

Predominant Value.   Housing patterns tend to be homogeneous. Homes worth $100,000 are in $100,000 neighborhoods; $50,000 properties are in $50,000 areas, etc. For appraisers, it is important for properties to be within the general pricing patterns of their neighborhoods because over-valued homes, even though they may have exceptional features, are difficult to sell at full market price.

Buyers, it is said in the real estate industry, seek the least expensive property they can find in the most expensive neighborhood they can afford. A home with a pool and five bedrooms in a neighborhood of conservative three-bedroom homes will be difficult to market at full economic value and therefore a lender will want to limit the size of a loan made against such property.

Facilities.   The existence—or lack—of community improvements, such as sewers and sidewalks, will influence property values.

Improvements.   Anything other than raw ground, such as houses, apartment buildings, garages, pools, etc., is regarded as an *improvement*. An appraiser will evaluate each improvement in terms of its age, condition and modernization. The improvement's remaining economic life will be estimated. Extra value will be given for modernized baths and kitchens, additions, and energy-efficient items such as enhanced insulation, wood-burning stoves and even landscaping that reduces energy usage.

Once all the variables have been considered (the items above are but part of a far longer list), an appraiser will calculate a property value using one of three systems. With the *market data* approach an appraiser will compare the subject property with other neighborhood sales. This is the most common form of appraisal for residential property.

The *income* system can be used to determine values for investment properties. Here the analysis is based on revenues and rates of return.

A third type of approach, *cost valuation*, estimates the value of materials and labor needed to erect a similar improvement on comparable property. This form of appraisal is valuable for specialized structures, such as churches and synagogues.

Using one or more forms of analysis, an appraiser will provide an estimate of value to the lender who may then elect to make a loan commitment. However, since the lender views the property as economic security, a conventional, uninsured loan for the property's full value will not be granted.

Instead the lender will provide a loan for only a portion of the property's value, say 80 percent, and the purchaser will put up the balance in cash, as a second trust or both. For the lender, a limited loan commitment plus the buyer's equity contribution both have the effect of reducing risk.

Not everyone can put up sufficient cash or secondary financing for a property purchase. In such situations a lender may provide more than 80 percent financing when there are promises of repayment by a third party, such as the VA, FHA or a private mortgage insurer.

KNOWING THE PLAYERS: WHO MAKES
LOANS, WHO HELPS

Savings and Loan Associations.   S&Ls are specialized financial organizations which have traditionally been the largest source of residential mortgages.

It is not surprising that S&Ls have been and are so active in the mortgage market. Historically S&Ls have been able to attract savings from the general public because governmental regulations once gave them the right to pay slightly more interest than commercial banks. Federal rules also guided the use of those savings: to get maximum tax benefits S&Ls have traditionally been forced to invest most of their available funds in mortgage loans.

Changes in the rules during the 1980s allowed S&Ls to venture outside their historic area of expertise and the results for some were devastating. Many S&L officers proved they did not understand how to finance commercial office buildings and other major projects, and institutions failed in many states.

Although numerous S&Ls have gone under, it should be clearly stated that those S&Ls which carry on are often excellent mortgage sources. In particular, S&Ls that have acted conservatively and continued to specialize in home loans remain a mortgage storehouse in virtually all communities, a source of financing which should not be ignored.

Commercial Banks.   Mortgages are an important, but secondary, activity for commercial bankers. Unlike S&Ls, the prime focus of commercial banks is demand deposits (checking accounts) and short-term loans, particularly business financing.

Commercial banks, however, have also seen an opportunity as S&Ls have failed. If done right, the residential mortgage business is a good, conservative lending opportunity, something many banks need at a time when the banking industry is under fire for its share of imprudent loans and weak management.

Mortgages are thus increasingly attractive to commercial bankers, especially if the borrower also happens to be a potential client who can bring business and personal accounts to the bank.

Savings Banks.   About 800 institutions known as "savings banks" exist, but there is now little to distinguish a "savings bank" from a "savings and loan association" because under federal rules, an S&L can be converted to a savings bank and a savings bank can be converted to an S&L. Historically, though, the two forms of institutions were different because at one time savings banks could issue checks and S&Ls could not. That subtlety largely disappeared with the development of NOW accounts that effectively gave S&Ls a checking capability. (When savings banks are owned by depositors they are often known as "mutual savings banks," especially in New England.)

Life Insurance Companies.   The nation's insurers are a substantial mortgage source, though much of their lending is used to finance major projects such as office buildings, apartment complexes, and shopping malls rather than single-family homes.

While some insurance firms deal directly with the public, most make residential loans through mortgage bankers and mortgage brokers. For this reason it is possible to have a home financed with insurance dollars even though the loan seems to come from another source.

Credit Unions.   Since 1978 federal regulations have allowed credit unions to make first mortgages and trusts, but with one important stipulation: loan amounts were limited by prevailing housing prices in given areas. The loan size restriction was lifted in 1982 and now credit unions are emerging as solid mortgage choices. Of the nation's 14,000 credit unions, about 35 percent offer first mortgages according to Jerry Karbon of the Credit Union National Association. Karbon points out, however, that those credit unions which offer mortgages represent about 70 percent of all credit union members nationwide, a big number since more than 60 million people are credit union members.

Mortgage Bankers.   Individuals and institutions who use their own capital as well as money from such sources as pension funds, insurance companies, and savings and loan associations to create mortgages. Mortgage bankers locate borrowers who meet standards established by investors and often "service" the loans they make. "Servicing" the loan means collecting monthly payments from borrowers and, if necessary, foreclosing.

Mortgage Brokers.   Individuals and institutions who match those who need money with interested investors. Commercial real estate brokers often perform this function.

Sellers.   There are always deals available in which some sellers will hold financing; however, when interest rates soar, the character of seller financing changes. In such times seller financing is not an occasional matter—it is a wholesale substitute for the commercial lending system. In 1980 and 1981, for example, it was estimated that when interest rates exceeded 16 and 17 percent, more than 60 percent of all residential resales involved some seller financing.

Lawyers.   Attorneys play an important role in the lending process because complex rules govern mortgages.

Lawyers are commonly employed to review real estate agreements prior to final acceptance and to write specialized legal language required for the sale. Attorneys often conduct *settlement (closing)* and in those cases where lawyers do not conduct settlement they frequently review settlement papers for a client, either the buyer or the seller, to assure that settlement follows the understandings described in the contract between the parties.

In the lending process directly, lawyers write and review agreements between buyers and sellers, such as equity-sharing arrangements. They also write and review mortgage documents for lenders generally and for sellers in those cases where a seller *takes back* financing (makes a loan directly to a buyer). An attorney will want to assure that the loan conforms with all appropriate rules and regulations—items such as usury limits, payment terms, the naming of trustees (if any), insurance requirements, etc.

SHOULD BROKERS MAKE LOANS?

Brokers and their agents have several important functions within the lending system even though they are not lenders per se.

First, brokers are a central source of mortgage information. Buyers and sellers commonly depend on brokers to locate real estate financing and to advise them on current rates, points, and loan formats.

Second, brokers look at the finances of prospective buyers to determine, in general terms, the level of financing they can afford. While this basic qualifying process does not guarantee financing, it does provide valuable information and guidance to buyers.

Third, brokers keep abreast of the mortgage market and may be able to locate "special" investor funds, money at below-market rates or with other advantageous terms. Knowing where the money is often spells the difference between a sale and no deal.

Although brokers have largely been passive loan sources in the past—recommending lenders rather than taking mortgages directly—many have begun to offer loan services in direct competition with other mortgage suppliers.

Brokers are a potent competitor in the lending field because they are best positioned to meet a buyer at the point of sale. Since many lenders rely on broker referrals for business, the growing role of brokers in the mortgage field has displeased many lenders. Now there is an ongoing war between brokers and lenders, and the cause—not surprisingly—is money, and who gets it.

When individuals finance or refinance real estate they enjoy certain protections as a result of the Real Estate Settlement and Procedures Act (RESPA). Among other benefits, RESPA outlaws "naked" referrals to lenders, deals where a real estate broker receives a fee just for giving a lender the name of a potential borrower.

Everyone agrees that naked referrals should be banned because no work is involved. Less clear is what happens if brokers and salespeople do some of the work (or all of the work) normally performed by mortgage loan officers, or if brokers make their facilities available to lenders.

The government's position on this matter has evolved over time.

- In 1984, the Department of Housing and Urban Development (HUD) allowed brokers to create in-house mortgage information services. Brokers could list lender rates and information, and they could charge lenders a fee for providing space on their information systems.
- In 1986, HUD ruled that brokers could charge borrowers a fee to access loan information, providing the charges were "voluntary."
- In 1990, brokers were allowed to offer loans, provided all fees were disclosed and borrowers were made aware that other loan sources were available.
- In 1992, HUD went all out and said that brokers could originate loans, be paid for such services, and work with as many—or as few—lenders as they liked.

We now have a situation where real estate brokers can effectively act as mortgage brokers. But if realty brokers were simply other lenders trying to obtain business no one would care. Instead, real estate brokers are in a very unique position, one which is now being reexamined in Washington.

Realty brokers are at the right place and the right time to generate loans. They are at the point of sale the very moment someone elects to buy a home. A buyer may know a broker, think highly of a broker, and regard the broker as an authority figure. And if the broker, a trained professional, says that he or she can smooth the home-buying process by finding a loan for the buyer, why not?

As it turns out there are several "why nots." A HUD review published in the *Federal Register* (July 21, 1994) outlines substantial questions regarding the right of realty brokers to originate loans.

HUD says that when it called for comments on loans and brokers it received 1,526 responses—1,473 against broker loan originations, 24 in favor, and the remaining 29 in the middle.

The issue for mortgage brokers is fairly clear: if real estate brokers originate loans there is less work and fewer dollars for mortgage brokers. But mortgage brokers were not the only ones opposed to broker-originated loans.

Sixteen state attorneys general, several federal agencies, and a number of title companies and law firms were also in the "anti" camp.

Why? Three factors stand out.

First, while fees cannot be paid to outside parties for mortgage referrals, the rules allow fees to employees. This means that if a brokerage firm owns an affiliated mortgage subsidiary, a brokerage employee might obtain a fee by referring a buyer to the captive lender. Note that only "employees" can receive a fee, not brokers and salespeople, who are usually "independent contractors."

Second, the HUD document states that if a broker originates a loan, it could "create a conflict of interest and a 'potentiality for fraud' for the broker or agent, whose fiduciary duty is to the seller." In English, this means there is a potent conflict when a broker represents a seller and is also paid for obtaining a loan.

As an example, suppose Broker Jones represents owner Smith and says a buyer can pay $150,000 for the Smith property with a loan through the broker. If the buyer can pay $155,000 by going to another lender—one not paying a fee to Broker Jones—then Broker Jones has big problems. The buyer is getting the house at discount (which is *not* why broker Jones was hired), and owner Smith is getting less than he should for the property (again, another reason why Broker Jones was not hired).

Third, commentators were concerned about steering—brokers who send borrowers to some lenders but not others in exchange for a fee. Lenders who pay a fee may not offer the best rates, thereby raising consumer costs.

Many brokers argue that they provide a consumer service by originating loans, that they do not make naked referrals, and that it is unfair to create requirements for them which do not also apply to mortgage lenders.

But if HUD has its way, several refinements may evolve.

- Brokers will have the right to originate mortgage loans.
- Referral fees related to specific transactions will be banned in most instances.
- Brokers will have to tell consumers that better loans may be available elsewhere.
- If brokers operate a computerized loan-origination system (CLO), then all lenders on the system must have equal access—no special favors for that certain lender who just happens to be a brokerage affiliate. Or the broker's cousin.

For borrowers, the rules for dealing with brokers who offer loans are the same as dealing with any other lenders. If a real estate broker can provide the best rate and terms, then there is no reason to go elsewhere. The catch, of course, is that borrowers will never know who offers the best possible rates without shopping around.

Also, it should be said that since real estate brokers commonly represent sellers, and since borrowers are typically buyers, the financing information given to a broker can be shown to a seller. Such disclosure can work two ways. If the borrower's finances are limited a seller will quickly understand that a higher price and a better deal are not possible from one particular buyer. If the buyer is well-heeled and has the capacity to pay more, then the seller may use such information to take a tougher stand if price or terms are still being negotiated.

In no case can a buyer/borrower be *required* to use a broker's loan system to obtain a property. Such a demand by a broker would raise serious questions involving such matters as steering, conflicts of interest, and licensure violations—topics most brokers strive mightily to avoid.

SECONDARY LENDERS: WHO THEY ARE
AND WHAT THEY DO

Anyone who has ever applied for a mortgage is familiar with primary lenders—local institutions such as S&Ls, mortgage bankers and commercial banks that make loans and collect monthly payments. Less well known are secondary lenders, multibillion-dollar organizations that play a key role in the mortgage financing system.

Suppose a local lender has $5 million available for mortgages. Fifty home buyers, each in need of a $100,000 loan, apply for financing and every loan application is approved. This is great news for the first fifty people, but what about future borrowers? Has the primary lender run out of money?

Fannie Mae was originally a governmental agency that was spun off to the private sector. It buys conventional, FHA, and VA mortgages as well as second trusts and adjustable rate mortgages. The publicly held organization maintains a loan portfolio which included mortgages worth $205 billion as of mid-1994. In addition, Fannie Mae had mortgage-backed securities worth $512 billion outstanding at the end of May 1994—securities that can be purchased and resold directly by investors.

Ginnie Mae, part of the Department of Housing and Urban Development (HUD), assembles and guarantees pools of FHA and VA mortgages. Investors may participate in such pools by purchasing *pass-through* certificates, on which they receive monthly payments for both interest and principal. As of May 1994, Ginnie Mae had guaranteed pass-through certificates worth $976 billion.

Freddie Mac is a part of the Federal Home Loan Bank Board, the regulatory agency that oversees federally chartered savings and loan associations. Freddie Mac purchases conventional, VA, and FHA loans that meet its standards and finances such purchases through the sale of mortgage-backed bonds to private investors. Freddie Mac made commitments to purchase mortgages worth more than $99 billion in the first five months of 1994.

In addition to the three major secondary lenders, there are smaller firms as well. The advantage of having a variety of players in the secondary market is that each is likely to have somewhat different loan standards. Local lenders can have more flexible loan policies than might otherwise be possible because a mortgage which does not conform to the requirements of one secondary lender may be acceptable to another.

While the sale and ownership of residential property is usually seen as a local matter, real estate financing is clearly within the stream of interstate commerce. The mortgage on a small house in Houston may well be owned by a pension fund in Boston, a situation that is plausible because secondary lenders have effectively created a national market for mortgage-backed securities and through those securities a market for mortgages themselves.

To have a national mortgage market investors must be able to buy, sell and trade standardized loan products, the value of which can be measured against alternative investments. The secondary lenders have created such products by developing guidelines that define which mortgages they will accept from local lenders.

To have an acceptable, or "conforming," loan which can be resold, primary lenders will tailor their lending practices to meet the standards established by secondary lenders. For instance, one guideline may suggest that no more than 28 percent of a borrower's gross monthly income can be devoted to mortgage principal payments, mortgage interest payments, taxes and insurance, what is known generally in the real estate industry as PITI. Such a guideline might then have a series of exceptions which allows local lenders some flexibility.

While there are major differences between secondary lenders—for example, one is private (Fannie Mae), one deals only with FHA and VA loans (Ginnie Mae) and only one has a major loan portfolio (Fannie Mae)—the national mortgage market collectively created by these secondary lenders has profoundly influenced the entire process of real estate financing. Here's why:

First, the existence of a national mortgage market allows money to readily move from capital surplus areas to regions and lenders that require additional funding. A national mortgage market prevents the "Balkanization" of the housing industry, a situation where mortgages can be available in one region or state but not others.

Second, the guidelines established by secondary lenders for conventional loans have proven to be in the public interest. Financial qualification standards, for example, protect borrowers, sellers, lenders and mortgage investors alike, since they assure that loans will be made only to financially able purchasers. In contrast, it is worth noting that so-called creative financing arrangements—in which similar guidelines are generally not employed—have resulted in significant numbers of foreclosures and, it can be surmised, substantial numbers of "house poor" homeowners, individuals who can afford to pay for little more than their mortgage.

Third, a national marketplace creates an element of liquidity, the ability to quickly convert mortgages to cash at a reasonable value. Without a national marketplace, a common ground to buy and sell standardized products, today's liquidity could not exist.

Fourth, a national mortgage marketplace allows local lenders to view their mortgage portfolio as a potential profit center, since loans may be regarded as a commodity to be bought, sold or held advantageously. Moreover, primary lenders can also reap profits by servicing the loans of others—collecting monthly payments for a fee, usually three-eighths of a percent of the remaining principal balance. The servicing business can be highly profitable and in some cases local lenders may offer loans at especially attractive rates to build up service portfolios.

HOW TO APPLY FOR FINANCING

As complex as the mortgage system may seem, its inconsistencies are largely superficial. Mortgage lending actually proceeds on a predictable basis and is governed by observable principles. By knowing the rules and understanding how the system works, buyers and sellers can develop both money-making and money-saving strategies.

Every real estate loan, regardless of the dollar amount involved, has traditionally required an appraisal and credit report ordered directly by the lender. In the case of larger homes—those costing $500,000 and up—lenders are likely to want two appraisals.

Lenders will also want the *original* sales agreement, including all contingencies and addenda. Note that the term "original" in this context means the final agreement signed and dated by both buyer and seller, not a copy.

By closing, lenders will want a professional inspection showing that the property is free and clear of termites and other wood-boring insects. Termite inspections are commonly ordered by purchasers and the inspection reports are then sent to the lender or presented at settlement, depending on lender requirements.

Another administrative chore concerns insurance. At or before settlement, borrowers must present an insurance policy which provides sufficient coverage to meet lender guidelines, commonly protection equal to at least the loan's value.

Most lenders use a basic application form developed jointly by the Federal National Mortgage Association (Fannie Mae) and the Federal Home Loan Mortgage Corporation (Freddie Mac). This form seeks information about the new property as well as the borrower's income, present housing costs and job situation as well as assets (cash, cars, etc.) and debts (mortgages, credit card balances, etc.).

The basic application form raises special issues that should concern borrowers. In particular:

- Lenders will want a full explanation if you've gone bankrupt or been foreclosed in the past seven years.
- If you're now a party to a lawsuit or have a judgment against you, lenders will want all details.
- If part of the down payment is borrowed, lenders will want to know how much, from whom, and under what conditions. Note that various loan programs often require purchasers to contribute 5 to 10 percent of the sale price *from their own funds.* Borrow too much for the down payment and you will be unable to qualify under certain programs.

Supplemental Information

The basic application should be seen as nothing more than a starting point in the information collection process. Given the presentation of certain information, the lender will seek to document each claim made by the prospective borrower.

First, lenders will ask for bank statements, cash management reports and similar documents dating back at least three months.

Second, lenders will want evidence that a deposit was made when the contract was ratified. The evidence sought at first is typically a receipt showing how much was paid and to whom, plus a copy of the check. Later, lenders will often require a copy of the cancelled check's front and back to show that it was actually cashed. Why? Because without a canceled check it's possible that no deposit was given or that the deposit was supplied by a third party.

Third, your current housing costs or mortgage situation will greatly interest lenders. With renters, lenders may speak to landlords or request rent checks from the past year, or both. For property owners, lenders will typically ask for canceled checks (originals, not copies) showing timely payments over the past 12 months plus a coupon or letter from the old lender showing a current balance.

Fourth, if you're receiving alimony, child support or separate maintenance, you need not declare such income to a lender. However, many borrowers report such income to qualify for the largest possible loans. Conversely, those who pay alimony, child support or separate maintenance must report payments since they represent debt. In a related matter, final divorce papers are often required to show who owns property, who doesn't, and who is responsible for given bills.

Fifth, if a gift is being used to purchase a new property, the lender will want an irrevocable gift letter from the donor to assure that the gift is not disguised debt. In some situations, lenders will go further and ask for evidence that the donor has the financial capacity to make a gift. Such evidence might include a deposit in the purchaser's account or a bank statement from the donor.

Sixth, if a current primary residence has been sold, the lender will want a settlement sheet from the sale presented *prior* to closing the loan. If the current property is not sold by closing, the current mortgage, taxes and insurance will be counted as debt by many underwriters, monthly expenses which can mean you won't qualify for a new loan. The logic of this approach is that if settlement on the current residence has not occurred by closing, it may never happen.

Seventh, if your current home is not sold but is being marketed, the lender will want a copy of a listing agreement with a broker to show that a good faith effort is being made to sell the property. Again, if the property has not been sold by closing, lenders will commonly view the old mortgage, tax bills and insurance costs as current expenses. Such expenses, in turn, will limit a homebuyer's ability to borrow.

Eighth, standardized application forms provide that prospective borrowers can add information which may influence the underwriting process. If you have income or debt from an unusual source, be prepared to provide appropriate documentation.

Ninth, if the property is part of a condominium, co-op or private unit development (PUD), lenders will want documentation such as by-laws, incorporation papers, budgets and letters from ownership associations showing the percentage of investor-owned units and insurance coverage.

Verifying Employment

While assets and debts are important, lenders also want to know how you earn a living.

For those who are employed, W-2 statements for the past two years plus pay stubs from the past 30 days typically represent adequate documentation, especially when the pay stubs show year-to-date income.

Individuals who expect a raise, or who receive bonuses or overtime on a consistent basis, should report such information to the lender.

For the self-employed, lenders will want tax returns for at least the past two years (in some situations, returns for a three-year period may be sought), a year-to-date profit and loss statement (if available and appropriate), a current balance sheet and a business credit report (again, if available and appropriate). Those individuals who work on commission should also provide all 1099 forms issued during the past two or three years.

For those who have been self-employed less than two years, lenders will look for business continuity. For instance, an accountant who moves from a firm to his own private practice will be viewed as having ongoing experience and stability. However, someone who opens a donut shop after ten years in the auto repair business may not meet underwriting standards—the new business activity is simply too recent to evaluate in terms of current and potential income.

Additional information will be required for those individuals who receive some or all of their income from either partnership or corporate interests.

In the case of partnerships, K-1 forms will be required. Such tax forms show the applicant's percentage of ownership as well as income and liabilities. However, full partnership returns (Form 1065) may not be available to lenders because other partners may not want their income disclosed. Most lenders will accept K-1 forms for the past two years as well as personal tax returns for the same period.

Corporate returns are important when an applicant holds a substantial ownership position, say 25 percent or more. Lenders will commonly seek Form 1120, coupled with personal tax returns for the past two years, when dealing with corporate owners.

Rental Properties

It's not unusual for applicants to own investment property, a subject which greatly interests lenders. Typically tax information found on Schedule E over a two-year period plus copies of current lease agreements will satisfy all information requirements.

Lenders and investors, however, are likely to view rental economics from radically different positions. To an owner, revenues are typically described in terms of income plus tax benefits less expenses. Lenders, however, are likely to allow only 75 percent of all rents as a credit. That revenue, less principal, interest, taxes and insurance, is considered income to most lenders. However, while only 75 percent of gross rentals are counted, no deduction is made for repairs. Once rental revenues are calculated using underwriting standards, depreciation is then *added back* to an applicant's overall income.

While the formula typically used by underwriters makes calculating rental income easy, it discriminates against properties with few repair costs. Conversely, properties that need extensive repairs benefit from common underwriting standards.

FULL DOCS VERSUS REDUCED PAPERWORK

It's clear from the previous discussion that a salaried worker who uses savings to buy a single-family house is likely to breeze through the application process with few paperwork or verification problems.

The self-employed, however, and those with extensive and complex income arrangements often face burdensome paperwork requirements. And unfortunately, the prospective borrowers most likely to encounter onerous paperwork demands are also the very people most likely to purchase expensive properties.

But whether individuals are buying small cottages or great mansions, there are strategies which can significantly reduce paperwork demands. In essence, the trick is to look for mortgage programs which offer not only attractive rates and terms, but also the fewest verification requirements.

Lenders are often willing to "trade" verification demands for larger down payments. If prospective borrowers put more equity into a property, the lender's risk is reduced and therefore the need for extensive paperwork declines.

In general terms, one might define mortgage programs within four basic verification categories:

Full Documentation.   Loans issued under full documentation guidelines require underwriters to verify virtually every fact and figure asserted by prospective borrowers.

Alternative Documentation.   Less rigorous than full docs, alternative docs require as much paperwork in many cases but less verification, a trade-off that can produce faster processing. For example, under some alternative documentation programs, if borrowers provide their three most recent *original* bank statements, lenders will not seek written verification of the account from a bank.

Low Documentation.   Under typical low doc programs, much paperwork is eliminated, especially for those who are self-employed or derive income from partnerships and corporations.

No Documentation.   Borrowers may have heard about "no doc" financing, but in absolute terms, such programs do not exist. All loan programs require some paperwork; happily, no doc programs require far less documentation than others. With no doc financing, lenders will require large down payments to offset risk and will often use credit report information to confirm borrower data rather than separate verifications from employers, lenders, banks, stock brokers, etc.

Pitfalls and Cautions

Through substitute documentation programs, borrowers can often avoid many hassles and complications. However, as good as substitute documentation programs may sound, there are five issues which should concern prospective borrowers.

First, there is no general agreement concerning how terms such as "alternative doc," "low doc" and "no doc" are defined. Different lenders have different definitions even for programs which seem to have the same description. In other words, the standards for one "low doc" mortgage may be entirely different from those of another "low doc" program.

Second, *even with reduced documentation, underwriting standards still apply.* For example, suppose Mr. Green needs $6,000 a month to qualify for a given loan. Suppose further that his monthly income is $5,000. Without an "exception" from an underwriter, he will not get the loan.

Third, low doc and no doc loans rely on borrower data rather than verified information, but now many lenders are requiring certified statements from borrowers declaring that the information supplied is correct and complete. There is no additional verification, just another piece of paper to use in the event of fraud or material misrepresentations.

Fourth, at a time when lenders of every stripe are reporting massive losses, no doc loans have become less common. No doc mortgages— loans where few facts are checked—suggest big fees and little work for lenders, a suggestion which is causing many lenders to back away from no doc financing.

Fifth, loans are complex transactions and it's entirely possible that some borrowers may encounter even more paperwork than the basic items we have listed. If additional verifications are required, make a point of getting needed information to the lender as quickly as possible to speed the application process.

QUICKIE APPLICATION PROGRAMS

In the past, lenders have been criticized for the lengthy and complex process borrowers faced when applying for loans. Now experience, competitive pressures, and the use of computer programs have caused lenders to drop many old paperwork requirements, especially in those cases where borrowers make large down payments.

One approach to reducing application hassles has been the development of pre-qualification programs. Pay a minimal fee, say $75, and a lender will review your finances before you buy a house and then make an actual loan commitment that's good for 60 to 90 days, subject to an adequate property appraisal and survey. Quickie pre-qualification programs can produce commitments in as little as three days.

A second approach is the instant loan. In this situation you apply for a loan, figures are run through the lender's computer, and in as little as 15 minutes you have a loan commitment, again subject to an adequate appraisal and survey.

Pre-qualification programs and quickie applications are typically available to borrowers willing to put down 10 to 20 percent of the purchase price. And while such applications programs are surely fast, there is no evidence that they always represent the best possible deals.

- Not all pre-qualification programs guarantee both rates and points. If rates are set but points can vary, then a true loan cost has not been locked in.
- Some pre-qualification programs are not loan commitments. Instead, they merely estimate your borrowing power.
- Some quickie loan application programs do make nearly instant loan commitments, but at rates and terms higher than those of other lenders. With such programs, borrowers trade speed for cost.
- Not only are some quickie loan programs more expensive than similar or identical programs offered by other lenders, they are often more expensive than *identical* programs offered by the same lender that require more time to process.

		Application Checklist			
Number	Requirement	Full Docs	Alt Docs	Low Docs	No Docs
1	Appraisal	YES	YES	YES	YES
2	Personal Credit Report	YES	YES	YES	YES
3	Ratified Final Sales Contract	YES	YES	YES	YES
4	Standard Application Form	YES	YES	YES	YES
5	Condo, PUD or Co-op Papers	YES	YES	YES	YES
6	Termite and Insurance Papers	YES	YES	YES	YES
	DEPOSITS				
7	Receipt for Deposit	YES	YES	ST	NO
8	Bank Statements (3 Months)	YES	YES	ST	NO
9	Stock and Bond Accounts	YES	YES	ST	NO
	MORTGAGES				
10	Current Mortgage Balance	YES	YES	ST	VC
11	Mortgage Payment Record	YES	YES	ST	VC
	IF DIVORCED				
12	Final Settlement (If Required)	YES	YES	YES	YES
	IF A GIFT IS PROVIDED				
13	Irrevocable Gift Letter	YES	YES	YES	NA
14	Evidence of Donor's Ability To Make Gift	YES	YES	ST	NA
15	Show Relationship, If Any	YES	YES	YES	NA
16	Donor's Name and Address	YES	YES	YES	YES
	IF CURRENT HOME MUST BE SOLD				
17	Evidence of Sale	YES	YES	YES	YES
18	Or, Copy of Current Listing	YES	YES	YES	YES

Number	Requirement	Full Docs	Alt Docs	Low Docs	No Docs
	IF EMPLOYED				
19	W-2 Forms (2 Years)	YES	YES	NO	NO
20	Pay Stubs (Last 30 Days)	YES	YES	NO	NO
21	Verification of Year-to-Date (YTD) Income	YES	YES	NO	NO
	IF SELF-EMPLOYED				
22	Business Credit Report	YES	YES	YES	ST
23	Income Tax Returns (2 or 3 Years)	YES	YES	NO	NO
24	Form 1099 for Commissions	YES	YES	NO	NO
25	YTD Profit & Loss Statement	YES	YES	NO	NO
26	Current Balance Sheet	YES	YES	NO	NO
	IF PARTNERSHIP				
27	Form K-1 (2 or 3 Years)	YES	YES	NA	NA
28	Partnership Return (If Available)	YES	YES	NA	NA
29	Personal Tax Return (2 or 3 Years)	YES	YES	NA	NA
	If Corporation				
30	Personal Return (2 or 3 Years)	YES	YES	NO	NO
31	Form 1120 (2 Years)	YES	YES	NO	NO
	IF RENTAL PROPERTY IS OWNED				
32	Lease and tax information	YES	YES	ST	ST

Notes: "ST" = Sometimes; "NA" = Not Applicable;
"VC" = Verify via Credit Report

- Some quickie loan programs guarantee attractive rates, but only if borrowers pay expensive lock-in fees. If you've paid a lock-in fee and then find a lower rate, you'll lose the fee if you switch programs. Conversely, paying a lock-in fee will at least assure that financing is in hand if nothing better is available.

WHAT LENDERS LOOK FOR

With all the information being supplied for a loan application you may well wonder how lenders are going to evaluate the material they receive. In essence, lenders will consider objective criteria such as income ratios and net worth as well as subjective issues that may not show up on paper, matters such as the potential of a borrower to bring in additional business. Here are the key items that lenders normally consider when reviewing a mortgage application:

Front and Back Ratios.   Ratios refer to the percentage of income used to pay various debts. Ask a loan officer "What are your ratios for a fixed-rate loan with 20 percent down?" and you may be given a short-hand figure such as "28/36." Here's what these numbers represent.

The "28" is a *front* ratio. To qualify under the lender's guidelines, no more than 28 percent of your income can be devoted to mortgage principal, mortgage interest, property taxes, and property insurance—what the lending industry calls "PITI."

The "36" is the *back* ratio. This figure means that under the lender's guidelines as much as 36 percent of your monthly income can be

---

What Ratios Do You Need?

1. What is your regular annual income from wages, self-employment, interest, dividends and other sources?_____
2. Divide the figure in item 1 by 12._____
3. What are your regular monthly payments for:
   Car Loans?_____
   Credit Cards?_____
   Personal Loans?_____
   Alimony, Separate Maintenance, and Child Support?_____
   Other Debt?_____
4. What are the total payments in item 3?_____
5. What are your monthly costs for principal, interest, taxes and insurance?_____

   To calculate your front ratio, divide item 5 by the monthly income shown in item 2._____

   To compute your back ratio, add item 4 to item 5. Divide this total by the monthly income shown in item 2._____

devoted to PITI plus other monthly debt payments for such items as credit card bills, auto loans, student loans, etc.

To figure your ratios, follow the same pattern as the Campbells. First, the Campbells took their $60,000 gross annual income (pre-tax) and divided by 12. This gave them a monthly income of $5,000.

Second, to find their front ratio they multiplied $5,000 by 28 percent. Using this figure they have $1,400 a month available under lender guidelines for principal, interest, taxes and insurance.

Different lenders use different guidelines and different programs also use different guidelines. Individual lenders are likely to have many guidelines, depending on the loan product you want. For example, fixed-rate loans and ARMs are each likely to have different guidelines.

To make matters even more complex, it's entirely possible that lenders will have different ratios for one loan. They may have 28/36 ratios for those making a 10 percent down payment, but 33/38 for those who put down 20 percent. With federal programs, FHA qualification standards are based on 29/41 ratios while loans made to VA borrowers are qualified with 41/41 ratios.

Secondary Income.   The wages that many people earn do not represent their entire income. Many individuals have secondary incomes from part-time jobs, dividends, trusts, etc. As long as such income is regular and continuing, lenders are likely to regard it as part of a person's income base.

Debt.   In addition to housing costs, most of us have other continuing obligations such as auto payments, alimony, credit card debt or child support. Lenders are likely to set a ceiling here, saying perhaps that no more than 36 percent of an individual's gross monthly income may be set aside for ongoing expenses. To fall within the guidelines, it may be necessary for an applicant to reduce credit card bills or finish monthly auto payments ahead of schedule.

Employment.   Steady employment is a major concern of all lenders. By "steady," lenders do not mean holding a single job for forty years. Job changes are considered normal and healthy as long as they provide a consistent pattern of upward income growth. Changing jobs and moving up the career ladder are normal events and lenders typically will give credit for experience in the same field. Thus someone who changes from the accounting business to ice cream retailing is held in less favor than someone who changes jobs within either accounting or retailing.

Lenders are also concerned about job obsolescence and self-employment. In the first case, a meteoric rise to the top of the buggy whip industry, unlike a good career in computers, medicine or whatever, is not likely to enthrall many lenders. In the second case, self-employment raises questions about income regularity and size. Most lenders require tax returns for at least two years before they will consider an application from a self-employed individual.

Net Worth.   One index that lenders value is a strong *net worth*—that is, the value of assets over liabilities. By definition, borrowers who have accumulated extensive holdings of property, stock, cash and other resources while holding down their debts have demonstrated a basic credit-worthiness.

Credit History.   Having a sound income is of little benefit to a lender if a borrower's funds are not used to meet credit obligations. A lender will want a credit report showing that a borrower has repaid monthly debts on a timely and regular basis.

While these categories describe general areas of interest to lenders, they do not discuss exceptions. The reality is that many borrowers fail to meet one or more criteria, yet obtain financing anyway. This happens because lending is as much art as science.

An individual may not earn enough to meet a lender's income-ratio requirement but that same person may be a physician completing a residency or a couple with one spouse returning to the work force. On paper such individuals may not qualify for financing but in the real world they are likely to have rising incomes which lenders cannot ignore.

Despite these guidelines, it should be understood that lending criteria change, sometimes overnight.

Suppose you apply for a loan when interest rates are 9 percent and during the few weeks when the lender is processing your application rates rise to 10 percent. While your income may have allowed you to

---

Loan ABCs

If you don't have the best credit in the world, you may hear lenders refer to "A paper," "B paper," "C paper" and sometimes even "D paper."

There are no universally-accepted definitions of these expressions, but in rough terms here is what they mean:

A paper. A loan application by someone with stable employment, a good income, excellent credit, an acceptable downpayment, and a property which appraises for the full sales value. Such applications, called "cookie cutter" deals because they instantly meet general standards, result in speedy loans and are readily sold in the secondary market.

B paper. Situations where the loan applicant has a blemish or two, such as late credit card payments or too much debt. Such applications are marginally harder to process but usually lead to financing.

C paper. A "financially impaired" applicant, someone with miserable credit, little income or a recent bankruptcy. While poor credit and minimal income can be a problem, the same is not always true about a bankruptcy. Conventional financing is clearly available to those who have been bankrupt, depending on the facts and circumstances involved.

D paper. A application from an individual with rotten credit, no income, and no prospects to do better. A very unlikely loan candidate, but if financing is available it will be at sky-high rates.

---

borrow $100,000 when rates were at 9 percent, a higher interest level will cut your ability to borrow. It may be that at the higher rate a lender will lend only $91,685—a big enough difference to kill many deals.

EVOLVING LENDER STANDARDS

The loan guidelines established by Fannie Mae and Freddie Mac are not absolute. Exceptions are permitted, but many local lenders prefer to interpret guidelines with literal precision, much to the detriment of borrowers.

The reason local lenders are often so hardnosed is that if loans purchased in the secondary market are later found to violate general guidelines, the local lender can be forced to buy back the offending mortgage. Sticking to basics, not taking a chance, limits lender risk.

A major problem with lender guidelines is that as society evolves, so do financial considerations. The nation is no longer composed—if it ever was—of nuclear families with a working Dad, a homemaker Mom, and two adorable children. The result is that guidelines are evolving to meet newly-emerging conditions.

- As part of their effort to meet Community Reinvestment Act standards, lenders may allow liberal standards for certain borrowers. As an example, instead of requiring 5 percent down, a buyer might put up 3 percent and the lender can then supply the additional 2 percent.
- Related persons who have lived together for at least a year can pool funds to buy property.
- The value of sweat equity—up to 2 percent of the purchase price—can be allowed in certain community lending programs.
- Even though a neighborhood has a fair or poor rating, according to Freddie Mac, mortgages can still be made as long as a viable housing market exists.
- Because minority and low-income communities are often underserved by lenders, many individuals do not have checking or savings accounts. They instead have loose cash, money which has traditionally been banned from use as a downpayment or for closing costs. Lenders may now allow cash-on-hand, says Fannie Mae, "if the borrower customarily uses cash for expenses and that usage is consistent with the borrower's profile and financial status." Freddie Mac says cash is acceptable, as long as the source can be verified.
- Seasonal income can count, as long as the same work has been done for the past two years and is likely to continue.
- With regard to credit ratings, Fannie Mae states that, "we emphasize that excellent credit does not have to be a perfect or spotless credit record since certain circumstances that are beyond a borrower's control can affect his or her intent to have excellent credit." "Generally," Fannie Mae says later, "a history that consists of a minor, isolated instance of poor credit or a late payment can be considered as meeting the intent of excellent credit—as long as it is satisfactorily explained and the borrower has other credit accounts with excellent payment records."

- Alternative credit references may be developed by showing the payment of utility bills, telephone charges, and rental costs.

WHAT ARE THE LENDER'S POLICIES?

Few people search for a new car by visiting only one automobile dealer and the same concept holds true for mortgage financing: to get the best deal one must shop around. This is an enormously useful activity because the mere process of speaking to mortgage loan officers, real estate brokers and others is both educational and potentially profitable.

To market their product—the rental of money—lenders disseminate vast amounts of information through advertising, direct public contacts, advisories to the real estate community and general press coverage. While the availability of information should certainly be regarded as beneficial to the general public, the sheer volume of data is often difficult to absorb or fully analyze. Not only is there a lot of information but it is forever in flux—today's interest rates and terms at fifty different community lenders can easily change by tomorrow.

The information problem is compounded by the issue of imprecise definitions. What, for example, is an *adjustable rate mortgage* (ARM)? Basically it is a mortgage in which the lender has the right to change the rate of interest in accordance with a specific index. But the number of ARM formats, each with its own distinctions, is virtually endless.

Not all loans, even those with identical labels, have identical terms and the differences can be financially significant. As an example, Fannie Mae has defined several standard—"conforming"—ARM formats but the huge secondary lender has also purchased at least 125 non-standard mortgage products.

Information on new financing is available from loan officers at S&Ls, commercial banks, mortgage bankers, credit unions and other lenders as well as local real estate brokers, who are usually familiar with current market information.

Have a notebook with a separate page for each lender contact and record the phone numbers and names of each loan officer with whom you speak for future reference. While some information will remain current, some will change. If you are in the market for financing over several months it will be necessary to check with lenders on a regular basis, say once every week or two, to keep current.

"Keeping current" is a relative term. Checking every week or two may be desirable while looking for property, but once a buying decision has been made it then pays to check rates even more frequently. The reason is that rates for many loan products change daily. While daily changes tend to be relatively small, the differences seen over several days can be large enough to make a deal easier. Or to kill it.

Questions to Ask Loan Officers:

Are you making new mortgage loans? If not, can you recommend any local lenders who are now active?

What is your current rate of interest for conventional financing—that is, a loan for 80 percent of the purchase price on the property?

In general terms, given an annual income of so many dollars, how much mortgage can I afford? Tell the loan officer that you are looking for a general figure only and that you understand that individuals can be qualified only after the lender has had a chance to review written applications.

What front and back ratios does the lender use for fixed-rate financing? For ARMs? For deals with 5 percent down? For deals with 10 percent down? For deals with 20 percent down? For deals with 25 or 30 percent down?

Is the rate quoted the nominal level of interest or the annual percent rate (APR)? Use the APR, a figure which tends to be higher because of compounding, as a standard when comparing rates.

Does the APR figure include the value of points? Note that in those cases where the expense of points is divided between buyers and sellers, the effective loan cost to purchasers should be calculated only on the basis of points actually paid.

Does the lender offer FHA or VA financing? Graduated payment loans? Growing Equity Mortgages (GEMs)? Adjustable rate mortgages? Other formats?

As a matter of policy, does the lender reserve the right to change the rate of interest between the time the loan application is received and the date of settlement? Are the rates locked in or does the lender reserve the right to change the rate of interest between the time a loan is approved and the date of settlement? Some lenders closely follow the market, while others guarantee that the rate quoted at the time of application or approval will be in effect at settlement. There are lenders who also have a limiting policy; that is, the rate of interest will be no higher than the rate established at the time the application was made or approved. If the market rate drops, so does the interest level on your loan but in no case does it go higher.

Is there a prepayment penalty if the loan is repaid early? Is the lender currently enforcing prepayment clauses?

Is the loan assumable? Loans today are either not assumable or assumable only by borrowers who, in the lender's eyes, are deemed "qualified." Older FHA and VA loans are often assumable by any purchaser and at little cost.

Does the lender offer *private mortgage insurance* (MI)? This is a form of insurance in which a third party guarantees a portion of the loan's repayment to the lender. This guarantee plus the property's equity value and the borrower's down payment reduce the lender's risk and for this reason a smaller down payment, say 5 to 15 percent, will be acceptable to the lender. For its part in the transaction, the private mortgage insurer is paid a fee by the borrower.

Will the lender *escrow* money—hold money in trust—to assure payments for property taxes, MI fees or other liabilities? Escrow funds must be paid at settlement and represent an additional cash expense to borrowers. Lenders commonly escrow money to assure the payment of local property taxes, a claim which takes precedence over any mortgage obligations. Questions to ask about escrow accounts: What rate of interest is paid on such funds? When are escrowed monies refunded?

What fees are required by the lender? For example, what is the cost of a mortgage loan application and is all or part of the money returned if the application is not accepted? In addition to an appraisal, which is required for virtually all mortgage loans, will the lender need a property survey or photos? If buying a condo or co-op, will the lender require a legal review? If so, at what cost?

These questions concern lender policies and they are important because different lenders approach loan applications independently. The policies of one lender may make you ineligible for financing, while those of another may allow you to borrow far more than you need.

Many borrowers feel somewhat uncomfortable about asking direct questions of a lender, but the reality is that real estate financing is a business deal and direct questions must be asked to get the best terms. If asking tough questions is uncomfortable consider the alternative: higher mortgage payments for the next 15, 20 or 30 years.

3
Financing and Ownership

When looking at real estate we often associate a form of property with a type of ownership. Townhouses, for instance, are frequently seen as condominiums when they can be cooperative units or part of a planned unit development (PUD).

For lenders, and consequently for owners, buyers and investors, ownership is a central financial issue. It is entirely possible to have two identical apartments in two identical buildings in a single city, each worth $100,000, yet because one is a condominium and the other a co-op, the ability to readily finance or refinance each property will vary dramatically. Different forms of property ownership mean more or less risk for lenders and thus a greater or lesser willingness to lend.

The ownership of real estate may be compared to a shopping basket of rights and the biggest shopping basket is associated with the outright possession of property, real estate held in *fee simple* ownership, or *severalty*. Basic rights associated with fee simple ownership include:

- You can sell your property to anyone at any time.
- You have the right to finance your property in any manner you choose, refinance it at any time or pay off all liens and own the property free and clear.
- You pay property taxes directly. If a neighbor does not pay his or her taxes there is no possibility that your property will be foreclosed.
- You can rent all of your property or you can rent a part of it.

- You can paint the front door cherry red and your neighbors will have no right to complain (though they do have a First Amendment right to snicker).
- You can sell individual rights, such as mineral rights or a right-of-way.
- You can have pets or children or both.

What you can't do is violate *zoning codes,* public policies established for the benefit of the general community. If you live in a suburban area, for example, you may own the backyard outright but you can't turn it into a shooting gallery.

Fee simple ownership does not necessarily require that only one person holds title. Fee simple ownership, as well as other ownership interests, may be held by several people or by entities such as partnerships or corporations. Ownership groupings can include:

- Lone individuals.
- Husbands and wives as *tenants by the entirety,* a form of ownership reserved exclusively for married couples. With this form of ownership there is an automatic right of survivorship; that is, with the death of one spouse title to the property automatically passes to the other.
- Unmarried individuals. There are times when unmarried individuals wish to own property with a right of survivorship and they can do so in many states by establishing a *joint tenancy with a right of survivorship.* In the event of death, title to the property can pass automatically to the surviving owner.
- General owners. A *tenancy in common* can be formed in those cases where joint ownership is merely a business deal. Each owner has an undivided interest in the property which can be sold, exchanged or willed. There is no automatic right of survivorship.
- Entities. Property rights can not only be held by people but by entities as well. Real estate can be owned by partnerships, corporations and trusts. Thus it is entirely possible to have 20 people or 20,000 people through a single corporation owning real estate on a fee simple basis.

Additionally, an endless number of ownership combinations—corporations and individuals, partnerships and trusts, trusts and corporations, etc.—can join together to form *syndicates* organized to buy, sell and manage real estate generally, and *joint ventures* established for a specific real estate deal such as the construction of a particular shopping mall or the ownership of an apartment complex.

Holding title is a potentially complex matter made even more complicated by the fact that ownership rules vary in each jurisdiction. Because holding title to real estate is complex, and because real estate ownership is related to a variety of other matters such as taxes and estates, consult with an attorney about any title questions you may have.

For example, what happens if husband and wife die simultaneously in a car crash? Who gets the property if there are no children? The husband's relatives? The wife's relatives? The state? A correctly drawn will is necessary to properly resolve such potential issues which, as odd as they may seem, do occur. Speak to your lawyer for complete information regarding wills.

While fee simple ownership is the ultimate form of real estate possession because it gives owners the largest number of rights, it is not the only way to own property. You can also possess property through other ownership formats: condominiums, PUDs, cooperatives and timesharing—forms of ownership with unique characteristics and thus separate financing requirements.

CONDOS, PUDs AND CO-OPS

In the 1960s few people had ever heard of condominiums and almost nobody owned one. Today the situation is different. Condos are everywhere and what had once been a wrinkle in the marketplace is now an accepted and popular alternative to fee simple ownership.

What is condominium ownership and what makes condos unique in the eyes of a lender? Condos have these characteristics:

- Condo ownership means that you possess a specific unit within the condominium project plus an interest in the common areas—

possibly the land under the condo, the pool, the hallways, etc. You may also have an interest in certain limited common elements such as a balcony or patio. Limited common elements are owned by the condominium association but their use is reserved exclusively for a particular unit owner.

- There is a separate recorded deed for each condo unit.
- Condo units are bought, sold, taxed, financed and refinanced independently. This is important to lenders because the failure of one condo owner to make mortgage payments will not cause the foreclosure of other units.
- All unit owners are voting members of the condominium association, often called the "council of unit owners," and may be elected to the association's board of directors.
- The condo association as well as all common costs are funded by a monthly condo fee levied against each owner. Failure to pay this fee can result in foreclosure.

While a condo owner does have exclusive title to and possession of a given unit, condos do not offer the same shopping basket of rights as sole ownership. To assure the comfort and safety of all owners, there must be certain rules, understandings, compromises and financial allocations which govern the condominium regime, information contained in these key documents:

Declaration.   Describes the condo and how it works, including such matters as the location of units and the definition of common areas. Shows how voting will be conducted, usually one unit/one vote or votes based on the square footage of each unit—the bigger the unit the bigger the vote. Once in place matters established in the declaration are almost impossible to change. The declaration is usually packaged with an engineering report, paid for by the developer, which describes the physical characteristics of the improvements being sold.

By-Laws.   Outline the condo's general management; for example, how often the board of directors is required to meet. By-laws can usually be changed by majority vote.

Rules and Regulations.   Directives established by the board of directors, items such as how long the pool will be open and how much the monthly condo fee will be increased next year.

Budgets.   A condo budget is developed each year to show projected expenditures based on past projections and experience. Included in the budget is a reserve fund, money set aside for future capital needs such as the repair of a cracked pool or the replacement of a new roof.

Public Offering Statement.   When a condo is first offered for sale to the public the developer must provide a public offering statement, a lengthy document which usually includes the declaration, by-laws, a projected budget, the terms of any maintenance or management agreements and an engineer's report describing the project's condition and estimating future repair and replacement requirements.

Even though condo units are owned and financed independently, lenders generally view condos as representing more risk than fee simple ownership. You may be a wonderful person and well entitled to a mortgage but what about other condo members? Will a lender be able to get full value for your unit at a foreclosure if the condo association decides to save money and defers needed maintenance? What happens if a large portion of owners rent out their units? Will investors want to allocate association money for elective expenses such as fixing up the tennis courts or redecorating the lobby? If there is a large portion of investor/owners, is the lender then making a loan for residential or investment property? Investments represent more risk to the lender than owner-occupied units.

Investment condos greatly trouble lenders. Many won't make investor condo loans if other investors already own 30 percent or more of the units in a given project. A related policy provides that when investors own many units, owner-occupant financing is available only when buyers put down 25 percent of the entire purchase price.

If a project has too many investors, it may be impossible to sell your unit to an investor if new financing is unavailable. If there are too many investors, the pool of potential owner-occupants may be limited by the 25 percent down policy.

By any standard, these lender policies create difficulties for owner-occupants who merely want to finance or refinance their units, but who live in projects which have attracted investor interest. These policies may also complicate refinancing for those who live in condos and then decide to move elsewhere and rent their old units. Refinancing in such situations may not be available.

If you buy a condo (or a PUD or a co-op, for that matter), in the lender's eyes you will have fewer dollars to support a mortgage.

Suppose you can afford monthly mortgage payments of $800 for a single-family house. At 9 percent interest that $800 can underwrite a 30-year conventional mortgage for $99,425. But if you buy a condo there may be a monthly condo fee which is a lien against the property. If the condo fee is $100, lenders might figure that you can only set aside $700 a month for mortgage interest and principal. In turn, $700 will only underwrite a 30-year, 9 percent mortgage worth $86,997.

Condos also present another dilemma for lenders: all those documents. Is there something in the by-laws or rules that will reduce the lender's security? The only way to find out is to have the papers reviewed by the lender's attorney—an additional loan application cost.

New condo buyers can generally get financing through the lender who financed the project's construction. Since the lender is familiar with the project there is little if any need for a new review of the condo papers.

Resale unit buyers can eliminate the documents problem by talking to lenders who previously financed units at the project. Such lenders have already reviewed the basic papers, so there is no need for an additional review. Real estate brokers and condo association officers can name those lenders who have made loans at the project.

All forms of financing can be used to finance condos but borrowers may find that processing is more complex than with fee simple properties. Get a list of lenders who already have made loans to unit owners since they will be familiar with the property, but don't hesitate to contact other lenders who may offer better terms and rates.

The additional cost of an application for a *new* lender must be viewed in context. If it costs an extra $100 to process a loan but you can save one-fourth of a percent interest, it pays to spend the additional $100 to get financing from a new lender. With a 30-year, $50,000 loan, the difference between a 9 percent rate and a rate at 9.25 percent is $9.03 per month, a difference which means that the $100 extra fee will be saved within a year.

A second type of ownership is a *planned unit development*, or PUD, a cross between condo and fee simple ownership with these characteristics:

- With a PUD you may own a townhouse, condo or single-family home.
- You and the other project members belong to an owners' association that takes care of mutual needs such as the mowing of common areas, snow removal, pool management, etc.
- PUD units are taxed and financed separately.
- Since PUDs are owned separately they have separate utility meters.
- The level of financial risk represented by a PUD unit is usually equated with that of a condo.

PUDs have proven popular in many suburban areas because they often combine planned growth with a variety of housing styles. Some PUDs are actually entire "new communities" where the owner's association is nearly the equivalent of a town government. Other PUD projects are quite modest. For instance, one stand of PUD townhouses consists of only 11 units, and the sole common activities of the owners' association are snow removal and lawn cutting. The monthly PUD fee is just $5.

Co-ops, a third form of ownership, are generally perceived as a far more restrictive form of possession than fee simple, condo or PUD ownership. If you own an interest in a co-op you do not own real estate directly. Instead, you own stock in a corporation and that corporation owns the entire project. In addition to stock, you also have an exclusive right to the use of a particular unit as well as a right to use all common facilities.

Because it is an organization rather than an individual which actually owns the property, the co-op has great power over the project's day-to day operations.

A co-op—much like a selective country club—has the right to assure that new members are compatible with current owners. New buyers must be approved by the co-op board, a process that can be tinged with highly subjective criteria. Thus to sell a co-op one must not only find a purchaser who is ready, willing and able to buy the property but one who is also acceptable to the co-op. Conceivably, if no buyer is acceptable to the co-op, one's interest in a co-op will not be marketable. Co-ops also have these unique features:

- The sources of authority in a co-op include the articles of incorporation of the cooperative association, the association by-laws and the house rules. These documents should be reviewed by prospective buyers to determine how the co-op is organized.
- Co-op projects are financed with an underlying, or blanket, mortgage. For instance, a single project may be built with 200 units and financed with a $10 million mortgage. Assuming all units were the same size, each unit will then have a pro rata mortgage obligation of $50,000. If the underlying mortgage is not paid the entire project can be in default, in which case all units may be foreclosed.
- Co-op units are not taxed individually. The co-op project, since it is a single corporate entity, receives a single property tax bill. If this bill is not paid, the entire co-op is in default and all units can be foreclosed.
- Because co-op ownership is in the form of stock, co-op buyers and sellers may be able to avoid property transfer taxes when they buy or sell units.
- If the co-op conforms with IRS regulations, deductions for mortgage interest and property taxes may be passed through to individual unit owners.

In terms of financing, lenders—except for those in the New York area where co-ops are widely accepted—have not been rushing to make resale co-op loans. Here's why:

If you are a lender and someone applies for a condo or PUD loan, it is clear that a definable property will be pledged as security for the mortgage. The actions of other unit owners, such as the non-payment of taxes, will rarely, if ever, affect the unit you finance.

With a co-op the situation is different. If 10 percent, or whatever number, of the co-op members do not pay their taxes, then ownership of the entire project is threatened. Since a lender has no right to check the credit of other unit owners, there is no way of knowing the overall financial condition of the shareholders as a group—an important consideration, since the actions of other owners can have a direct bearing on the borrower's interest. Moreover, the borrower is pledging a stock certificate rather than property as a security for the loan, a certificate bound to the fortunes of the entire corporation.

Co-ops also present interesting financial questions when re-sold.

Suppose you buy a unit when a building is first erected or converted to co-op status. Your unit costs $55,000 and of that amount $50,000 is represented by the underlying mortgage. Five years later your unit is worth $85,000 and you want to sell your interest. What do you do about financing? Since the underlying mortgage is for all the units at the project, your buyer cannot simply get a new first trust.

One approach is to have the buyer assume the unit's underlying mortgage and to then pay the difference between the underlying mortgage and the sales price in cash. A second choice is for you to become a lender, to *take back* some financing above the value represented by the underlying mortgage. However, if you take back financing from a buyer, where will you get the cash to buy a new residence for yourself?

While buying for cash and seller take-backs represent traditional approaches to co-op refinancing, new lending practices have made buying and selling co-ops far easier than in the past.

So-called "share" financing, essentially a second mortgage option for co-ops, is now available. If a unit is worth $100,000 and the underlying mortgage has a $60,000 balance per unit, then with a $20,000 share loan 80 percent financing is available; a $30,000 share loan will give 90 percent coverage. In the case of loans with coverage over 80 percent, be aware that such loans require mortgage insurance and that such financing may not be available outside large metropolitan areas.

Share loans are attractive because lenders can sell them to investors in the secondary market, something that was impossible several years ago. For information, write to the NCB Savings Bank, SFB, 1401 Eye St. NW, Washington, D.C. 20009. The phone number is (202) 336-7700.

Another approach to co-op financing has been through the use of so-called recognition agreements. With recognition financing, ownership documents are assigned to lenders who then have certain rights in the event borrowers default or the unit is sold. Check to see if a co-op in which you are interested has recognition agreements.

Lastly, borrowers might ask about the FHA 203(n) program, which can be used to insure co-op loans for individual units. This program is so obscure, and so complex, that there is not one known example of an individual who has obtained financing under this program in recent years. Still, it's on the books.

Because of their corporate nature, condos, PUDs and co-ops raise a variety of questions that in many cases would not be asked when buying or financing fee simple real estate.

Critical Issues to Review:

What is being sold? In some cases, certain parts of the property, such as pools or underground parking spaces, have been retained by developers and the result is that these facilities are available only at extra cost.

What is the current condo fee? Condo fees are subject to change and normally go up over time. Look at past budgets and see if there have been radical fee increases from year to year. If so, it may be that the budget is not well planned.

What is the current co-op fee? Note that the co-op fee will include a payment for the underlying mortgage. With a condo or PUD unit, monthly fees and mortgage payments are paid separately.

If you are considering a new project, how was the condo, PUD or co-op fee estimated? What other projects has the developer completed? Visit past projects and speak to unit owners there. Has the developer made a good-faith effort to keep all promises? Has all promised work been completed? What would the unit owners do differently?

Are any major capital repairs expected within the next two years? If so, are adequate reserves being built up to handle repair costs? Be aware that public-offering statements contain a wealth of information regarding potential repairs. For instance, an engineer's report may say that unit air-conditioning systems have a projected life of 15 years. If the building is 12 years old you can expect to make replacements fairly soon.

To cite another example, a public-offering statement may show that a roof has a life expectancy of 20 years and the building is 23 years old. In such cases the developer has honestly and openly declared where a potential cost may be found. In the event of a claim against the developer because of roof leaks, the developer can justly say that the problem had been disclosed to purchasers and that the units were bought by informed buyers. The moral: It pays to read condo, co-op and PUD documents closely.

Have reserves been set aside? Check the budget to assure that reserves are being collected for future repairs and improvements. The alternative to reserves are special assessments, possibly huge, budget-wrecking fees charged to each unit owner when an emergency repair must be funded. Failure to pay a special assessment can result in foreclosure.

Has there been a special assessment in the past two years or are any expected within the next two years? If you are a buyer and a large special assessment looms in the near future you should adjust any purchase offer downward.

How are utility bills paid? In many projects utility costs are included in the fee. The problem with paying utilities as a group is that individual unit owners are not directly responsible for their gas and electric costs, and utility expenses at such projects tend to be far higher than at condos or co-ops with separate meters. Also, it invariably happens that while you are willing to conserve fuel, a neighbor runs a sauna or model steel smelter twenty-four hours a day. Resolve the problem before it develops by avoiding projects without separate meters.

How large is the unit? The size of a unit is generally expressed in terms of square feet but the definition of a unit may vary. Some developers measure from the middle of one common wall to the middle of the next common wall, while others measure wall to wall. Some developers include balconies and patios in their calculations.

What is standard? Are the appliances in the model the ones being sold with the unit or are they extra-cost options? What about carpets, tiles, kitchen floors, and cabinets? Do they come with the unit or are they extra-cost options? Items sold with the unit are items which will not have to be bought or upgraded later.

How much parking is available? Are spaces assigned? Do you pay extra for parking?

If you are buying a co-op unit, is the sale contingent on the board's approval? If so, on what criteria is approval based?

Are there any new lawsuits or judgments currently outstanding against the condo association or co-op? If so, what is your potential responsibility as an owner?

Are there now or have there been any lawsuits by the condo association, co-op, PUD or individual owners against the developer? Suits can arise for many reasons, not all of them justified, but in many cases they concern allegations of incomplete work, which should be of interest to prospective borrowers because they may require special assessments if not settled.

Is there any alteration or improvement to the unit which violates the condo declaration, master deed, by-laws, rules, regulations or insurance coverage? Is there any alteration or improvement that violates the co-op's rules, regulations or insurance coverage?

Are there any outstanding building or health code violations against either the unit or the project? In particular, ask whether pools have been shut down for health code violations.

Is the unit now leased? If so, what are the lease terms? *Leases remain in effect even when ownership changes, unless the lease provides otherwise.* If the property is in an area governed by rent control, does the tenant have an automatic right of first refusal to purchase the property? Consult with an attorney when buying leased property.

Are many units rented? Are large blocks of units owned by investors? This can be a serious problem, since resident owners may be more willing to make repairs and improvements than non-resident investors. Also, lenders may not be overjoyed by the prospect of making a loan in projects with a large portion of investors, a factor that may reduce resale values.

Is the project on a land lease? With a land lease the ground under the project is leased for a given term, perhaps 75 or 100 years. At the end of that period title to the improvements on the property—the entire project— reverts back to the owners of the land lease. With land leases, the land owners may typically renew or not renew at their option. In all cases, the unit owners—land tenants—face the possibility of new costs and the loss of their lease and thus their unit.

A land lease may be attractive initially because acquisition costs are reduced—you are buying a unit but not the ground under it. The problem is that as time goes by there is less and less incentive to maintain the project. After all, why repair the roof ten years before the reversion date? Also, a land lease is much like an apartment rental. When the rental period ends, not only may you be required to leave but you will have no equity in the property.

Much can also be learned about condos, co-ops and PUDs by speaking with past and current presidents and treasurers of owner associations. Also, why not speak to prospective neighbors? They will certainly have an interest in meeting a potential owner and it's a good opportunity to evaluate the project on an informal basis.

TIMESHARING

Few of us vacation year-round so why own or pay for resort property 52 weeks a year or hassle with ever-increasing resort rental costs?

That basic question is behind the large and growing "timesharing" concept, an idea which involves some 1,000 projects and one million owners nationwide.

Until recently most property was sold on a fee simple basis; you bought a home or vacation property and owned it outright. Within the limits of zoning and public safety you can rent it or keep a dog the size of a heifer and answer to no one about your taste or style.

As choice locations in both urban and resort areas grew in value, condominiums increasingly replaced fee simple ownership. While people paid more per square foot for condo units than for fee simple property, condos had fewer square feet and thus cost less per unit.

One result was that condos made the ownership of real estate more affordable for buyers who were otherwise unable to purchase. Higher prices per square foot also generate more dollars per project to developers, an economic factor that should not be overlooked.

Timesharing goes a step further. A timeshare project is not only a condo, it is a condo where multiple owners have access to a given living space, albeit at different times. With the timeshare concept, what you get is the use of a furnished condo unit for a specific period of time, say the first week of February in Miami or the second week in December in Aspen. Units are available year-round, however, so that prices for timeshares in a single project can vary extensively.

The timeshare concept raises four central questions: What are you buying? How do you pay for it? What happens if you can't use your unit? Are timeshare units a good investment?

Timeshare units are sold in two formats. Many projects sell units on a fee simple basis—that is, the full ownership of a condominium interest. These units may represent a recorded, legal interest that, within the condo's rules, can be sold, rented, traded or willed.

Timeshare units are also marketed on a *right-to-use* basis, where purchasers are not actually buying real estate. Instead, they receive one of three types of right-to-use leases, including *club memberships,* which allow for the use of facilities but are not generally easy to re-sell, *vacation leases* that can be sold or rented, and *vacation licenses,* which cannot be sold but typically give access to hotel facilities. Right-to-use programs generally have a set time frame, say 12 to 40 years, after which the unit reverts back to the developer.

If you're interested in purchasing a timeshare unit don't expect to get a mortgage from your nearby friendly lender. Since 1980, lenders have been able to make loans for timeshare purchases, but usually as unsecured (personal) consumer credit loans.

The catch with funding a timeshare purchase with a personal loan is this: mortgage interest is usually tax deductible, interest on personal loans is no longer deductible.

A second catch concerns rates. Mortgages are generally viewed as among the most safe and secure loans that can be made. Personal loans are less secure and therefore rates are higher. Combine higher rates with a lack of write-offs and the true cost of such financing is substantially greater than a home loan.

For instance, if someone has a 9-percent mortgage and their combined federal and state tax rate is 33 percent, for each $100 they spend on mortgage interest, their tax bill declines by $33. Viewed another way, their true interest rate is 6.7 percent and the true out-of-pocket cost is $67.00.

With a personal loan the numbers work differently. First, the rate is likely to be higher than interest levels associated with mortgages, perhaps 12 or 13 percent rather than 9 percent. Second, pay $100 for personal interest and there is no deduction.

For the borrower who pays state and federal taxes equal to 33 percent of his income, he actually must earn $149.25 to pay a personal interest bill of $100 ($149.25 less 33 percent = $100.00). In this scenario, the true interest rate for a personal loan is 14 percent and the true cost is $149.25—twice the effective amount paid for a deductible mortgage.

According to Charles R. Wolfe of Gaithersburg, Maryland, a consultant to timeshare projects nationwide, most timeshare purchases are paid for this way: The developer first finances the entire project through a commercial lender. Individual purchasers, in turn, put down 10 to 20 percent of the cost of their units in cash and the balance is then financed by the developer. The interest rate for such financing, according to Wolfe, is usually at a slightly higher level than currently available second trusts.

In many cases, timeshare units are purchased on an *installment loan* or *land contract* basis; that is, ownership in the property is not conveyed until all or most of the loan has been paid. Conceivably, if a single payment is missed the loan can be in default but most developers, according to industry sources, have a liberal late payment policy.

The "advantage" of the installment loan system, at least to developers, is that lengthy foreclosure procedures are avoided. This is necessary because a single timeshare project may encompass thousands of interval units, each with a relatively small mortgage balance. For instance, a project with 50 units can sell 2,500 intervals (50 units × 50 weeks)—as many transactions in a single building as may occur in small cities!

Foreclosure in such circumstances is costly and impractical, so installment sales are often used to reduce the developer's financial risk. If a buyer won't pay the mortgage, at least the developer can resell the unit without too much difficulty. Foreclosure may also result if annual maintenance fees are not paid. This is a charge for the management and upkeep of both the project and the unit, particularly cleaning between intervals. Maintenance fees typically range from $150 to $250 per unit week.

Since the developer will be managing the project and providing financing, many states now require developers and sales organizations to be registered and bonded. For more information about a particular developer, contact such authorities as consumer affairs offices, real estate commissions and state attorneys general.

Because timeshare units provide rights only during specific time periods they may seem useless if you are not free for a given week. However, units may be exchanged, a unique timeshare concept. It works this way:

You register your unit with an exchange service at least ninety days before you use your interval. They will then suggest possible units for which you can trade, units that may be in different parts of the country or even overseas. In general, like units are traded for like units but it is sometimes possible to trade an inexpensive unit in one location for a prime unit elsewhere. In addition, many units are exchanged within projects.

Whether or not timeshare units are a good investment is a matter of opinion and the view here is that right-to-use units have little profit-making potential and are best viewed as a hedge against future vacation costs. Fee simple units, however, may have investment value, particularly as the timeshare movement becomes more widely accepted.

As the timeshare industry has grown, the number of units that have become available for resale has also increased. If timesharing seems attractive, prospective buyers should consider resale units typically available at a substantial discount when compared with new units. Although resale units represent the same financial and ownership considerations as new ones, they may offer the advantage of far lower prices, sometimes as much as 50 percent below new timeshares. To find the latest timeshare resale prices check the classified ads in your local newspapers and magazines as well as the "Timeshare-Resale" classified section published by *USA Today*.

The American Resort Development Association publishes *Resort and Urban Timesharing: A Consumer's Guide*. Copies may be obtained by sending a stamped, self-addressed business envelope to ARDA, Suite 510, 1220 L St. NW, Washington, D.C. 20005.

Questions to Ask:

What form of timesharing ownership is being sold?

If a lease interest is for sale, how long is the lease?

Are there any resale intervals available in addition to intervals available through the developer? If so, at what price and at what terms?

How is the interval unit financed?

If installment financing is used, what happens if a payment is late? Is there a penalty or does the loan automatically terminate?

Will your local lender, or a lender where the project is located, provide a personal loan to cover the unit's cost?

What is the current maintenance fee?

What is included with the unit (furniture, dishes, etc.)?

Does management have an in-house exchange program? If so, is there a fee to unit owners? How much? Are re-sale units available? If so, look for discounts.

Have there been complaints to the Better Business Bureau, local consumer offices or the state real estate commission concerning either the project or the developer? If so, what are the complaints about and how have they been handled?

How is timeshare financing treated under tax reform? Ask a CPA or tax attorney whether interest on timeshare financing can be deducted if the mortgage is a personal loan not secured by real property.

Knock on a few doors and ask current unit owners what they think about the project and the developer.

4

How to Pick the Right Mortgage

The most difficult problem in real estate financing is not in finding a mortgage. Real estate financing is always available in every market and in every community—if you are willing to pay the price. Simply stated, there is no shortage of people and institutions that will gladly loan all the money you need at premium rates and terms.

The real dilemma is choosing one loan from among the essentially limitless number of financing options available at any given time. The issue here is not confined merely to interest rates and monthly payments, rather there is the broader problem of finding the best financial package within the context of your needs, income, assets, financial potential and personal goals.

Many of the questions regarding loan selection are academic in the sense that borrowers often have few realistic choices. It would be great, for instance, to have a zero-interest loan but if you don't have the up-front cash such financing is out of the question.

Since we must each work within the bounds of our financial positions, the best way to find a loan is to see which mortgage format best meets our needs. If we lack cash we will want financing that requires little money down. If we lack income we will want financing with small monthly payments. If our financial position is stronger we can opt for a loan with a low interest cost but high monthly payments. Here is how common lending forms can be divided according to borrower requirements.

Benchmark.   Since borrowers are going to compare loan rates and terms we need a standard against which mortgages can be measured. The best benchmark is the "conventional" loan financing, which features a 30-year term, self-amortization, market interest rates, 20 percent down and level monthly payments.

Although conventional financing is the most consistent benchmark, FHA ARM loans are useful when comparing adjustable rate mortgages since they offer uniform terms nationwide. Rates and fees, of course, may differ.

Low Down Payment.   Many buyers cannot afford to make a 20 percent down payment, so there is a need for financing that requires few dollars up front. Such loans include FHA, VA, no-cash deals, and loans backed with private mortgage insurance (MI), as well as loans through such plans as NeighborWorks, FannieNeighbors, and the Community Home Buyers Program. In addition, growing equity mortgages (GEMs) often require small down payments because they represent relatively less risk to the lender than many other loan formats. *Pledged-account mortgages* (PAMs) and *reserve-account mortgages* (RAMs) do not require much cash in the form of a down payment, but someone, possibly the buyer, must deposit funds with a lender.

Much Cash Up Front.   All cash deals mean 100 percent of the purchase price must be paid up front. Zero-interest loans usually require one-third down. The 20 percent down required for conventional financing seems high in today's market. Also, it should be said that buyers can elect to put down additional cash when financing property with any loan format.

Low Initial Monthly Payment.   As monthly payments drop it becomes easier to qualify for financing, and several loan formats—graduated payment mortgages (GPMs), front-loaded interest-only plans (FLIPs), GEMs and buy-downs—all have low initial payments. Adjustable rate mortgages (ARMs) and *graduated payment adjustable rate mortgages* (GPARMs) usually feature low monthly costs at first but, unlike the other loan formats in this category which have programmed monthly increases, future ARM payments may rise or fall in a random manner.

Random Variable Payment.   When loans, such as ARMs and GPARMs, have monthly payments that can rise or fall according to an index they require more budget planning than loans with set monthly costs.

Low Rates and Terms.   Blend loans feature below-market interest rates. Assumed loans, except for ARMs and financing requiring lender "consent" for assumption, often have both below-rate interest and a shortened term. Second trusts and wraparound mortgages can have both low rates and terms, depending on the particular deal and market conditions.

Low Interest Cost.   Low interest "cost" does not necessarily mean a low interest "rate." Instead these are loans which over their terms require relatively few dollars for interest expenses. *Zero-interest plan* loans (ZIP) have—not surprisingly—no direct interest expense. GEM mortgages are programmed to have short terms and low interest costs. Second trust and wraparound loans, depending on individual rates and terms, can often cut interest costs significantly.

Short Loan Terms.   If 30-year financing is a "standard" loan term, then shorter mortgages include 15-, 20- and 25-year loans, GEM mortgages (15 years or less), and virtually all second trusts. Wraparound loans have terms of less than 30 years, depending on the remaining term of any existing financing.

Assumable Loans.   ARMs, FHA and VA financing can be assumed by qualified borrowers in most cases. Older conventional loans are frequently assumable at original rates and terms.

Monthly Payment to Borrower.   A home can be seen as a storehouse of value and one way to get cash from that storehouse is with a reverse mortgage. Another approach may be to have regular withdrawals with a home equity loan or reverse mortgage.

Balloon Payments.   Balloon payments are a common feature of second trusts, ARMs and roll-over loans. Some GPMs also have balloon notes.

Loans to Avoid.   There are three loan formats that are difficult to justify from the borrower's perspective: land contracts, roll-over loans and
40-year mortgages. The first two mortgage formats are hazardous,
while the latter is needlessly expensive. In addition, certain ARMs—
those without interest caps, those with negative amortization or those
that feature monthly payment changes—should be avoided.

HOW TO COMPARE LOAN FORMATS

Because needs differ there is not a single, magical mortgage formula
that will somehow resolve the loan problems of all borrowers. Different strategies work well for different people and it is therefore necessary to have a sound selection process before one can have a sound
selection.

Variety has always been part of the real estate financial system
because conventional loans simply don't work for all purchasers—too
much down is required, initial monthly payments are too high, financing is too long and total interest costs are too great. To get around
these problems, and in many instances to simply make a better deal,
buyers routinely use alternative mortgage formats.

Just because a sale is not based on conventional financing does
not suggest that a deal is "abnormal" in some way. Alternative mortgages are perfectly legitimate forms of financing that can cut interest rates, reduce monthly payments, lower down payments, and
drop overall mortgage costs. Alternative mortgages can also feature
large down payments, negative amortization, changing monthly payments and interest rates that rise and fall randomly during the term
of the loan.

The fact that alternative loans are different from conventional
financing does not imply that such distinctions are necessarily negative. All loans are merely financial tools which are useful in some cases
and inappropriate in others. Deciding whether or not to use a particular loan format depends on the needs of the buyer and the facts and
circumstances in each sale.

Loans should be compared individually—the second trust of one
lender versus the second trust of another—as well as format against

format—zero-interest mortgages versus graduated payment loans. Here are thirteen central points of comparison.

1. Does the loan require fewer dollars down or more dollars down than other mortgage formats? Small down payments mean maximum leverage—the use of OPM to finance as much of the property as possible. Unless mortgage rates are "high" relative to other investments, it pays to seek leverage when buying. Once a loan is in place you can then look at restructuring and refinancing opportunities. FHA and VA loans are examples of financing that require few dollars up front.

2. Are monthly payments subject to change during the term of the loan? If changes occur, are they pre-planned or random? How often are changes permitted? Pre-planned changes, such as monthly payment increases found in graduated payment loans, allow borrowers to budget their incomes. Random changes, such as those associated with ARM financing, are more difficult to project.

3. Are the initial monthly payments larger or smaller than other mortgage formats? The lower the initial monthly payments the easier to qualify for a loan of any given size. Graduated payment loans are attractive because they often feature significantly lower initial payments than will be required for conventional financing. In many cases loans offer below-market interest rates initially as an inducement to borrowers. ARMs, for example, usually have initial rates below conventional financing levels but such rates are not guaranteed for the life of the loan.

4. Are monthly payment changes limited? Is there a cap on the amount your monthly payments can rise, say, not more than 7.5 percent annually?

5. Is there a cap on the maximum amount of interest that can be charged? Is there a minimum? If there is no interest cap, rates can rise with the market. Will the lender agree to an interest cap in exchange for an up-front fee? Note that if increased interest costs are not passed through to borrowers through higher monthly payments or occasional cash injections, negative amortization may be permitted.

Basic Mortgage Checklist

What is the down payment required compared to other loan formats? Larger_____Smaller_____

Are monthly payments subject to change during the term of the loan? Yes_____No_____

How often are payment changes permitted? Monthly_____Semi-annually_____Yearly_____Biannually_____Other _____

If changes occur, are they pre-planned or random? Pre-planned_____Random_____

Are initial monthly payments larger or smaller than other mortgage formats? Larger_____Smaller_____

Is there a cap on monthly payment changes? Yes_____No_____

Is there a cap on the maximum amount of interest that can be charged? Yes_____No_____Is there a minimum? Yes_____No_____

Is negative amortization allowed? Yes_____No_____

If negative amortization occurs, can the loan term be extended? Yes_____No_____

If interest payments are related to an index, which index is used? Name of index:_____

Can the loan be assumed at its original rate and terms by a qualified purchaser? Yes_____No_____

Can the loan be prepaid in whole or in part at any time without penalty? Yes_____No_____If not, what are the conditions of prepayment?_____

---

6. Is negative amortization allowed? If negative amortization occurs early in the term of the mortgage is it automatically corrected later with higher scheduled payments, that is, without additional infusions of cash?

7. If negative amortization occurs, can the loan term be extended? With adjustable rate loans there is often a provision to extend the loan term from 30 to as many as 40 years. This provision benefits the borrower in the sense that it is not necessary to refinance the property if any loan balance remains after 30 years. It also means larger interest payments and slower amortization over the life of the mortgage.

8. If interest payments are related to an index, which index is

used? The longer the span of events being measured the better the index from the borrower's perspective.

9. Can the loan be assumed at its original rate and terms by a qualified purchaser? This may be of value in the future when today's borrower becomes tomorrow's seller.

10. Can the loan be prepaid in whole or in part without penalty? This is a key question because if a loan can easily be prepaid in part and without penalty then the borrower can unilaterally restructure the loan at any time.

11. What are the tax consequences of the loan? Speak to a CPA, tax attorney, or enrolled agent for specific advice.

12. When all factors are considered, which loan format is best within the context of your needs today?

13. Which loan format will best meet your needs five years from today? Ten years? Will your income decline as a result of retirement or a job change? If so, be wary of loans with rising monthly costs, such as graduated payment mortgages, or loans which may have random monthly increases, such as certain adjustable rate loans.

COMPUTERS AND THE SEARCHING PROCESS

When searching for real estate financing it pays to consult as many local lenders as possible—savings and loan associations, mortgage bankers, credit unions, banks, insurance companies and even relatives and employers. Use the questions found in the section on lender policies (Chapter 2) as a guide and keep careful notes showing how each potential lender responds to your call.

In addition to local lenders, we are now at the beginning of a new phenomenon: the computerized mortgage information service.

Mortgage information can be easily assembled, digested and displayed with a computer. In fact, the fast turnover of rates and terms makes computers ideal for keeping up with industry changes.

If you've ever shopped for a mortgage you know that finding a loan is not a calm or casual adventure. But now computers have arrived and with them the possibility of one-stop mortgage shopping and the chance to find bargain financing from among hundreds of loans.

Ideally, a computer system should allow you to fill in some blanks, press a few buttons and have the best mortgage in town pop up like morning toast. While computers have yet to become that efficient, they are radically changing the way we shop for mortgages and buried within those changes are both new opportunities and potential pitfalls for borrowers.

Borrowers have traditionally sought mortgage money from such sources as savings and loan associations, mortgage bankers (individuals and companies that bring lenders and borrowers together and then "service" loans), commercial banks, insurance companies and, more recently, credit unions. Multiply the number of loan sources in a given community by the variety of available mortgage products and you can see that hundreds of loans are available at any time.

Although in theory there are many choices, few borrowers have the time or stamina to contact every local loan source. Choices are often made on the basis of recommendations from real estate brokers, proximity to a lender, long-standing financial relationships or in response to advertisements.

Once a lender has been found, it is necessary first to choose the right mortgage instrument and then apply for financing. The lender will have the property appraised, get a credit check, verify the application and complete all necessary paperwork, a process known generally as "origination." Application charges to borrowers usually total $200 to $400 while the total cost of originating a mortgage is generally calculated as 1 percent of the loan's value, a fee incorporated into the up-front charges paid at settlement (closing).

How do computers change the system? On a basic level, computers can be seen as an electronic shopping mall where lenders hawk their latest products. Want an adjustable rate mortgage (ARM)? Feed in the amount needed and the computer can show interest rates, monthly payments, adjustments and caps for every ARM in the system. How will an ARM compare with VA financing or a conventional loan? The computer can make point-by-point comparisons within a few minutes.

As an electronic shopping center, a computer listing loans from many lenders is really nothing more than a glorified database which cuts the number of phone calls borrowers need to make. Since information about various loan options is in one place and in a single format, it is possible to compare hundreds of mortgages. Looking at so many loans provides some sense of market trends and helps distinguish the good deals from the dogs.

Just as important, information in the electronic shopping center is current. A lender offering a new loan or changing a rate can update the computer at any time.

By itself, a vast amount of data may be incomprehensible. How do you sort through so many loans choices? Should you just pick the mortgage with the lowest initial rate or are there other factors to consider?

Mortgage choices today can be fine-tuned to mesh with changing incomes, retirement programs, tax brackets and alternative investments; in other words, mortgages can be part of a complete financial planning effort. Trained advisors can explain how different mortgages work, the meaning of industry terms such as "negative amortization" and "wraparound" financing, as well as the relative costs of various loan alternatives.

From the borrowers' viewpoint, it is advantageous to have several hundred loan choices displayed in one place. But as many loans as a given system may contain, no system contains all available mortgages and it is entirely possible that the best loan is not in the system. For this reason borrowers can still benefit by calling various local lenders if only to assure they are getting the best deal.

Computer systems also present the problem of rigidity. Loans may be processed within guidelines: if you need so much income to afford a certain mortgage, you may not get financing if your income is marginally low or your debts are marginally high. In contrast, a lender you know may be more flexible, particularly if you are a long-time client with a respectable credit history.

Although computers produce copious volumes of information, one has to ask about utility: How useful is the data you receive? For example, when comparing ARMs it is not enough to look at interest rates. There is a considerable potential difference between two ARMs with equal interest rates when one permits negative amortization while the other does not. Clearly the latter loan is a better deal.

Lastly, there is the issue of locking-in rates. Mortgage rates change constantly and if you apply for a loan July 1, the interest rate can be 2 percent higher by the time you settle in August. Some lenders guarantee rates as of the date of application, others as of the date of approval and some only as of the moment of settlement. Borrowers would do well to see if rates quoted as of the date of application can be locked in; otherwise interest quotes have little, if any, value.

LOANS ONLINE

The computer revolution has allowed mortgage lenders and realty brokers to follow mortgage rates with electronic speed and to greatly accelerate the application process. Now, the next step in the computer revolution is coming into play, the opportunity for consumers to directly access mortgage information.

It is estimated that 180,000 electronic bulletin boards are now in place nationwide (60,000 public, 120,000 private), boards that allow individuals with computers, modems, and the right software to trade information and download software. And some of that information, not surprisingly, involves mortgages and real estate.

As an example of how the system works, consider the real estate area associated with America Online (AOL), a national electronic bulletin board where I act as the real estate adviser.

In the real estate area, AOL members without additional charge can list a home for sale, rent or exchange in the MLS (a system that is open to brokers and nonbrokers alike), download software from the library, review articles in the "reading room," debate the latest commentary, and have a question answered on the area bulletin board.

It is important to understand that AOL is an interstate information exchange, essentially a communications medium of general circulation or coverage not primarily engaged in the advertisement of real estate. AOL is not a real estate brokerage, not a mortgage broker, and not a mortgage banker.

Why is this important? It means an enormous range of views and opinions appear online—sometimes with great heat. There is no monopoly for one firm, company, or set of ideas. By providing an open forum, there is much that can be learned in private and at minimal cost.

You can also do something else. If you want to know about mortgage rates, you can find up-to-date lender listings. You can check ARM index levels to assure that your lender is using correct information to calculate loan adjustments. You can compare rates found online with the offerings of local lenders. Questions about mortgage choices, practices, and policies can be answered online. And if you see a loan you like, just contact the lender with the listed 800 number or send a note to the lender on AOL's electronic mail.

Systems such as AOL's—which have reached more than 1.25 million people nationwide—will become increasingly important as more people use such networks and as a growing number of lenders post daily rates. Already, according to 1992 National Work-at-Home Survey conduced by LINK Resources Corporation in New York, there are 16.5 million households with computers and 44 percent of all home-based computer users own modems. Lenders cannot possibly ignore such huge numbers, the very reason more and more mortgage providers are going online.

As of early 1995, an AOL membership costs $9.95 per month, a fee that includes five free hours on the system. The rate for additional time is $2.95 per hour. To obtain free software for any major computer system, and to obtain the latest rates and details, call 800-827-6364, extension 5764. *Be certain to mention the extension number to obtain new-subscriber discounts and benefits.*

5
No-Cash and All-Cash Deals

Buying real estate would certainly be much easier if no cash was required up front. Not only are such deals possible but they are commonplace—millions of veterans have bought property with 100 percent financing, and similar deals by non-vets are made daily.

Properties can be bought without cash in a number of ways and a short list of alternative approaches might include purchases in which:

- The seller or a third party takes back a self-amortizing mortgage for the property's entire value plus all closing costs.
- The purchaser assumes a first trust and the seller or a third party finances the balance with a second trust. At the end of the term a balloon payment is due.
- The purchaser gets a new mortgage and the owner or a third party takes back a second trust with a balloon payment.
- The buyer assumes or gets a new first mortgage, a second trust from the seller and a third trust from still another source.
- The purchaser assumes a first trust or gets a new loan and trades a 1947 Rolls Royce in mint condition for the balance due.
- The purchaser is a veteran and gets 100 percent financing with a VA-backed mortgage.
- A rich aunt pays for the property.
- The buyer trades a house in Tampa for the seller's home.
- A property is bought and before settlement the purchaser resells the house to another buyer at a profit.

• A property is bought and, coincidentally with settlement, a portion is sold to pay all costs above financing.

In every case the term *no money down* can be substituted for the words *deferred liability*. The buyer owes money in the future or paid money in the past (for the purchase of the Rolls, the house in Tampa, public service to earn VA benefits or the psychological cost of his aunt's good will) or devalued the property by selling off a portion.

Deals with no money down make great sense in those cases where enormous balloon payments can be avoided and purchasers can afford monthly carrying costs—the precise arrangement used by the VA. The problem is that some borrowers equate the idea of "no cash" with "no responsibility." They forget that not everyone can afford high monthly mortgage payments or raise enough cash to pay off balloon notes. (See table below.) The best time to make a no-cash deal is when interest rates are low, because there are probably better places to invest money. When interest rates are high purchasers are often best advised to invest in their own mortgage. If rates later fall the property can be refinanced.

No-Cash Deals	
Money down	None.
Loan size	100 percent financing.
Monthly cost	Largest possible for property.
Balloon note	None with VA but balloon payments are common with conventional no-cash deals.
Loan term	30 years with VA but often far shorter with investment deals, say 3 to 5 years.
Pros	No-cash deals allow borrowers to acquire property with no initial capital. Large loans mean large tax deductions for interest payments, no points and reduced settlement costs.
Cons	No-cash deals mean high monthly mortgage bills and the possibility of huge balloon payments.

No-cash financing is often used by investors and in such cases monthly mortgage payments often exceed rentals, a situation known as "negative cash flow." This polite term means that each and every month the investor must make cash payments to keep the property. Negative cash flow is not a serious problem for many investors because they can afford to pay the negative cash flow from their general income and the tax and appreciation benefits of ownership offset monthly cash losses.

For example, suppose Harding buys a four-unit apartment building which produces rentals worth $2,000 a month. Harding's costs for first and second mortgages, property taxes, repairs, maintenance, etc., total $2,250 per month. Harding thus has cash losses of $250 per month, or $3,000 a year, a sum Harding can readily pay from other income.

Where Harding benefits in this deal is that his income tax deductions for mortgage interest, property taxes, electricity, depreciation and other items total $15,000 annually. In his tax bracket, these deductions reduce Harding's tax bill by $4,200. In addition, each month the mortgage is being paid down and so the equity in the property rises even if market values remain stagnant.

Moreover, Harding takes steps to reduce his losses. He paints the hallway and plants new shrubs to make his property more attractive. Rather than raising rents directly at first, he invests $4,000 and installs individual utility meters so that electric bills are paid directly by the tenants. With the new meters in place Harding air-conditions each unit. A year after he bought the property, Harding raises monthly rentals by $35 per unit but the tenants stay. Why? Because the property is a better place to live.

The problem is that not every Harding—or Smith or Brown—can afford $250 in cash each month. Not everyone can invest an additional several thousand dollars in a rental property or is in an income bracket that will produce the same tax savings as Harding's.

To be successful, investment deals with no money down must be affordable in the event property income does not rise, vacancies occur or major repairs are required. Buyers must also have a clear, reasonable plan to both carry and repay all debt, particularly short-term balloon payments, which are a frequent feature of investment no-cash sales. Without such planning no-cash deals are a sure prescription for financial disaster.

Questions to Ask:

What is the interest rate for conventional financing?

What is the interest rate for the first trust? Second trust? Third trust? Etc.

Does the no-cash deal include financing to cover the cost of closing?

Are balloon payments part of the deal? If so, exactly how will they be repaid?

Are you making a no-cash investment with the expectation of raising rents? If so, why is it that you will be able to raise rentals, while the present owner has not? How will a rent increase affect vacancy rates?

Do you have sufficient income to cover negative cash flow?

Do you have enough capital to make repairs or cover vacancy losses, if any?

Is it possible to subdivide the property? Since the property is security for at least one loan, will the lender(s) allow you to subdivide?

How will a no-cash deal affect your tax position? Speak with a tax advisor for further advice.

Is your financing assumable?

Can your financing be repaid in whole or in part without penalty at any time?

BUYING FOR CASH

The least cumbersome way to buy real estate is to pay cash. If you've got the money, paying cash will save dollars by eliminating loan discount fees (*points*), mortgage application charges and origination fees (generally 1 percent of a mortgage). Settlement costs will also be reduced, since there is no need to set aside escrow funds for the payment of taxes, FHA, VA or private mortgage insurance or other expenses.

But if buying a home with cash has attractive aspects, there are also problems. The most basic difficulty is that few people have the dollars needed to buy a home without financing. But even when the dollars are available, buying for cash is not always a sound financial choice. A home without a mortgage is a home without a major tax deduction. A home without a fixed-rate mortgage is a home which cannot fully profit from inflation.

Given the balance of benefits and problems, when should real estate be bought for cash? The answer depends on alternative investments and your personal situation.

First, have you devised a personal financial strategy? Have you set aside funds for retirement plans, placed cash in a savings account or other liquid asset and bought sufficient health and life insurance? Are you making high-interest credit payments for credit cards, cars or furniture? If so, paying cash for property is not likely to be your best financial choice.

Second, are you about to retire? Selling a large home may generate enough dollars to buy a retirement property for cash. Buying for cash, in turn, will cut monthly living costs. If you pay cash will you have enough income from other sources to live in the style to which you are accustomed?

Third, what is your tax situation? When you sell a personal residence and buy another personal residence of equal or greater value, any tax on the profit made from the first property's sale is deferred. Note that buying a house of "equal or greater value" does not mean you must pay cash for the second property—you can get a mortgage and invest the cash earned from a first home sale. Also, after age 55 you are entitled to a one-time profit exclusion from the sale of a personal residence of up to $125,000 at this writing. (This means if you only claim $100,000 you forfeit the right to claim the balance.) Check with a CPA or tax attorney for an update on current tax regulations and for advice concerning your specific situation.

Fourth, what about liquidity? Traditionally it has been difficult to get cash out of a house without selling or refinancing. This tradition has changed with the ready availability of home-equity loans. Still, real estate is not a liquid investment in the sense of a savings account or mutual fund where access to your assets is ultimately guaranteed. After all, you can apply for a home-equity loan and be rejected.

Fifth, how does a mortgage look as an investment? If mortgages are available for 10 percent, by paying cash you are getting an effective, pre-tax return of more than 10 percent; the exact return will depend on your tax bracket. How does investing in a mortgage compare with

The All-Cash Deal	
Loan size	None.
Interest rate	None.
Monthly payment	None.
Down payment	100 percent of the purchase price.
Pros	No monthly payments, lender fees or interest charges.
Cons	No tax deduction for interest payments and no leverage.
Central issue	Is your money best invested in a house to avoid mortgage payments or in other "investments" such as lower credit card debt? Is your money put to better use with stocks, bonds, retirement plans or other investments?

stocks, bonds, mutual funds, and retirement plans in terms of both return and risk?

One attraction of paying cash for a prime residence is that you can finance property at a later date, perhaps when rates have come down or you have a specific need for capital. However, paying cash requires some element of crystal ball gazing. What if you pay cash today and interest rates rise? Will you qualify for all the new financing you need or want at a later date?

Paying cash for real estate is a strategy which assures control over real estate dollars. Some people who never pay cash for investment property have homes free and clear of any debt. Why? Because home ownership—as distinct from investment real estate—implies certain psychological values. It may be that buying for cash is not a sound financial choice in many cases but it is an alternative which some people find more comforting than high rates of return, a feeling that cannot be measured in dollars and cents.

Questions to Ask:

What is the prevailing interest rate for conventional mortgages in your community?

What is the current return you can expect from the conservative investment of your funds?

How large is the one-time profit exemption from the sale of a personal residence? (Speak to a CPA or tax attorney for current information.)

Do you anticipate reduced income as a result of retirement in the next decade?

Do you expect to move to smaller housing within the next ten years?

Do you believe that home mortgage rates will generally rise or fall from current levels over the next several years?

As a matter of personal preference would you want to own a home which is free and clear of all mortgage debt? While this may not be the best choice in terms of dollars and percentages, it is a choice that comforts many people.

6

The Conventional Loan

Until the mid-1930s, the most common form of real estate financing was the *straight,* or *term,* mortgage with a five-year life and semi-annual interest payments. Straight loans were attractive years ago because interest rates were low and plenty of cash was available when refinancing was necessary.

But the Depression and harsh weather in the Midwest—the Dust Bowl—brought out the worst features of the term loan system. People who were unemployed could not make semi-annual interest payments, farms where crops no longer grew were not acceptable collateral for new financing and many lenders failed, shutting off valued sources of community cash and credit. The inevitable result was a rash of foreclosures and calls for a new system of home financing.

That new system arose in the 1930s when the Federal Housing Administration popularized the long-term, self-amortizing home loan, a concept we today know as *conventional* financing.

A conventional loan is the benchmark against which all other mortgage concepts should be measured and such loans are distinguished by five central features:

Set Monthly Payments. Each month the borrower makes payments which are substantially equal during the life of the mortgage.

Set Interest Rates. The interest rate is established at the time the loan is first created and remains unchanged during its life.

Fixed Loan Term.   Most conventional loans are designed to be repaid over an extended period of time, usually 30 years.

Self-Amortization.   Conventional financing is arranged so the entire loan, including all interest and principal, will be completely repaid when the mortgage ends. As a result there is no *balloon* payment—a huge sum of money due at the end of the loan term—associated with conventional loans, so refinancing is unnecessary.

Coverage.   Conventional loans are equal to 80 percent of the purchase price. A buyer must put down cash or additional financing for the balance.

With these factors in mind, a conventional sale might look like this: Buyer Stevenson purchases a new home for $100,000. Of this amount, $20,000 is represented by the cash down payment paid by Stevenson at settlement, and the remaining $80,000 is in the form of a 30-year mortgage from a local lender. At the end of 30 years, Stevenson owns the property free and clear of any mortgage debt.

The Conventional Loan	
Sale price	$100,000
Cash down	$20,000
Loan size	$80,000
Loan term	30 years
Monthly payments	Level, $615.13
Balloon payments	None
Interest rate	Fixed, 8.5 percent
Total payments	$221,447
Total interest	$141,447

Conventional loans are appealing to lenders because such financing assures limited risk. The buyer's down payment creates a deep cushion which protects the lender in the event of foreclosure. With the $100,000 home above, for instance, the buyer has invested $20,000, leaving the lender with less risk worth than if the home was bought with $5,000 down or nothing down. If the house must be foreclosed, the lender's interest will be completely protected if the property sells for $80,000 plus the cost of the foreclosure action. Since $80,000 is considerably below the property's market value, the lender has only the most limited financial exposure.

Conventional loans are a useful index against which individual lenders can be compared. Unlike other forms of financing, conventional mortgages are commonly offered by all community lenders and since the terms and conditions of conventional loans are standardized, it is an easy matter to determine which lender has the best available rates and terms.

Conventional loans also have another value. In most cases to qualify for a conventional loan borrowers must have 28/36 ratios. Using these ratios it is easy to provide a *conservative* estimate of borrowing power.

For example, payments for an 8.5-percent, $80,000 mortgage will be $615.13 per month. If insurance is $25 per month and taxes are an additional $75, then we know the total cost for principal, interest, taxes, and insurance—PITI—is $715.13. If lenders qualify borrowers by allowing 28 percent of our gross, pretax income for PITI, then to afford a monthly cost of $715.13 we need an income of $2,554.04 a month, or $30,648.48 per year.

We also know that if the back ratio is equal to 36 percent of our gross monthly income, then in addition to housing costs we can spend as much as $204.32 on credit card debt, auto payments, etc. We obtained this figure by multiplying $2,554.04 by 36 percent. The answer is $919.45. If we subtract the amount of money allowed for housing expenses ($715.13), we are left with $204.32 ($919.45 less $715.13).

Conventional loans raise a serious issue today: Is a 30-year loan the best mortgage format? For some portion of all borrowers, conventional loans remain the best deal in terms of interest rates, monthly costs and down payments. But for many borrowers, conventional financing is far from the best arrangement. Other mortgage formats, as we shall see, feature less money down, smaller initial monthly payments, and interest savings that can top $100,000 for loans of comparable size. While conventional financing may have been a great idea fifty years ago, it is the mortgage of choice for fewer and fewer people today.

Questions to Ask:

What is the current rate of interest for conventional financing? (This question should be asked when considering any loan format, since it provides a baseline from which to measure alternative mortgages.)

What portion of the home can be financed with a conventional loan?

Can I get conventional financing if a second trust is used to finance a portion of the purchase?

In addition to the current interest rate, are "points" or loan discount fees being charged? If so, how many?

In general terms, how much income will I need to qualify for a conventional loan of X dollars?

7

Second Trusts

Real estate sales which are not made entirely for cash involve the use of at least one mortgage or deed of trust. However, a large number of transactions involve more than one loan and in those cases where a single property is used to secure multiple loans an important question arises: Who gets paid first?

An order of repayment among private lenders is established in the loan papers created between property owners and lenders. Claims will be fully settled in order; that is, the claims of the first mortgage or first trust holder will be completely repaid before any claims by a second loan holder are addressed. In turn, the claims of the second mortgage or second trust holder must be fully satisfied before the debt of a third lender can be addressed, and so on.

The catch for junior trust holders is that there may not be any cash remaining once prior claims have been satisfied. Second trusts and mortgages thus represent more risk than first loans and therefore command higher interest rates. Here is an example illustrating why secondary financing has inherently more risk than primary loans.

A home is bought for $106,250 and Cleveland, the buyer, knows he can get a conventional, 30-year loan for $85,000 at 9 percent interest. The rest of the money will come from Cleveland, who has $8,000 in cash, and a $13,250 loan from Uncle Bob. It's agreed that the $13,250 will be in the form of a second trust secured by the property, that the loan term will be five years and that there will be no balloon payment.

Cleveland, with Uncle Bob's money in hand, gets an $85,000 first mortgage from a lender. After two years, Cleveland defaults and the property is sold at foreclosure for $85,000. The first mortgage holder takes the $85,000, leaving nothing for Uncle Bob. (See table below.)

Second Trusts: Mr. Cleveland's Loans	
Purchase price	$106,250
Cash down	$8,000
First trust	$85,000 at 9 percent interest
First trust term	30 years
First trust monthly payment	$683.93
Second trust	$13,250 at 12 percent interest
Second trust term	5 years
Second trust monthly payment	$294.74
Total monthly payment	$978.67
Balloon payment	None in this example

Note that the first trust holder had no economic incentive to sell the property for more than $85,000 plus foreclosure costs. Thus, while a lender with a second trust can seek to foreclose on a property in the event his loan is in default, consideration must be given to the idea that by triggering a foreclosure a second mortgage holder may do little more than satisfy the claims of a prior lender. In effect, the threat of foreclosure by a second trust holder, and the protection offered by foreclosure, is greatly reduced by the prior claims of another lender.

Also, it should be said that Cleveland had steep monthly payments totaling $978.67 in this example. His monthly payments could have been lower if he had a second trust with a balloon payment. In that case, his cost for a second trust could have been, say, $100 per month rather than the $294.74 he agreed to pay his uncle. Perhaps with lower monthly costs he might have avoided foreclosure.

If second trusts represent enhanced risk why are so many sellers, lenders and investors willing to hold such paper? One answer might be that the element of risk is offset by a higher rate of return. Another response is that some sales are possible only with second trusts. For example, when interest rates are high borrowers may not qualify for financing from local lenders and if sellers don't take back second trusts their properties won't be sold.

It is possible that a junior loan can resemble a first trust in all particulars but this is not likely. In a typical situation, several distinctions are common.

Loan Term.   While conventional loans may have a term of 30 years, second trusts are generally for a shorter term, say 2 to 10 years with most terms being 5 years or less. If you are a borrower you will want the longest possible term because long terms mean lower monthly payments for self-amortizing loans and more time to refinance if a balloon payment is due when the loan ends.

Amortization and Monthly Payments.   Because secondary loans have a short term they can only be self-amortizing if they have large payments. For example, a 30-year, $85,000 loan at 9 percent interest requires monthly payments of principal and interest of $683.93. A 10-year, 9 percent self-amortizing loan for this amount will require monthly payments of $1,076.74, and a 5-year note will call for payments of $1,764.46 per month.

Instead of being self-amortizing, however, secondary financing is likely to feature relatively small monthly payments. Such payments have two effects: they make the loan affordable to a borrower and they create a balloon note, a huge final payment at the end of the loan term. Indeed, if the interest rate is sufficiently high and the monthly payments are sufficiently low, *negative amortization* may occur, a situation in which the balloon payment will be larger than the original debt.

Coverage.   With a conventional loan, the purchaser typically makes a 20 percent down payment in cash, while a lender puts up the rest of the sale value in the form of a mortgage. With a second trust, the buyer's cash contribution is frequently less than 20 percent. For example, if a buyer puts down 10 percent of the purchase price in cash and gets a second trust for 10 percent then the balance of the purchase price, 80 percent, can be financed with a conventional loan.

In those situations where a seller or other party takes back a second trust, lenders will often accept such arrangements as long as the buyer is financially qualified to make both first and second trust payments. Some lenders, however, will not make loans where second trusts are involved. Others will make loans, but only if buyers put down at least 5 to 10 percent of the purchase price with their own money.

Questions to Ask:

What is the interest rate for conventional financing?
What is the interest rate for second trusts?
Can you get a lengthy second trust, say 10 or 15 years?
If you're a buyer, the longer the second trust the better.
Will second trust financing involve a balloon payment?
If so, how large a payment?
If you are getting a new first mortgage will the lender allow second trust financing to be used to acquire the property? This is a question that should be satisfied before being committed to a purchase agreement.

HOW TO CUT HOUSING PRICES WITH SECOND TRUSTS

Second trusts can be regarded as a kind of financial ball of putty, loans that can be stretched, compressed, pulled and flattened into any shape acceptable to both borrower and lender. In those cases where it is the seller who becomes a lender by taking back a second trust, second trusts can be molded to favor either buyer or seller.

Imagine a situation where the prevailing rate of interest for a conventional loan is 10 percent while second trusts are available for, say, 12 percent interest. In a particular sale, a property is sold for $120,000. By adjusting the cost, size and terms of a second trust different results—and advantages—can be produced from a single core transaction.

- Case 1. The property is sold for $120,000 and a lender puts up $80,000 for a first trust. The seller takes back a $16,000 second trust at 12 percent interest and the buyer puts up the balance ($24,000) in cash. In this illustration there is market financing for both the first and second trusts, 80 percent of the deal is financed and 20 percent is paid in cash by the purchaser. This is an essentially neutral deal with no advantage to either buyer or seller, assuming the property has a market value of $120,000.

- Case 2. The property is sold for $120,000 and a lender puts up $80,000 at 10 percent interest for a first trust. The seller takes back a $16,000 second trust at 10 percent and the buyer pays the $24,000 balance in cash. Here the buyer has an advantage because the interest charge on the second trust is less than the prevailing market rate for such financing. Alternatively, a deal with the same financial result can be arranged by lowering the sales price.

- Case 3. The property is sold for $120,000 and a lender puts up $80,000 at 10 percent interest for a first trust. The seller takes a $40,000 second trust at 14 percent. In this example, the buyer is trading costlier financing for the opportunity to purchase property with no money down. This scenario works for buyers with enough income to support enlarged monthly mortgage payments and who are in the upper tax brackets, a factor which partially offsets high mortgage costs. The seller here is getting $80,000 in cash from the first mortgage plus a note with an above-market interest rate, a good deal for owners who don't need the cash represented by the second trust, $40,000 in this illustration.

Second trusts can be manipulated in terms of size as well as interest. It often happens that a buyer or seller has an intense ego commitment to a particular dollar figure. For example, a seller may want $120,000 for a given property, not because the home is worth that much but because the owner feels the $120,000 figure conveys a certain social status. Similarly, a buyer may not want to purchase real estate for more than a particular dollar value, say $110,000.

- Case 4. A property is sold for $120,000 and a lender finances $80,000 with a mortgage. The buyer is willing to pay the $120,000 price, which he feels is excessive, only if the deal can be negotiated further. In this instance the buyer asks for, and gets, a $30,000 second trust from the seller at 9 percent interest and pays $10,000 in cash at settlement. The true economic value of this transaction is far less than the recorded price of $120,000 may indicate.
- Case 5. A home is marketed for $120,000 but a buyer will only offer $115,000, his "limit." The seller agrees to a deal with an $80,000 first trust from a local lender, $10,000 in cash from the buyer and a $25,000 second trust at 16 percent interest held by the seller. The buyer has not exceeded his paper limit, but the value of this package is worth more than a cash deal for $115,000.
- Case 6. A home is marketed for $120,000 with $20,000 in cash from the purchaser, $80,000 from a local lender and a $20,000 second

trust from the seller at 12 percent interest. If the second trust is self-amortized over three years, the payments will be $664.29 per month. If the payments were set at $200 monthly, a far more affordable figure for most purchasers, there will be a huge balloon payment due when the loan ends. To avoid a balloon payment and still have reasonable monthly payments, the loan term can be extended. For instance, a 15-year second trust (a rather long second trust) will only require monthly payments of $240.03 to be self-amortizing.

To negotiate second trust alternatives it is necessary to calculate the costs, benefits and disadvantages of a series of possible loan arrangements. One useful way to make such comparisons is to create a chart showing monthly payments, the length of the loan, the loan's total cost (the number of payments × the monthly expense), any balloon pay-

Comparing Second Trusts			
	Deal 1	Deal 2	Deal 3
Sales price	——	——	——
Cash down	——	——	——
First trust	——	——	——
Interest rate	——	——	——
Term in years	——	——	——
Monthly payments	——	——	——
Second trust	——	——	——
Interest rate	——	——	——
Term in years	——	——	——
Monthly payments	——	——	——
Total monthly payment for both loans	——	——	——
Balloon payment	——	——	——
Points	——	——	——
Total cost°	——	——	——
Total interest	——	——	——

° It is probable that the first and second trusts will have different terms; to figure total loan costs multiply first and second trust monthly payments by the number of months each will be outstanding. For example, a 30-year first trust will have 360 payments, a 5-year second trust will have only 60 payments.

ment, etc. To find total interest, subtract the original balance from the loan's total cost and then add the value of any balloon payments. Using such a chart will allow you to compare second trust alternatives and see which is best for you.

SELLERS AS SECOND TRUST LENDERS

The concept of "real estate financing" usually implies that an institution such as a savings and loan association, mortgage banker or bank will somehow be involved in the mortgage process. However, sometimes second mortgages are seller "take-backs," direct arrangements between buyers and sellers in which sellers make loans to purchasers and thus assume a new role, that of lender.

While commercial lenders are in the business of processing loan papers and making mortgages, individual sellers rarely have an equal level of expertise. For this reason sellers who wish to hold second trusts should examine such financing carefully before making commitments. Buyers too should review loans from sellers to assure that they do not contain unworkable or unfair provisions.

The rules governing second trusts are established in the jurisdiction where the property is located. Different jurisdictions have vastly different approaches to second trusts and both buyers and sellers should investigate such financing with care before ratifying a real estate sales agreement. Here are the major areas to consider:

Interest. What is the proposed rate of interest? Many states have usury laws which establish maximum rates of interest for various kinds of financing. If the interest rate exceeds the usury level, the lender may suffer severe penalties. In some cases, a distinction is made between the rate allowable for residential second trusts and for second trusts that are part of an investment purchase and so the purpose of a loan may influence the rate allowed.

When money is tight, market conditions may require high interest levels to justify a second trust. But what happens if the usury limit for second trusts is 20 percent and a fair market return is 22 percent? In such instances either the loan will not be made or the terms of such financing will be adjusted so that usury rules are not violated. For example, rather than having a $20,000 loan at 22 percent, buyer and seller may agree to other terms, perhaps a $23,157.90 loan at 19 percent interest ($20,000 × 22 percent equals $4,400; $23,157.90 × 19 percent also equals $4,400).

Payment.   Second trusts are usually designed so that borrowers can make relatively small monthly payments. These payments, plus the short term which second trusts generally feature, often require a balloon payment when the loan ends. How much is the monthly payment? How large is the balloon payment? Where, specifically, will the borrower get the money to repay the balloon payment? By refinancing? Through an inheritance? Savings? If savings, why not structure a self-amortizing loan initially and avoid the whole issue of a balloon payment?

Format.   Standardized real estate contracts commonly call for the precise wording and terms of a loan to be "in the lender's usual form." This means commercial lenders get to make the rules. If you are a seller/lender, then surely you should insist on the same right and have your attorney draw up or approve all loan documents.

Servicing.   Commercial loan payments can be made at the institution where the loan originated, by mail, or electronically from one commercial lender to another. But what about loans which are made by property owners? In many cases, borrowers simply mail monthly payments to second trust holders, a system that may be disrupted if payments are delayed or lost in the mail. To assure that payments are being made—and received—in a timely manner, it may be best to make payments to a local lender who can date and verify the payment and then forward the money to the second trust holder. For more information about establishing such accounts, speak to officers at local savings and loan associations or banks.

Restrictions.   Local rules concerning second trusts may contain a variety of conditions, requirements and restrictions. In the District of Columbia, for example, the right to make a second trust with a balloon payment may vary according to whether or not the seller is an owner/occupant or a non-occupant (investor) owner.

Insurance.   Sellers making second trust loans should be concerned with two insurance issues:

First, commercial lenders insist on title insurance, of which they are the beneficiary, to at least the value of their loan so they will be protected in the event title to the property is faulty. Junior note holders often require similar protection so they can be repaid in the event of a title dispute.

Second, commercial lenders routinely require property owners to maintain adequate fire, theft and liability insurance. Seller/lenders should also get copies of the original policy (at settlement) as well as updates showing that the policy remains in force and that timely premium payments are being made.

Continuation.   If a situation develops where a borrower cannot repay a balloon note, serious questions arise for both the buyer and seller/lender. Should the property be foreclosed? Is there a way the note can be refinanced or extended? One approach to this problem has been developed in Maryland, where certain borrowers who made balloon notes after July 1, 1982, may unilaterally extend the term of their notes for up to two years, a situation which means that monthly payments will continue but the balloon payment is postponed.

Default of the First Trust.   Since first and second mortgage holders are often paid separately, the maker of one note may not know if payments on the other loan have been missed. Many second trusts contain a provision that they are automatically in default if the first mortgage is not properly paid.

Taxes.   Seller/lenders will certainly want to know that taxes on the property are being paid in a timely manner, and borrowers may be required to present proof of payment.

Trustees.   If the junior note is a "trust" and not a "mortgage," then the seller/lender should have the right to name the trustee or trustees.

Credit.   The willingness of an owner to hold a second trust should be contingent on a review, satisfactory to the seller/lender, of the borrower's finances and credit. A lender should have the right to see a borrower's credit report and, if the borrower is self-employed, past tax returns as well. It may be wise to have all credit information evaluated by a CPA.

The areas above clearly suggest that second trusts contain a host of potential problems for the unwary. To avoid needless difficulties, it is essential to consult with an attorney familiar with such financing in the jurisdiction where the property is located. Note also that many issues which concern second trusts are also important in those instances where sellers are creating first mortgages.

Questions to Ask:

What is the rate of interest for conventional financing?

What is the interest rate on savings accounts and money market funds?

What interest rate is available if you make a second trust?

What is the usury rate in the jurisdiction where the property is located?

Will the second trust be a self-amortizing loan or will it require a balloon payment?

What portion of the purchase price is in the form of cash from the buyer?

Are there legal restrictions which limit the use of a second trust in your transaction? Speak to an attorney for complete advice.

Can you meet your financial needs in the event your borrower fails to make timely payments?

Can you meet your financial needs in the event your borrower stops making all payments?

Can you meet your financial needs if you must spend several thousand dollars in a foreclosure procedure?

Can you meet future obligations, perhaps a balloon payment of your own, if your borrower fails to make his or her balloon payment to you?

Does the buyer have a unilateral right to continue the note and not make the balloon payment? Does this type of regulation govern balloon notes in your area? If you are a seller, how will the deferral of a balloon payment affect your personal finances? Would such a regulation make a second trust unworkable?

What will a local lender charge to service your loan?

What are the tax implications of deferred payments? Speak to a CPA or tax attorney for complete information.

HOW TO SAVE $100,000 WITH SECOND TRUSTS

Second trusts can be used effectively both to acquire real estate and to refinance property. When compared with 30-year conventional loans, second trusts are often a bargain even when they have higher interest rates.

Second trusts can be surprisingly cheap in terms of actual interest costs because they have short terms. Combined with an assumable first trust in a sale, or added to an existing loan when refinancing, second trusts can save borrowers thousands of dollars in many cases.

Mr. Hansen's Loan Choices		
	New First Trust	**First Trust/Second Trust**
Loan principal	$70,000	$25,000 loan balance $45,000 new financing
Interest rate	9 percent	6 percent old loan 12 percent new loan
Monthly payment	$563.24	$210.96 old loan 645.62 new loan $856.58 Total
Number of payments	360	180 old loan 120 new loan
Total payment	$202,765	$ 37,973 old loan 77,474 new loan $115,447 Total
Total interest	$132,765	$45,447
Interest saved	none	$87,318
Points	$700	$450

Suppose Hansen has an assumable, 6 percent mortgage with 15 years to run. He needs $45,000 to pay his daughter's college tuition and so he looks at refinancing alternatives.

The Hansen home is worth $100,000, the present mortgage balance is $25,000 and monthly payments are $210.96. (The original loan balance was $35,187.)

Hansen can go out and refinance the entire property by getting a $70,000 loan at the current rate—9 percent in this example. That loan will require 360 payments of $563.24 each. Or Hansen can get a $45,000 second trust at 12 percent interest. If this was a 10-year second trust, 120 monthly payments of $645.62 will be needed for a self-amortizing loan. The table above shows how Mr. Hansen can cut his interest bill by $87,318.

In addition to interest costs, one must also consider up-front fees. If a single point is charged in each case, a point for the $45,000 second trust will cost $450, while a point for a new $70,000 first mortgage will cost $700. Loan origination fees are likely to be far less expensive with the smaller second trust. Fees for appraisals and credit reports should be identical.

For Hansen, the use of a second trust will save more than $87,000 in interest costs. If the additional cost per month, $293.34, is more than he can afford, Hansen can work out some arrangement to offset the expense, such as postponing the purchase of a new car or eliminating a vacation. Alternatively, his daughter might agree to pay the additional money by working part-time.

Notice that Mr. Hansen would have been just as far ahead if he were buying rather than refinancing property under similar circumstances. For example, suppose a house was available for $85,000 and that a $25,000 first trust at 6 percent interest was assumable. Hansen can pay $15,000 in cash and get a conventional loan for $70,000, or he can assume the existing mortgage and get a second trust for $45,000. If the rates and terms were the same as with the refinancing example, Hansen will still save more than $87,000 in interest costs by choosing the second trust.

8

How to Pay Off
a Balloon Note

Whenever balloon loans are discussed great attention should be paid to the risks of such financing, mortgages that feature huge payments at the end of their terms. Borrowers who fail to make this large final payment may lose their property through a foreclosure action. Yet, despite the potential risk, balloon payments are a common feature of many real estate transactions because they offer advantages to savvy borrowers.

While balloon notes have traditionally been associated with second trust financing, they are becoming more common with first mortgages as well. Roll-over loans have huge balloon payments. Graduated payment mortgages (GPMs) and adjustable rate mortgages (ARMs) can have balloon payments also.

Balloon payments result from one of two situations. In the first case, monthly payments are too low to amortize the loan. For example, it will cost $703.93 a month to have a $50,000 loan at 10 percent interest amortized over 9 years. If the monthly payments are only $400, the table at the top of the next page shows what happens.

With this loan there is no amortization whatsoever because monthly payments are always less than $703.93. After 9 years, a borrower will owe $52,900.90.

In the second case, balloon payments can develop when monthly payments are large enough to produce a self-amortizing loan but the loan term is too short. For example, to amortize an $85,000 loan over 30 years at 10 percent interest will require monthly payments of

	Low Monthly Payments		
End of Year	Principal ($)	Interest ($)	Loan Balance ($)
1	-209.43	5,009.43	50,209.43
2	-231.36	5,031.36	50,440.78
3	-255.58	5,055.58	50,696.36
4	-282.34	5,082.34	50,978.71
5	-311.91	5,111.91	51,290.62
6	-344.57	5,144.57	51,635.19
7	-380.65	5,180.65	52,436.35
8	-420.51	5,220.51	52,436.35
9	-464.54	5,264.54	52,900.90

$745.94. The table below shows what happens to the loan if the payments were set at $745.94 but the loan term is only 5 years.

In this case the principal balance at the end of 5 years is $82,088.17,

	Short-Term Balloon Schedule		
End of Year	Principal ($)	Interest ($)	Balance ($)
1	472.50	8,478.73	84,527.50
2	521.97	8,429.26	84,005.53
3	576.63	8,374.60	83,428.90
4	637.01	8,314.22	82,791.89
5	703.72	8,247.51	82,088.17

an amount somewhat lower than the original note. With payments large enough to produce self-amortization, the principal value of this loan—or any loan—will always decline.

Borrowers should distinguish between balloon arrangements that result in smaller principal balances and those which actually increase the debt. Growing balloon payments take more money to refinance from borrowers who have not made—or who have been unable to make—amortizing monthly payments. Such borrowers may require more income to refinance their property than to acquire it initially because they are seeking larger loans, depending on interest rates. In addition, as the size of the debt rises one has to wonder if there is enough value in the property to justify a growing loan.

The balance between the risk and benefit of a balloon payment must be carefully weighed by individual purchasers and lenders. Buyers without adequate financial means, discipline or planning should clearly stay away from balloon financing. Those who do use balloon loans must develop a rational repayment strategy, possibly one of the eight listed here.

Strategy 1.   Loan term. In general, borrowers should seek the longest possible term when using balloon financing. More years mean more potential opportunities to renegotiate loans, refinance property or sell real estate if necessary.

Having the longest possible term does not necessarily mean that borrowers should wait to the last minute before refinancing. As time passes interest charges accrue and balloon payments grow. More dollars, even dollars devalued by inflation, will be required to satisfy the note and so the problem of repayment should be examined as soon as the loan is made.

Strategy 2.   Refinance in part. In those situations where the first mortgage has a balloon payment it may be possible to raise needed cash by obtaining a second mortgage, hopefully a loan without a balloon requirement.

Strategy 3.   Get a new balloon note. This may not resolve the ultimate problem of a balloon payment but at least it will defer the issue for a while. With the new balloon financing at least try to get better terms, that is, a longer note if possible, lower interest or better monthly payments.

Strategy 4.   Refinance completely. If you have been making regular payments on your current mortgage and have a good credit record you may be able to refinance with a new, self-amortizing loan from a commercial lender.

Strategy 5.   Get an extension. If you have a good payment record, a lender may want to continue the loan, particularly if the rate of return is at or above current market levels. Borrowers will have the most leverage if they couple an extension with an interest increase long before the balloon payment is due.

Strategy 6.   Sell part of the property. It may be possible to subdivide your property and sell off some portion to meet a balloon payment. Be aware that since the entire property is secured by both the first and second trusts, if you want to subdivide and sell off a piece to pay only the second trust you will need permission from the first trust holder.

Strategy 7.   Sell an interest in the property. Enter into an equity-sharing arrangement with a cash-rich buyer. This will result in eliminating the balloon payment while diluting your interest in the future profits, benefits and losses associated with property. Again, check the first trust to see if an equity-sharing arrangement is permitted.

Strategy 8.   Sell the property. Investment buyers will frequently acquire property financed with a balloon note with the intention of marketing it before the balloon payment is due. The proceeds from the sale can then be used to pay off all liens against the property, including the balloon note. In considering this approach, one must wonder what happens if the property's value does not appreciate or if the cost of marketing eliminates all profit.

An increasing number of five year, seven year, and 10-year balloon notes have recently become available. Such loans can be attractive because they have a marginally-lower interest rate than conventional mortgages with 30-year terms.

Lenders sometimes argue that they will continue balloon notes providing the borrower has made timely payments. Even in the best circumstances, however, lender assurances should not be seen as a substitute for the greater certainty of a 15 or 30-year loan commitment.

While it may be true that a balloon note can be refinanced, it is also likely that refinancing will involve another loan application and closing—two inconvenient and expensive events. No less important, who can tell where interest levels will be in five or 10 years. If rates are sufficiently high, then obtaining a new loan to replace balloon financing may be better than foreclosure, but it may also mean huge monthly payments.

Questions to Ask:

How large is the balloon payment? (Always get an amortization schedule to determine principal and interest costs.)

What is the rate of interest?

When is the balloon payment due?

How long will the process of refinancing take? Be certain to allow extra time in case an application is delayed or rejected and additional weeks or months are needed to process a new or revised application.

What are the tax implications of subdividing property, particularly land which is part of a personal residence? What are the tax implications of entering into a shared-equity arrangement? Speak to a tax consultant for current advice.

Can you subdivide property while keeping the first trust? In many instances subdividing is prohibited by the terms of the first trust.

9

How to Save Money with Assumable Mortgages

The largest single source of below-market financing is the multibillion-dollar pool of existing mortgages, where payments may be continued by real estate buyers without a change in interest rates or other conditions. Known broadly as *assumable* mortgages, such financing is available in every community and represents a source of significant dollar savings for many purchasers. An assumable loan situation can look like this:

Mr. Pace likes a $45,000 house in the country and offers to buy the property with $5,000 down. The sale also includes assuming a first trust with a $20,000 balance and getting a $20,000 second trust from the seller.

The reason Pace wants to assume the first trust is that it has a 6 percent interest rate. His payments on the note total only $150 per month and the loan has a little more than 18 years to go. The second trust, a 10-year, self-amortizing note at 12 percent interest, costs $286.94 per month.

As an alternative, Pace can get a 30-year, $40,000 first trust at 9 percent interest with monthly payments of $321.85. While the assumption/second trust arrangement costs $85.91 extra per month when compared to new financing, Pace will save $58,897.50 by using the combined financing package.

Assumable mortgages offer three major advantages to borrowers. First, assumable mortgages offer the possibility of below-market financing. When you can take over a loan with 6 percent interest in a 9 percent market, you're ahead.

	Mr. Pace's Loan Choices	
	New Loan	Assumption and Second Trust
Money down	$5,000	$5,000
Loan balance	$40,000	$20,000 first trust 20,000 second trust $40,000 Total
Interest rate	9 percent	6 percent first trust 12 percent second trust
Number of payments	360	$220.27 first trust $120 second trust
Monthly cost	$321.85	$150.00 first trust 286.94 second trust $436.94 Total
Extra monthly cost		$85.91
Total payments	$115,865.66	$33,040.50 first trust 34,432.80 second trust $67,473.30 Total
Extra cost	$48,392.36	

Second, buyers who might otherwise be frozen out of the real estate market by high interest rates can often find affordable housing when they locate property with assumable financing.

Third, assumable mortgages produce faster equity growth. In their first years, monthly mortgage payments are heavily tilted toward interest costs and only a limited number of dollars remain to reduce the principal balance of a loan. Over time, the balance between interest payments and principal reductions changes, with more and more money going to pay down the loan's principal balance.

Since loans are typically assumed several years after they originate, buyers who assume benefit from larger equity reductions each month. For example, a 30-year, $85,000 mortgage at 9 percent interest will require monthly payments of $683.93. Of this amount, only $46.23 will be used to reduce the principal balance in the first month. If such a loan were assumed after 60 payments, the monthly cost would be the same but the principal reduction would rise to $72.15.

Within the pool of assumable mortgages are loans with interest costs of 6, 7 and 8 percent. As a rule, the lower the rate of interest the older the loan. Older mortgages, in turn, have smaller remaining principal balances, so buyers will need more cash or secondary financing to obtain such loans. A $100,000 home may well have an assumable loan at 6 percent interest but the principal balance may be just $20,000. To buy this property a purchaser will have to come up with $80,000 in cash or credit, financing which is not available to everyone and which may be better invested elsewhere even when it is available.

While low interest assumptions are clearly something for which buyers should search, the benefits of assumable financing are not always certain.

Consider a situation where a property is available for $100,000. There is a $50,000 assumable first trust at 8 percent. The buyer has $20,000 in cash and asks the seller to take back a $30,000 second trust. The seller will do this, but only if the buyer pays 11 percent interest.

If accepted, the result of this arrangement will be a blended overall interest rate of 9.13 percent. The question is whether the combined rate and monthly payment required for the two loans is a better or worse deal than simply refinancing the property on a conventional basis. It is entirely possible that an assumption with a second trust will have both a higher interest rate and a higher monthly payment than a new loan.

In addition to comparing interest rates and monthly payments, financing costs must also be weighed. Is there a modest assumption fee or is a large payment required? How does the expense of an assumption compare with the expense of new financing, including loan application fees, points, and origination costs?

The element of time must be considered when comparing assumptions with alternative financing arrangements. An assumed mortgage plus a second trust may have higher monthly costs than a new conventional loan but the combination package may have a term which is considerably shorter. If you intend to hold property for many years, the higher payments may actually be a bargain if there are fewer of them.

Questions to Ask:

What is the assumable loan's remaining mortgage balance?
What is the assumable loan's interest rate?
What is the assumable loan's remaining term?
How much cash is required to take over an assumption?
What is the prevailing interest rate for conventional financing?
What is the prevailing interest rate for a second trust?
How large is the assumption fee?
In comparison, what is the cost of new financing in terms of a loan origination fee, points, title insurance, legal fees, etc.?

WHERE TO FIND ASSUMABLE LOANS

For many years home loans were freely assumable because interest rates were relatively stable and the value of money was not rapidly eroded by inflation. Lenders who paid 4 and 5 percent for savings accounts and other short-term deposits could profitably loan money for 30 years at 6 and 7 percent interest. Assumptions, in such conditions, were practical because the interests of neither lenders nor borrowers were harmed.

This system worked well until the late 1970s. At that time the cost of short-term borrowing began to rise above the return lenders were receiving from mortgage portfolios and huge losses were the natural result.

Why did the system change? With inflation the public could no longer preserve the spending power of its dollars by making short-term deposits at low rates. Mortgage interest rates went up as lenders were forced to pay more interest to attract short-term deposits and accounts.

Just as important, dollars which at one time would have been deposited with mortgage lenders were now diverted elsewhere. The "lending" industry was transformed into the "financial services" industry, where more players competed for the public's money. Billions of dollars, for example, were shifted from banks and savings and loan associations to money market funds and other new investment choices, a process known as "disintermediation" in the jargon of the financial community.

The fact that short-term funding costs rose meant that lenders had multibillion-dollar mortgage portfolios paying 4, 5, 6, 7 and 8 percent interest which were underwritten by short-term borrowing at rates of 12, 13 and 14 percent and even higher. As part of their strategy to limit losses, lenders began to restrict the assumability of new loans. New mortgages made in the "lender's usual form" began to commonly include a *due-on-sale* clause (also known as an *alienation* clause), which provided that the entire loan would be payable at the time the property was sold or, alternatively, that mortgages could be assumed but only with the prior written "consent" of the lender.

As restrictive clauses became more common, lenders were able to reduce their portfolio of outstanding assumable mortgages and thus lower their exposure to changing market conditions. While original borrowers with fixed-rate mortgages can get loans at current market rates, such rates are not freely passed along to future buyers. In effect, the burden of inflation had been shifted from lenders to borrowers.

Not surprisingly, due-on-sale clauses raised and continue to raise a number of issues. Are such clauses in the public interest? If not, can lenders enforce them? Are there ways to evade due-on-sale restrictions? A variety of lawsuits have resulted from efforts to avoid such limiting clauses. What must one do to get the "consent" of a lender? In many cases lenders will not agree to an assumption under any conditions, while in other situations lenders will approve assumptions when interest rates are raised, new fees are charged, or both.

While new mortgages routinely contain due-on-sale clauses, the pool of loans which are assumable encompasses millions of mortgages. Here, in general terms, is a catalogue of loans that are commonly assumable:

FHA Mortgages.   Traditionally one of the most important sources of assumable financing, FHA loans today may or may not be freely assumable, depending on who is selling the property, who is buying, and the loan's age.

FHA loans made prior to December 1, 1986 are generally assumable with the exception of certain FHA-backed loans made through state and local housing programs. These special loans may only be assumed by those who qualify for related housing programs, usually individuals with low or moderate incomes who have not owned property in the past three years.

Assumptions for FHA loans made between December 1, 1986 and December 14, 1989 were restricted during the first year to qualified owner-occupants. Investors could only assume such financing after two years.

FHA loans made after December 15, 1989 are not freely assumable. Owner-occupants wishing to take over FHA mortgages must be financially qualified. As to investors, they need not worry about assumptions because they are barred from assuming loans made after December 15, 1989.

At this point the FHA assumption scoreboard looks like this:

- All loans made prior to December 14, 1989 are freely-assumable by owner occupants. The one-year waiting period no longer matters because all FHA mortgages issued during or before 1989 are at least 12 months old.
- FHA loans made before December 1, 1986 can be assumed by investors. FHA mortgages made between December 1, 1986 and December 14, 1989 can be freely assumed by investors because the loans are at least two years old.
- FHA loans made after December 15, 1989 can only be assumed by qualified owner occupants. Investors need not apply.

Despite the new rules, at the end of 1989 roughly three million FHA loans were outstanding and most were freely assumable at their original rates and terms.

VA Mortgages. VA loans issued before March 1, 1988, are freely assumable and borrowers who wish to acquire such financing must pay a $45 transfer fee. Loans made after March 1, 1988, are qualified assumptions and would-be purchasers must pass muster with both the lender and the VA before such financing can be assumed. Lenders are likely to charge from $300 to $500 for processing qualified assumptions, plus a .5 percent funding fee paid to the VA.

Millions of older VA loans are now outstanding and freely assumable. In addition, it should be said that while only veterans qualify to take out loans under the VA program, both vets and non-vets can assume VA financing.

Silent Loans.   Conventional loans not containing due-on-sale clauses or language to the contrary should be freely assumable at their original rates and terms.

Due-on-Sale Loans.   In some circumstances a lender may elect not to enforce a due-on-sale clause. For instance, if the loan has a 12 percent interest rate and the prevailing interest level is 10 percent, then the lender will logically want the loan to continue. When a loan has a due-on-sale clause which the lender elects to ignore, be certain to obtain a clear, written statement from the lender noting that the loan can be assumed and detailing all conditions.

ARMs.   Adjustable rate mortgages are commonly assumable at current rates by qualified buyers.

Estates.   When a borrower dies and the property is willed to a relative who lives on the property, then the new owner-occupant may assume the loan.

Divorce.   In divorces, loans may be assumed by spouses and children who live on the property.

State Bans.   In some jurisdictions due-on-sale clauses are prohibited. For specific information, contact a knowledgeable real estate attorney in the jurisdiction where the property is located.

Consent Loans.   In those instances when a loan is assumable with the lender's consent, such consent may be given, often in exchange for an increase in interest to the current rate, charging fees up front or issuing new mortgage documents that entail certain payments to the lender.

The question with both consent loans and ARMs is whether or not assumable mortgages with market interest rates are bargains. Since the rates for both conventional and assumed loans with current interest rates will be substantially the same, one must weigh the expense of an *assumption fee* (a charge made by a lender at the time of an assumption to at least cover the cost of paperwork and frequently to raise the lender's yield from the mortgage) and all other charges versus the cost of new financing, including items such as loan application fees, origination charges, points, etc.

Questions to Ask:

> Is the loan freely assumable?
> If the loan is assumable, is there an assumption fee? (As a matter of negotiation try to get the other party to pay this cost or at least share this expense.)
> If there is a due-on-sale clause, will it be enforced?
> What actions will be required to satisfy a lender whose "consent" is needed for an assumption? Will interest levels rise? Are new mortgage papers required?

ASSUMPTIONS AND RESPONSIBILITY

While the term *assumption* is used generally to describe mortgages passed from seller to buyer, more specific definitions are required to resolve an important issue: Who is responsible to the lender if loan payments are missed?

To determine the precise obligations of buyer and seller one must see if a property has been purchased "subject to" the mortgage or if the loan has been "assumed."

In those cases where property is purchased "subject to" the mortgage it is understood that the buyer is not responsible to the lender for the loan's repayment. If payments are not made by the buyer the lender will seek compensation from the original borrower. While the buyer may have little direct responsibility to repay the loan, it would take a truly irrational person to not recognize that default means foreclosure, the loss of any equity invested in the property and the total improbability of future mortgage borrowing. These are powerful financing considerations which no purchaser can reasonably overlook.

When mortgages are *assumed* and the buyer agrees to be responsible for the entire debt, the lender can pursue both the original borrower and the purchaser in case of default.

Properties purchased with assumed financing or bought "subject to" the mortgage represent deals between buyers and sellers rather than lenders and borrowers, except when the "consent" of a lender is given. It is possible for freely assumable financing to be passed from seller to buyer even when the purchaser is totally unknown to the lender.

Lenders may not be able to prevent the take-over of freely assumable mortgages but, in turn, they are not required to release original borrowers from the obligation to repay their loans. After all, if sellers could merely pass on the responsibility to repay mortgage debts it would be a simple matter to hurt the lender. Here's what can happen in the worst case.

Wainwright bought a property 10 years ago for $100,000 that was financed with $20,000 in cash and a freely assumable $80,000 mortgage. Because of flooding, the value of Wainwright's property has dropped substantially and to reduce his loss, Wainwright sells his home to a vagrant who agrees to assume the original loan. The vagrant makes no payments on the mortgage and the bank soon forecloses. The mortgage balance is $75,000, the foreclosure value is only $40,000 and so the lender suffers a loss of $35,000 plus foreclosure expenses.

How much liability, in real terms, do original borrowers have when a loan is assumed or payments are continued "subject to"? Since the overwhelming majority of all mortgages are never in default, there is only the most limited possibility that a lender will pursue an original borrower for compensation. Even when a loan is defaulted, original borrowers still benefit from several practical considerations.

First, the property's innate value is generally far greater than the balance of assumed financing.

Second, in those sales which feature large down payments and second trusts, the original borrower's liability for the first trust is well defended because all proceeds from a foreclosure sale will first be applied to the repayment of that debt before any payments are made for a second trust or to the purchaser. In "no cash" or "cash plus" sales, however, the seller's protection is limited if non-existent.

Third, there are some who argue that it is a good strategy to remain liable for a mortgage. If the buyer defaults, it is suggested, it may be possible to get the property back at discount by repurchasing it from a buyer faced with foreclosure.

Whether or not it will be possible for original borrowers to get a release depends on the lender's policies. Lenders, however, have little incentive to release original borrowers except in those cases where mortgage terms can be structured more favorably in their behalf. Several incentives may encourage lenders to release original borrowers, including:

Higher Interest. A lender may authorize a release for the original borrower if the interest rate on the loan can be raised.

Buyer Qualification. Lenders have a clear and understandable desire to assure that new borrowers will be creditworthy individuals. Raising interest rates is a useless exercise if the new borrower cannot afford monthly mortgage payments.

New Papers. In some instances lenders will release original borrowers if they can issue a new mortgage with the exact same terms as the first loan. A new mortgage, rather than a mere continuation of the old loan, will generate additional fees to the lender.

Fees. *Assumption fees* are charges made by lenders to cover the cost of processing new paperwork. However, some lenders see such charges as profit-centers and exact substantial payments to permit a release.

In addition to getting a release directly from a lender, original borrowers may also require a release from other parties. See Appendix B for detailed information regarding VA and FHA release policies.

Questions to Ask:

   If you are a buyer, are you assuming old financing or purchasing property "subject to" an old loan?
   If you are a seller and your loan is assumable do you want a release?
   What are the lender's release policies?

10
Assisted Loans

Cash is a key ingredient in many real estate sales and yet money up front is not always necessary to cement a deal; indeed, a number of real estate strategists recommend buying without cash if possible.

What happens if you're a buyer without dollars, someone with enough income to support mortgage payments but too little currency on hand? Or, how can you boost your credit standing if you have saved your dollars but have limited earnings?

A large portion of all real estate transactions may be described as *assisted* sales, deals in which a buyer without sufficient cash or adequate credit receives material aid from an individual or institution that has no claim against the future appreciation of the property. Families, friends, the VA, FHA and private mortgage insurers are among those that may be clustered in a discussion of assisted transactions. In addition, assisted sales can include equity-sharing arrangements, deals often made within families.

GIFTS AND CO-SIGNERS

The help of friends and family in a real estate deal most often comes in the form of cash gifts or the extension of credit, acts of generosity that must be viewed with some care.

For the protection of buyers, sellers and lenders, a "gift" should be seen as something more than a passing oral comment by Uncle Willard or whoever to come up with $15,000 if you ever purchase real estate. A gift commitment is truly a gift when it is:

Irrevocable.   A "gift" that can be taken back is not a gift.

Free of Consideration.   A "gift" on which one pays interest, where repayment in whole or in part is expected, or where other valued consideration is anticipated is not a gift.

Available.   A gift not in hand by settlement may cause the forfeiture of a deposit because the deal cannot be completed.

Binding.   What happens if a gift commitment is made and the donor dies before the gift is delivered? Gift commitments should be binding on heirs, executors, administrators, successors and assigns.

Contingent.   A purchase dependent on the delivery of a gift should be structured so that if the gift is not received by a given time and date, the sale is off and the deposit of the purchaser will be returned in full. Conversely, if it is the intent of the donor to provide a gift for the purchase of a particular property, that gift should be returned if for some reason the sale falls through.

Carefully Thought Out.   Sizable gifts may involve significant tax questions which should be reviewed by an attorney and/or tax authority prior to any commitment. For instance, will the donor be forced to pay a gift tax? How will a gift affect the recipient's tax basis in the property? It may be that an outright gift is not the best approach in certain cases. Rather than providing a large bundle of cash up front, some donors instead take back a mortgage which they then partially forgive each year.

There are some buyers who have managed to accumulate enough cash for a real estate purchase but lack sufficient income, at least on paper, to qualify for a mortgage. In such situations, co-signers with good credit may participate in a sale.

A lender will want a co-signer to repay any portion of a defaulted loan not re-captured in a foreclosure sale. In many instances, lenders will not only want a credit-worthy individual to be a co-signer but also to be on the deed as a co-owner. The reasoning is that in the event of default the lender can pursue the co-signer for foreclosure costs, which often amount to several thousand dollars, as well as any portion of the loan not satisfied in the sale.

The possible problem with a co-signer as co-buyer is that this is not truly the relationship which many families or friends envision. Also, a co-signer on the deed may endanger the ownership of the property—and the lender's interest—if the co-signer goes bankrupt or is forced to pay a liability claim. With a co-signer as a co-owner, both buyer and co-signer would be wise to have an attorney draw up an appropriate agreement outlining the relationship between the parties and resolving potential estate issues as well.

As with gifts, sales that depend on co-signatories should be made contingent on performance; that is, there is no deal if the co-signer refuses to sign documents, provide credit information or take such other steps as may be required to complete the sale. In addition, the actions of co-signers should be binding on heirs, executors, administrators, successors and assigns.

In the case of both gifts and co-signers, borrowers should be aware that not all prospective donors and co-signers can be regarded as capable individuals. The ability of habitual alcoholics, the legally insane, those with certain drug dependencies, minors, senile individuals, and bigamists to make gifts or co-sign documents may be subject to future challenge even when such personal difficulties are not immediately apparent. Be certain to obtain advice from an attorney in the event of competency questions.

Questions to Ask:

Can you reasonably expect a gift from any friend or relative? If so, are there any conditions?

Is the donor willing to sign all requisite forms?

What are the tax implications of a gift? Speak to an attorney or CPA for specific advice.

If friends or relatives are willing to act as co-signers will the lender also require them to be co-owners? If they are co-owners, what is your relationship? Is it an equity-sharing deal? Speak to an attorney about co-ownership issues.

VA FINANCING

In 1930 federal bureaus and offices concerned with veterans' issues were consolidated within a new entity, the Veterans Administration.

Home mortgages backed by the agency subsequently became known as "VA loans" even though the VA did not—and does not—make loans, it only guarantees a portion of their repayment. On March 15, 1989, the VA was promoted to Cabinet-level status and renamed the Department of Veterans Affairs, "DVA" for short. Because loans for veterans have long been known as "VA" financing, we'll continue to use the term "VA" generally, even though such loans may be backed either by the old VA or the newly-created DVA.

By their nature, programs developed by the federal government tend to be large and the no-money-down VA mortgage program is no exception. There are four million VA-backed loans outstanding and together they represent some of the best financing around.

What makes VA financing unique? There are several major factors:

- The VA is not a lender. Instead, the VA acts as a co-signer to assist qualified individuals who need home mortgages.
- Unlike conventional loans which require 20 percent cash down, there is no VA requirement for a down payment unless the purchase price of the property is greater than the VA's estimate of reasonable value or if a lender requires a cash down payment as a condition of the loan. Many VA buyers, however, elect to make a down payment even when one is not required to reduce their monthly payments.
- Mortgage amounts are not limited by the VA. Lenders, however, may elect to limit the size of VA loans that they will process. Under the current system, most lenders will provide up to $203,000 to qualified vets.
- Historically the VA mortgage program has been seen as a loan "guarantee" rather than insurance on which individuals pay premiums. In recent years, however, the VA has charged a "funding fee" to vets based on the amount put down to acquire a property. As a result of the 1993 budget bill, the funding fees now look like this: with less than 5 percent down, the fee is 2 percent of the loan value; with more than 5 percent but less than 10 percent down, the fee is 1.50 percent of the amount borrowed; with at least 10 percent down, the funding fee drops to 1.25 percent.

In the case of a veteran refinancing under the program to get a lower interest rate, the funding fee equals .50 percent of the loan amount. A vet who uses his or her eligibility a second time (perhaps to borrow more or to buy a new home) will pay a 3 percent funding fee for new financing.

As to National Guard and reservists who are now included in the VA program, they pay a .75 percent premium to use VA financing. For example, a reservist who uses VA financing to buy a home with nothing down would pay a 2.75 percent funding fee.

- A major attraction of VA financing has historically been the ability to freely assume such loans. That policy has now been replaced with a new standard which requires that would-be purchasers obtain the approval of both the VA and the lender who made the loan. The result is that new VA loans—those made after March 1, 1988—are no longer freely assumable. In addition, a small percentage of VA loans made through state and local housing agencies may be assumed only by individuals otherwise qualified to participate in such programs.

- VA rates float with the marketplace.

- Both fixed-rate and adjustable loans can be backed with VA guarantees.

- VA financing is self-amortizing if held for the complete loan term.

- VA-backed loans may be pre-paid without penalty. However, pre-payments must be made on the loan's due date, otherwise you may face a penalty of as much as one month's interest. Speak to your lender for details.

- VA loans are generally available to those with military experience. Individuals who served in peacetime prior to Sept. 7, 1980 are generally required to have 181 days of continuous active duty service to qualify for VA benefits, 90 days of such service in wartime. Those who have served since Sept. 7, 1980 are typically required to have at least 24 months of continuous active-duty service to qualify for VA benefits.

- Individuals with six years of service in the National Guard or Reserve may now qualify for VA mortgages.

- Certain other individuals such as officers in the Public Health Service may also qualify for VA benefits.

The VA mortgage program embodies a guarantee on which lenders rely to reduce their risk. The VA promises to repay a maximum today of $36,000, a figure which represents each veteran's "entitlement."

When the VA program was first established during World War II the initial entitlement was $2,000. By the end of the war the entitlement figure was raised to $4,000 and it has gradually risen ever since. For VA-qualified buyers the rise of entitlement means that it is possible to have purchased a home many years ago and still have some entitlement remaining. A purchaser who bought a home for $25,000 in 1960 when the entitlement level was $12,500, for instance, will now have a remaining entitlement balance of $23,500, essentially an unused line of credit from Uncle Sam.

It may be possible for a vet to have his or her entitlement reinstated in certain circumstances. A veteran's entitlement can be restored to the full current level when a previous VA-backed loan has been completely repaid as part of a sale or when a VA-qualified purchaser assumes a VA mortgage and substitutes his or her entitlement for that of the original buyer.

If VA interest rates decline, an owner/occupant vet can refinance an old GI loan without using any additional entitlement. The size of the new GI mortgage, however, can be no greater than the value of the old loan balance plus any settlement fees required to obtain the new financing.

The size of an entitlement becomes important when one considers that lenders usually seek a four-to-one ratio of entitlement credit to mortgage debt. With the $36,000 guarantee, a lender will generally loan $144,000 to a financially qualified buyer. However, the $144,000 figure is not a legal limit and a lender could—and many do—make far larger loans.

Beyond the $36,000 entitlement, the VA now guarantees 25 percent of loan amounts above $144,000, up to a maximum exposure of $14,750. Ginnie Mae—the big secondary lender—has agreed to buy VA mortgages from local lenders providing individual loan amounts do not exceed $203,000. Between the VA guarantee and the Ginnie Mae loan limitation, most VA lenders will provide loans up to $203,000.

How important is VA financing? Except for several West Coast areas, typical homes sell for substantially less than $203,000 throughout the country. In the Washington, DC area, for example, three bedroom, two-bath homes in nearby Prince Georges County (Maryland) are commonly available for $125,000 to $150,000. In Wichita, KS, three-bedroom houses with two baths and two-car garages sell for just $75,000 to $85,000.

Given the broad availability of good houses at reasonable prices, it is unlikely that the VA loan ceiling will be raised for several years. A vet with a good income can now buy a substantial home with no down payment—a terrific deal by any standard.

To qualify for VA financing, a veteran must possess DD Form 214, a form given out when leaving the service, and VA Form 26-1880, "Request for Certificate of Eligibility." These forms are used to get a "Certificate of Eligibility." For current information visit VA regional offices, write the VA, or call via toll-free phone lines.

While VA mortgages would seem to be limited to veterans alone, the VA program actually benefits a far broader scope of the population. Non-veteran purchasers can assume VA mortgages at their original rates and terms, a significant financial advantage in many cases.

Non-veteran sellers can participate in the program by offering their homes to VA-qualified purchasers. To get VA financing, a home must be evaluated by the VA to determine its economic worth. An appraisal, or "Certificate of Reasonable Value" as it is called may be ordered by contacting regional VA offices.

The VA points out that its Certificate of Reasonable Value is for financial purposes only and is not intended to be a structural inspection. It is therefore possible to buy a VA-financed house that is in something less than pristine physical condition.

The question of when to order a VA appraisal is an issue that should be of some importance to sellers. Clearly an appraisal will be required to get VA financing, but should an appraisal be sought earlier in the marketing process, before there is a purchaser with whom to deal?

By getting an appraisal just before a home is offered for sale sellers will at least have the VA's view of what their property is worth. This can be a valuable selling tool if the appraisal meets the expectations of the seller, since property advertising can then be directed toward VA buyers ("VA appraised at $139,900"). But what happens if the appraisal is low? Sellers in such situations have spent money for an appraisal they are not likely to publicize.

Sellers are best served by having the buyer get and pay for an appraisal as part of the loan application process after an offer on the property has been made. An offer is a product of the marketplace and is surely an important benchmark by which the value of the property can be measured, one that cannot be totally ignored in the appraisal process.

If it should happen that the VA appraisal is less than the sales value of the property, the VA will guarantee a loan equal only to the estimated worth of the home. When an appraisal is below the sales value, the VA requires that purchasers have the option to withdraw from the deal, in which case their deposit must be returned in full.

In the event of a low appraisal there are also two other strategies which can be employed. First, a buyer can pay the difference between the sales price and the estimated value in cash. Second, the seller can reduce the sales price to the appraised value. As a matter of negotiation, buyer and seller may meet somewhere between these two choices.

Another new direction from the VA concerns borrower liability in the case of an assumption.

In the past the VA has vigorously sought to recover money lost from defaults, even when the original veteran borrower was *not* involved in fraud, material misrepresentation, or bad faith. Since loans made prior to March 1, 1988 were freely assumable, it could happen that a vet sells a home, the loan is assumed, the vet is not released from liability, and seven years later the vet receives a letter saying the buyer—or the buyer's buyer—had defaulted on the loan, the property was sold at foreclosure, and now the vet owes Uncle Sam $12,000.

In an absolute sense the veteran surely does owe the $12,000 because no release was provided. But is it fair or reasonable to pursue a vet who acted in good faith, made his payments, and was not a direct party to the foreclosure?

The VA, with prodding from Congress, has come to the conclusion that there are times where VA loans fail, where vets are liable on paper, and yet circumstances are such that it is unfair and unconscionable to pursue all claims against the vet.

The VA has established a "Compromise and Waiver Committee" (also known as "COW") to aid veterans with liability problems stemming from loans issued prior to March 1, 1988. The committee has the authority to reduce or waive claims, depending on the facts and circumstances in each case. More details are available from local VA offices.

The VA policy does not effect more recent mortgages because VA loans issued after March 1, 1988 can only be assumed by financially-qualified individuals. After the assumption is made, the original borrowers no longer have liability.

Questions to Ask:

What is the current VA interest rate?

What is the largest VA-backed mortgage offered by most local lenders?

What is the current number of points sought by lenders making VA loans? Check with different lenders, as this figure may vary. When VA interest rates are similar or equal to conventional levels there should be few, if any, additional points.

What is the current VA entitlement?

If you have used your VA entitlement in the past do you have any remaining entitlement? Check with your local VA office.

If you are a seller do you want a Certificate of Reasonable Value? If so, how much is such an appraisal?

Can you substitute an FHA appraisal for a Certificate of Reasonable Value? This may be possible in some areas, so contact your local VA office for more information.

If you are a buyer, do you have a Certificate of Eligibility in hand? How long will it take to get one?

What are the latest assumption rules? Is there an assumption fee? If so, how much?

Is there a funding fee being charged at the time you apply for VA financing? If so, how much?

What course of action will you take if the VA appraisal is less than the agreed sales price for a property?

Are there new VA rules which will affect your ability to get VA financing? Check with your local VA office.

FHA LOANS

The Federal Housing Administration (FHA) is one of the oldest and largest sources of mortgage assistance available to the general public. While VA mortgages can be seen as a reward for public service, FHA-backed loans are an outgrowth of a different public policy—the view that readily available mortgage funds will stimulate the economy in general and the housing industry in particular.

What makes FHA financing so attractive? Traditionally the answer has been low down payments and liberal qualification standards. Simplicity has also been a hallmark, at least until the past few years. Today the program is increasingly complex and increasingly expensive, qualities not normally associated with financing for first-time buyers and moderate income households.

Like the VA program, FHA financing does not mean that a federal agency lends money to homebuyers. Instead, the federal government guarantees repayment to participating lenders. This guarantee is so potent that FHA borrowers can obtain loans with excellent terms and little down.

By "FHA financing" most people really mean loans developed under Sec. 203(b), the largest of many mortgage insurance programs available through FHA. Here's how it works.

Loan amount and down payment. For many years FHA loans had a basic down payment formula: 3 percent of the first $25,000 and 5 percent of anything else. That evolved into a more complicated system between 1991 and 1992, but now we are largely back to the original FHA schedule.

To determine the FHA down payment we must first ask what is being financed. Let's say that Ms. Ratner buys a home for $90,000. Let us also say that there are closing costs worth $2,000 that can be financed by the FHA.

Step 1. The maximum loan amount for single-family homes has been pegged at $152,362 as of late 1994. The catch is that this maximum only applies to so-called high-cost housing areas. If Ms. Ratner lives in a community where housing costs are generally lower, then the maximum FHA loan can be as little as $77,197 as of this writing.

Conversely, if the Ratner property is located in Alaska, Guam, or Hawaii, or if Ratner is buying a two-, three-, or four-unit property, then the maximum FHA loan limit can be significantly more than $152,362.

Step 2. The FHA down payment formula works like this: 3 percent of the first $25,000 (a maximum of $750), 5 percent of the next $100,000 (as much as $5,000), and 10 percent of everything higher (for a $152,362 loan the additional amount would total $2,736.20). For a $152,362 loan the down payment would be $8,486.20—5.55 percent of the total purchase price.

How to Calculate FHA Down Payments

Case #1: $60,000 property

Sale Price	$60,000
Less: 3 percent of $25,000	750
Less: 5 percent of $35,000	1,750
Total Downpayment	2,500
Total Loan Amount	$57,500

Case #2: $110,000 property

Sale Price	$110,000
Less: 3 percent of $25,000	750
Less: 5 percent of $85,000	4,250
Total Downpayment	5,000
Total Loan Amount	$105,000

Case #3: $145,000 property

Sale Price	$145,000
Less: 3 percent of $25,000	750
Less: 5 percent of $100,000	5,000
Less: 10 percent of $20,000	2,000
Total Downpayment	7,750
Total Loan Amount	$137,250

In the case of Ms. Ratner, her down payment will be $4,000 ($750 + $3,250), and her basic loan will amount to $86,000 ($90,000 less $4,000).

Step 3. Under current FHA rules all allowable closing costs can be financed and added to the loan. For Ms. Ratner, this means her total loan is now $88,000 ($86,000 + $2,000) if she finances her closing costs. Her down payment will rise somewhat because of the higher loan amount.

Insurance. For many years, the insurance premium of the most popular FHA single-family program, Sec. 203(b), was equal to .5 percent of the current mortgage balance, insurance that stayed in effect as long as the loan was outstanding. Since loan balances declined over time, FHA insurance costs also dropped each month.

Now, however, the FHA is using a two-pronged approach to insurance funding. Not only is there a monthly .5 percent premium, the FHA also requires a single, lump-sum insurance payment up front, an amount generally equal to 3 percent of the mortgage balance.

With an $85,000 mortgage, for instance, the up-front fee will amount to $1,912. While purchasers can pay this sum in cash at settlement, it's more likely that most buyers will opt to increase the size of their mortgage by the value of the up-front insurance fee and make somewhat higher monthly payments.

How does the new insurance payment plan compare with the old formula? If the FHA interest rate for a 30-year, $85,000 loan was 8.5 percent, the monthly payment will be $635.58. Add a 0.5 percent insurance fee and the effective cost to the borrower is 9 percent, or $688.99 the first month.

The up-front insurance fee will not change the amount of cash required for this deal, because the fee can be added to the amount borrowed. Adding the insurance fee to the loan, however, increases monthly costs.

If we borrow $85,000 and add on a $1,912 fee, the total loan amount is $86,912 ($85,000 plus $1,912), and the monthly payment at 8.5 percent interest is $668.28. In addition, we have to add the .5 percent monthly insurance premium, a cost which brings the monthly expense to $704.49. While up-front costs are lower when closing expenses are

FHA Insurance Plan				
Fiscal Year	Up-Front Fee	Loan-to Value Ratio	Annual Premium	Years In Force
1995	2.25	89.99 or under	.50	11 years
	2.25	90.00–95.00	.50	30 years
	2.25	95.01 or more	.55	30 years

added onto the loan, borrowers should be aware that there is more debt to pay off when the property is sold because more money has been borrowed—$86,912 rather than $85,000, in this example.

Refunds.   While the up-front insurance premium has represented a barrier to homebuyers, at least in the past any unused portion has been refundable.

For instance, if Griffin paid a 3 percent fee up front for a 30-year mortgage but sold the house after 5 years, fairness suggests that some or much of the insurance premium has not been used and therefore Griffin should get a partial refund.

As this is written FHA has two refund policies.

First, on loans where borrowers paid only *monthly* premiums, essentially loans made prior to September 1, 1983, refunds are no longer available.

Second, refunds are available on loans made after September 1, 1983 for borrowers who paid an up-front fee.

For information about possible refunds, first obtain your FHA case number from your lender at closing or as soon thereafter as possible. Second, save the case number. You may need it years from now. Third, when you sell or refinance, contact your lender for refund information. Fourth, if the lender cannot help, contact the FHA (703-235-8117) and provide your FHA case number. Be aware that it will be difficult, if not impossible, for FHA to help if you do not have a case number.

Prepayment.   Residential FHA loans may be prepaid in whole or in part without penalty. You can make prepayments at any time during the loan term; however, if a prepayment is not made on the monthly due date, it will be credited to the next due date. And you will owe interest for the month. For complete information on FHA prepayment planning consult with your lender. In some situations it may be best to make prepayments with two checks: one for the value of the mortgage payment and another for any additional monies. With two checks, borrowers will have a record of all prepayments.

Loan Limit.   Unlike VA or conventional financing, there is an FHA loan limit. This limit is established by the federal government and varies according to whether or not a region is considered a "high-cost" housing area. As this is written, for example, guidelines allow as much as $152,362 for single-family housing in many high-cost areas. Check with lenders and brokers for loan limits in your area.

In addition, be aware that HUD has actively sought to raise the FHA loan limit. It is possible that at the time this book is read the FHA loan limit may exceed $170,000 if HUD is successful.

Rates.   FHA rates float with the market and parallel the ups and downs of other mortgage products.

Assumptions.   FHA loans have traditionally been freely assumable, but this tradition is now ended. In basic terms, current FHA assumption rules look like this:

First, loans made prior to February 4, 1988 are freely assumable. Loans made between December 1, 1986 and February 4, 1988 originally were restricted for periods of one to two years after origination, but such loans are now sufficiently old and the restrictions have expired.

Second, FHA mortgages made between February 5, 1988 and December 14, 1989 were originally restricted. For owner-occupants, assumptions in the first year after origination were banned except to qualified buyers. For investors, there was a two-year ban on assumptions unless the borrower was qualified. Both bans have expired.

Third, FHA loans made after December 15, 1989 may only be assumed by qualified owner-occupants and no loans may be assumed by investors.

FHA policies stem in part from a rash of foreclosures in recent years. However, millions of loans issued prior to December 15, 1989 remain outstanding and assumable.

Properties.   Loans under Sec. 203(b) can be used to acquire not only single-family homes but also structures with two, three and four units. As the number of units increases, so does the maximum mortgage amount that the FHA will insure. As this is written, congressionally approved guidelines allow FHA loans up to $152,362 for a single-family home, $194,850 for a duplex, $235,550 for a triplex, and $292,800 for a four-unit property. Single-family homebuyers in Alaska, Guam, and Hawaii may be able to get even larger FHA loans under Sec. 214. Be sure to check with lenders for the latest loan limits in your area.

When used for the purchase of multiple-unit buildings, FHA loans can be an attractive financing tool, particularly for individuals with limited capital. As an *owner-occupant*, a purchaser can acquire property with a minimal down payment, thus preserving his or her capital for repairs and upgrading. While occupant-owners can get FHA loans at established rates, such financing is off limits to investors.

Qualification standards.   The FHA qualifies prospects on the basis of *gross* income, the amount earned before taxes.

When considering an FHA loan, borrowers are qualified with 29/41 ratios; that is, up to 29 percent of your gross income can be devoted to principal, interest, taxes and insurance (PITI). Up to 41 percent of your income can be devoted to PITI plus such consumer costs as auto loans and monthly credit card charges. In the case of energy efficient properties, 31/43 ratios are allowed.

To obtain FHA-backed loans buyers must be financially qualified and the property evaluated by an FHA-approved appraiser. If it is found that the FHA appraised value is less than the selling price, then either the sales price must be lowered or the purchaser must be willing to cover the difference in cash. The FHA will not permit the use of a second trust to bridge the difference between the sales price and the appraised value of the property. The FHA will permit the use of second trusts as long as the combined value of the first and second trusts does not top FHA loan limits or required loan-to-value ratios.

Note to readers: Check index as well as Appendix B for other specialized FHA loan programs, such as ARMs and graduated payment mortgages, which are discussed separately.

FHA FINANCING WITH SWEAT EQUITY

One of the most attractive ways to buy real estate is to trade labor for cash, a strategy that holds obvious appeal for those with solid monthly incomes but few dollars in reserve.

Until recently sweat equity deals financed with FHA guarantees have meant heavy loan fees up front. Under the FHA 203(k) program it is possible to borrow enough money to both acquire a property and then fix it up.

Suppose Robinson wants to purchase a property for $80,000. In addition he will need $20,000 for improvements. Under 203(k) Robinson would receive $80,000 at closing to purchase the property and then the lender will release the $20,000 balance as repairs are made.

The trouble with 203(k) loans, at least from the lender's perspective, is that they require a lot of work. While most loans are finalized at closing, that is not the case with 203(k) financing. Since loan proceeds will be released as construction is completed, the lender must assure that the work has been done. To compensate for their extra paperwork and on-site inspections, lenders under 203(k) are permitted to charge not only a 1 percent origination fee, but also a 1.5 percent supplemental lending fee.

In addition to more fees up front, 203(k) borrowers may also face higher interest costs. If you borrow with 203(k), expect to pay an additional .5 to 1 percent above most other FHA loans.

Given higher interest costs and more fees it is not surprising that 203(k) loans are rarely used. Only a few hundred loans a year have been made under this program, despite the fact that it does allow people to buy today and improve tomorrow.

A different and less costly approach to sweat equity is now emerging from HUD's Salt Lake City office. Rather than go through 203(k), why not use 203(b) to achieve many of the same results?

What happens in Salt Lake City (and now elsewhere) is that a builder works with a buyer to complete a home. The builder erects a structure and the buyer completes certain work, say painting, landscaping, or exterior concrete construction. In exchange for such labor, the buyer gets a credit at closing to offset FHA downpayment requirements.

The Salt Lake City concept is attractive because it eliminates the 1.5 percent supplemental fee lenders can charge under 203(k), does not require any additional interest expense, and allows lenders to make loans without excess paperwork, inspections, or hassles. The builder sells a property, the lender makes a loan, a broker earns a sales fee, and the buyer gets a property. Everyone is happy.

Can it work in your area? The folks in Salt Lake City deserve credit for pioneering a sane concept and there is no reason why the sweat equity idea should not be transportable. Before buying into this program however, borrowers should consider the following issues.

- Not all local FHA offices will approve sweat equity deals under 203(b). Before considering an FHA sweat equity deal, find out about the policies of your local FHA office. If they will approve sweat equity arrangements under 203(b), confirm such information in writing.
- Unlike 203(k), the borrower/buyer is doing work on a property that he or she does not actually own. Improvements are made prior to closing which means that if the deal falls through, the buyer can forfeit his or her work. With 203(k), in contrast, the borrower owns the property. At best with the Salt Lake City approach a would-be buyer has an equitable interest in the property prior to closing, but not title.
- The borrower must complete required work according to the builder's timetable, otherwise the builder might face a long wait to close the deal as well as unanticipated interest costs.

- The amount of credit a buyer can obtain is limited to the value of the FHA down payment. No cash can come out of the deal as a result of the borrower's work.
- Brokers, builders and lenders should clearly explain the risks represented by working on property to which one does not have title. It will undoubtedly be appropriate to include a full disclosure statement showing that the risk in such deals includes, but is not limited to, lost labor and the cash value of all improvements.
- The builder is responsible for the borrower's work. Under FHA rules, new home builders must provide a one-year warranty to qualify for FHA financing. Whether the work is done by the builder, the borrower, or gremlins from space, the property must be constructed and finished in a "workmanlike manner." Otherwise there can be no loan.
- Qualification standards under the sweat equity program remain liberal. While a conventional loan may require ratios of 28/36, the FHA allows borrowers to qualify for financing with 29/41 ratios—high ratios that allow buyers to borrow more than might otherwise be possible.
- While the 203(k) program is open to *both* owner-occupants and investors, the 203(b) plan is limited to resident owners. This means the sweat equity approach may be possible for owner-occupants, but it is off-limits to investors.
- FHA loans may have attractive ratios, but in high-cost areas the value of FHA financing is limited by maximum loan ceilings. Simply put, an FHA loan may not provide enough dollars to satisfy borrower requirements in certain cities and suburbs.

Sweat equity in exchange for down payment credits makes tremendously good sense, so why don't private-sector lenders adopt the same concept?

Lenders are forever looking for new ways to gain loan volume and for them the sweat equity concept is surely a potent marketing tool. The value of sweat equity is simple to assess with new homes, and the concept can easily be extended to existing properties. Just have two appraisals, one before the buyer begins working and one after.

Questions to Ask:

What is the current FHA interest rate?

What is the current FHA loan limit for single-family housing under Sec. 203(b)?

What is the current FHA down payment schedule for Sec. 203(b) loans?

What is the current FHA insurance premium? Is it due at settlement?

If you do not want to pay the FHA insurance premium in cash at settlement can you get a larger loan? If you elect to finance the premium, how much will your mortgage increase? What portion of the premium can be financed through a larger mortgage? How much additional cash will you need at settlement to cover the FHA premium, since less than the full value of the premium can be financed?

If you are selling an FHA-financed property on which you have paid the premium up front, will the buyer give you a credit equal to the remaining value of the insurance premium when you sell?

How many points, if any, are lenders generally seeking for FHA 203(b) loans today? How many points, if any, are being charged for other FHA programs? Contact several local mortgage loan officers to compare costs.

Can you use a VA appraisal when seeking FHA financing?

Are FHA loans freely assumable or not freely assumable? If FHA mortgages are not freely assumable, what qualifications must be met by a new borrower? How much will it cost to assume?

PRIVATE MORTGAGE INSURANCE (MI)

There are hundreds of thousands of sales each year that would not occur except for the availability of FHA or VA financing, loan programs that provide financing with little or no money down. Yet FHA and VA programs are not for everyone. Many buyers are not VA qualified and a large portion of all home sales require more money than can be insured by the FHA.

The FHA and VA programs, however, are not the only sources of institutional mortgage assistance or even the largest. When the success or failure of a sale depends on a small down payment, many buyers turn to a unique financial product called *private mortgage insurance,* or MI, as it is known in the real estate industry.

MI is nothing more than the promise of a private insurer to repay a lender in the event a low down payment mortgage is in default. Without this promise a lender will not make a low down payment loan because such financing represents an excessive level of risk.

If conventional financing is available at 8.5 percent interest with 20 percent down plus 2 points, conventional financing with MI will also be available at 8.5 percent interest plus two points but with only 5, 10 or 15 percent down plus the MI premium. It is the combination of conventional financing rates plus reduced down payments that makes MI loans popular. Indeed, in recent years more MI loans have been issued than either FHA 203(b) mortgages or financing backed by the VA, and in some years more than both government programs combined.

Because interest rates for conventional and MI mortgages are identical, there are no additional points to pay at settlement as is often the case with VA financing. And, unlike the VA program, MI has no regulations which require sellers to pay all points. With MI, deciding who pays points is a matter of negotiation.

The cost of private mortgage insurance is based on the size of the loan, the amount of coverage required by the lender, the type of loan (fixed or variable payment), the type of policy, the length of coverage and the proportion of the property's value represented by the down payment.

Private mortgage insurance can be purchased on either an annual basis or as a multi-year policy. With annual policies, buyers pay premiums monthly on the remaining loan balance, whereas multi-year coverage is paid with a single premium at settlement. Of the two policies, annual coverage is preferred by purchasers nearly 20 to 1.

MI premiums are determined in part by the size of the down payment. A larger down payment presents less risk to the lender, so there is a correspondingly lesser need for insurance coverage. With 10 percent down, for instance, there is usually 20 percent MI coverage. With only 5 percent down, there is 25 percent insurance coverage. Thus if someone puts down 5 percent on an $85,000 property and has MI coverage, the lender will be insured initially for at least $20,187.

In general, MI works like this: As down payments become larger, less coverage is required and therefore premiums are smaller. In reverse, as down payments become smaller, more coverage is required and therefore premiums are higher.

Also, MI rates are influenced by the type of loan being insured.

MI Premium Costs for 30-Year Loans		
Fixed-Payment		
Annual Premium		
Loan Amount	$85,000	$85,000	$85,000
Down Payment	5 Percent	10 Percent	15 Percent
Cost at Closing	.6 Percent	.36 Percent	.29 Percent
Annual Premium Rate°	.64 Percent	.36 Percent	.29 Percent
Fixed-Payment		
Annual Premium		
Loan Amount	$85,000	$85,000	$85,000
Down Payment	5 Percent	10 Percent	15 Percent
Cost at Closing	.70 Percent	.45 Percent	.34 Percent
Annual Premium Rate°	.74 Percent	.45 Percent	.34 Percent
Fixed-rate		
Single-Premium		
Possible Refund	4.30 Percent	2.95 Percent	2.30 Percent
No Refund	3.25 Percent	2.50 Percent	1.75 Percent
Adjustable-rate		
Single-Premium		
Possible Refund	5.05 Percent	3.75 Percent	2.65 Percent
No Refund	3.85 Percent	3.15 Percent	2.00 Percent

Source: GE Capital Mortgage Corporation. Fees and rates subject to change without notice.
Note: Lenders typically collect 14 months of premiums at closing when using an annual premium program — the equivalent of one year in advance which is paid to the mortgage insurance company plus a two-month reserve.

Since fixed-rate loans are less risky than adjustable-rate mortgages, premiums are lower for fixed-rate financing. The table on page 150 shows various premiums current at the time this book was written.

MI can be paid annually, in which case borrowers will make a small payment at closing as well as payments each month for as long as the lender requires coverage.

MI can also be paid in a lump sum, what the industry calls a single premium. Since most borrowers want to hold down closing costs, lump-sum MI can be added to the loan amount and paid out over time.

The catch to single-premium coverage is this: as a practical matter it's not available with 95 percent financing. For example, if Turner borrows $100,000 and puts down $5,000, she can then obtain single-premium coverage by paying a one-time lump sum fee of $4,300 (4.3 percent). Industry rules, however, will not allow Turner to just make a 5 percent downpayment and then finance the single premium over 30 years. She must pay the 4.3 percent premium in cash at closing, something not acceptable to most people who need or want 95 percent financing.

Lump-sum payments can be calculated in several ways. With 10 percent down, some single-premium programs allow borrowers to obtain a refund if they sell or refinance a home before the coverage runs out. Borrowers buying such MI might expect to pay a single premium equal to 2.95 percent of the loan amount. However, it's also possible to buy lump-sum MI where no refund is permitted. The advantage here is that the premium is far lower, just 2.5 percent.

In practical terms, if we have a fixed-rate, $85,000 loan with 10 percent down and an 8.5 percent interest rate, our MI premiums might look like this:

- With annual premiums, we will pay $340 at closing and approximately $297.50 in the first year. Actual payments will be based on outstanding monthly loan balances, so the first monthly payment will increase $24.79. Each month thereafter, monthly costs can drop slightly as the mortgage balance declines.
- With a 2.95 percent lump-sum premium we pay an additional $2,507.50 up front. If we add the premium to the mortgage balance, the loan will rise to $87,507.50 and the monthly cost will increase from $653.57 to $672.86, a difference of $19.28. Note, however, that when we pay off the loan or sell the property, a larger loan amount will remain outstanding than with annual premiums. If our goal is to buy property today, and if property values

increase, a larger loan balance may be less important than the ability to own an appreciating asset.

- With a no-refund, 3.15 percent rate, our up-front premium will be $2,677.50. Once again we can add the premium to the loan amount and pay the premium over a period of years. If we increase the loan amount by $2,677.50 we will owe $87,667.50, and the monthly payment will increase from $653.57 to $674.09. The no-refund approach costs an additional $20.52 per month when compared with a non-MI loan.

- As an alternative, if we use FHA financing, there will be a 2.25 percent insurance premium. If the FHA up-front fee is added to the loan balance, the principal will rise to $86,912.50. The monthly cost will jump from $683.92 to $699.31, an increase of $15.39. The FHA monthly payment is higher for two reasons: first, more has been borrowed; second, in addition to the 8.5 percent interest rate there is also a .5 percent monthly insurance fee. In effect, the FHA loan is priced at the equivalent of 9 percent interest.

For those borrowers who intend to own their property for a long time, lump-sum MI without a refund is likely to be the most attractive choice. If you intend to be a short-term owner, then annual premiums are likely to be cheapest.

Annual premiums, however, may require big payments up front—the premium for one-year in advance plus the equivalent of two month's in escrow. Such heavy closing costs have traditionally limited the use of annual premiums, but now a new program makes them more accessible.

In 1993, the GE Capital Mortgage Insurance Corporation came out with a program to reduce closing cost expenses. Under the plan, a lender collects the premium for one month in advance, rather than 12. The result is that closing costs can drop substantially.

As an example, GE says that a borrower who purchases a $100,000 home with 5 percent down would normally pay a mortgage insurance premium at closing of $570. Under the new monthly premium plan, the buyer's closing cost would drop to $51.

Lenders are willing to accept a lower down payment with MI-backed loans because they have less risk. If a MI buyer defaults, the lender faces one of two choices, either of which is far more attractive than an uninsured foreclosure.

A MI insurer may pay off the entire loan and thus gain title to the property. This happens in 30 to 40 percent of all MI defaults.

Alternatively, the insurer will pay 20 to 25 percent of the total claim. The "total claim" can include not only the outstanding mortgage balance but also such items as accrued interest, foreclosure costs, attorney's fees, and property tax payments made after the loan is in default.

It may seem that with only 20 or 25 percent MI coverage the lender still has considerable financial exposure but this is not the case.

First, the original size of the loan was less than the sales value of the property. The difference between the loan amount and the selling price is represented by the purchaser's down payment.

Second, over time the buyer has paid down the original loan balance with each monthly payment, except in the case of negative amortization loans where the value of the principal balance actually increases over time. As the principal balance declines, the proportion of the property's worth represented by the outstanding mortgage balance declines as does the level of the lender's risk.

Third, there is the possibility that the value of the property has increased over time. Again, as the gap between the loan balance and the market value of the property is enlarged, the lender has less risk.

Fourth, the property has a foreclosure value which may be equal to or greater than the outstanding loan balance plus related costs. If the foreclosure value covers 100 percent of the money due to the lender, then the lender will have no claim against a private mortgage insurer. If the foreclosure value fell short of the amount of money due to the lender, then the lender can make a claim against the insurer up to the value of the policy.

Although a private mortgage insurance premium is paid by the real estate purchaser, the lender is the beneficiary of the policy and determines whether or not it will be continued. This feature, as well as several others, makes private mortgage insurance and the companies which offer such policies unique. Here's why:

- Although real estate buyers pay the premiums, private mortgage insurance agreements are actually contracts between lenders and insurers. A common provision of such agreements is that lenders must foreclose when monthly payments are four months behind.
- Private mortgage insurance premiums are established at the time a policy is issued and may not be changed.
- Private mortgage insurance may be canceled by the insurer only in the event of fraud or unpaid premiums.
- Private mortgage insurance is not sold through general insurance brokers. Instead, policies are marketed directly to lenders who then make such policies available to borrowers as a condition of granting a loan. Lenders may not collect a sales commission for the placement of private mortgage insurance.
- MI helps lenders re-sell loans in the secondary mortgage market, an important consideration for lenders who continually roll over funds to make new mortgages. Because of the substantial reserves private mortgage insurers are required to maintain, MI-backed loans are regarded as secure mortgage investments. Secondary lenders such as Fannie Mae, Freddie Mac and private pension funds have bought millions of conventional loans backed with private mortgage insurance—estimated purchases worth $35 billion in a recent year.
- Private mortgage insurers benefit from high inflation rates. The reason: inflation reduces the worth of the dollar, so it takes more cash dollars to acquire a given piece of real estate. Since mortgages are valued in terms of cash dollars, it follows that mortgage insurers face fewer claims as property values rise, regardless of whether or not the increase in value is a product of inflation or real economic appreciation.

Those who pay private mortgage insurance on an annual basis should know that it is often possible to cancel such insurance—and to stop making premium payments—when the loan value is reduced to 80 percent of the property's value.

For instance, if you bought a home for $100,000, put down 5 percent, and received a $95,000 loan, then the loan-to-value ratio (LTV) is

95 percent. If property values rise for two years and the house is worth $118,750, the mortgage debt is likely to remain largely unchanged but the loan-to-value ratio will drop below 80 percent.

If your loan has been sold to a big secondary lender such as Fannie Mae or Freddie Mac and the LTV is 80 percent or less, then you may be able to cancel your private mortgage insurance. Other considerations include what is being financed (rental properties and second homes have tougher standards), late payments (it's bad news if you've had them), and how your home is financed (loans with rising monthly costs such as ARMs and graduated payment loans may not qualify).

Considering that private mortgage insurance can cost several hundred dollars a year, it can pay to check lender policies.

Private mortgage insurance is often mistaken for *mortgage life insurance*, a different product. Mortgage life insurance is designed to protect purchasers if they are unable to pay their mortgage as a result of disability or death.

Mortgage life insurance is available through many lenders as well as general insurance agencies. Policies obtained through lenders often name the lender as the beneficiary, while policies placed through insurance brokers allow the buyer to select the beneficiary. For further information about costs and coverage, speak to knowledgable loan officers.

Questions to Ask:

How much cash down is required?

What is the current premium for the first year of a private mortgage insurance policy and for each renewal year thereafter for loans with 5 percent down, 10 percent down and 15 percent down?

If buying a multi-year policy, how many years of coverage will the lender require? What is the one-time cost of a multi-year MI policy? Can you add this expense to the mortgage amount you are seeking?

What is the lender's general policy on renewing MI mortgage coverage? How many years can you expect to pay a premium?

As a condition of obtaining a mortgage, does the lender require the purchaser to place any money in an escrow account to assure that MI premiums are paid? If so, how much?

97 PERCENT FINANCING

Whether interest rates are high or low, limited savings have always been a major barrier to home ownership. Combine closing costs, reserve requirements, and down payments for conventional loans and the total may amount to 25 percent of a home's acquisition price.

Fortunately, not every deal requires conventional financing. VA loans are available with nothing down to qualified vets. FHA mortgages typically require 5 percent down or less in most cases.

But while everyone has been watching interest rates plummet in the past few years, another form of plummeting has also taken place: down payment requirements have been getting smaller and smaller, much to the benefit of buyers, sellers, and brokers.

The new shift toward lower down payments can be seen in the Community Home Buyers Program. Under CHBP you can borrow with 5 percent down, or perhaps 3 percent under the 3/2 option if another party such as a parent or community group will provide the additional cash.

The next step has arrived, loans that simply require 3 percent down and boast very liberal qualification ratios. GE Capital Mortgage Insurance now covers loans with 3 percent down for those with a household income that does not exceed 115 percent of the median household income for specific areas. Fannie Mae, aiming for low- and moderate-income borrowers, restricts its 97 percent loans to those with 100 percent of the local median household income.

GE estimates that 97 percent LTV loans will make financing available to an additional 750,000 buyers. If 10 or 20 percent of such buyers actually enter the marketplace and make purchases, the homes they buy are likely to be modest properties sold by people who will move somewhere, hopefully up to more expensive houses. The result will be a wave effect throughout the marketplace that increases the pool of potential buyers at every pricing level and thus competition for houses.

GE explains that under its program, a Chicago buyer with a 5 percent down payment would be able to purchase a home worth $98,543 under conventional guidelines. Under the GE program, the buyer would need just 3 percent down and could afford a home priced at $113,554. Interestingly, the 5 percent deal would require a $4,927 down payment while the more expensive home would require a down payment worth just $3,407.

Viewed another way, GE says that to buy a $125,000 home, a borrower would need a household income of $37,820 to purchase under CHBP with 5 percent down and $38,425 with 3 percent up front.

Since a deal with 3 percent down represents more risk than a purchase with 5 percent down, mortgage insurance costs are higher—.86 percent with an annualized monthly MI rate, versus .68 percent for a CHBP loan with 5 percent down, according to GE.

Part of the higher insurance cost results from a lower down payment, but another reason for the higher premium is that lenders have less exposure. For example, a lender who makes a 5 percent CHBP loan has exposure on 72 percent of the mortgage amount—insurance makes up the rest. With a 3 percent loan, the lender's exposure is 70 percent—in essence, a risk-free deal, or as close to risk free as a lender can get.

With the Community Home Buyers Program, GE and Fannie Mae have done much to open the housing market to low- and moderate-income households, especially first-time buyers who simply have not had enough time to accumulate savings. If you're looking for corporate social activism in the '90s, this is it, two companies taking a marketplace risk to extend credit in a new and innovative manner.

Deals with 3 percent down raise three important questions. First, how low can we go? Second, why can't such programs be open to everyone? Third, when will we reduce down payment requirements for small investors?

Loan mythology tells us that deals with 20 percent down and 80 percent financing are "conventional," the sense being—apparently—that deals with less money down are "unconventional," or somehow less valid. But the experience of the VA (with no money down and 41/41 ratios) and FHA programs (little down and 29/41 ratios) provides six decades of proof that lenders do not need 20 percent down from borrowers to limit risks. What lenders need is insurance to reduce exposure, something available in abundance.

The prediction here is that after a year or two with 97 percent financing restricted to low- and moderate-wage earners, the next step will be 97 percent mortgages for anyone with decent credit. And once at the 3 percent threshold, then why not go for nothing down? After all, how much more risk is there? You can bet that actuaries are making economic models every day trying to determine precisely how much risk is involved.

And if Mr. and Mrs. Buyer can purchase with little or nothing down, what about the small investor? Is not a requirement for 30 percent down ludicrous, especially when the buyer's property and the investor's property may well be identical homes in the same community?

REDUCED-EQUITY MORTGAGES

The trend toward reduced-equity mortgages—loans with 5 percent, 3 percent, and perhaps even nothing down—is not limited to new financing. In addition, refinancing increasingly requires less equity, good news for borrowers.

It used to be that when refinancing lenders wanted at least 10 percent equity. Now lenders increasingly allow refinancing with 5 percent equity, a substantial difference.

At first the difference between 5 and 10 percent seems marginal, but in reality the new standard will help many owners. To understand why, consider that a growing proportion of homes are being bought with less cash. The 1993 Chicago Title real estate survey, a look at major metropolitan areas around the country, shows that first-time buyers put down just 14 percent in 1993, versus 18 percent in 1976.

Now look at what happens when rates fall. Owners want to refinance, but if they put little down, then traditionally they do not have sufficient equity to get a new loan with lower rates.

Or, look at what happens when home values remain stable or actually fall. Owners again have an equity shortage that limits their ability to refinance with lower rates.

Or to cite another example, consider that mortgages typically produce little amortization in their first years. This means that even those who have owned for several years may not qualify for refinancing because their loan has not been paid down enough to produce the equity they need—a big problem if local home prices are stable or falling.

For instance, if a home is bought for $105,000 and $100,000 is financed, the owners have 5 percent equity—at least if we do not consider sales and marketing expenses. If the owners have a 30-year mortgage at 8.5 percent, it will take them more than five years to reduce the loan principal to $95,000 or less—the level of equity needed to refinance under the old standard.

By going to a 5 percent equity standard lenders achieve a number of advantages.

- More people can refinance, thus boosting lender activity (and revenue).
- More people can refinance, thus reducing investor returns when rates drop.
- People with the greatest refinancing need, those in tough markets and those with little equity, have a better chance to refinance.
- Owners are less likely to be locked into given rates. If rates change, it becomes possible to ratchet down and take advantage of lower interest levels even with limited equity.

The bottom line is that the new trend toward reduced-equity mortgages means that more people than ever are likely to qualify for new loans, particularly now that an old barrier has been halved.

3/2 LOANS AND EMPLOYER ASSISTANCE

Lenders are picky about many items and one that always draws their interest is the matter of money and where it comes from. Put down 10 percent on a home and a lender will want to be certain that the 10 percent is yours and not a secret loan from a third party.

Recently, however, a new trend has emerged. Some lenders are encouraging borrowers to find down payment money from relatives, employers, local governments, and non-profit groups.

There are now several programs which allow borrowers to purchase real estate with 5 percent. But while deals with 5 percent down have been available for many years, the so-called 3/2 loans are different. Instead of 5 percent down from the borrower, with a 3/2 loan the borrower puts down 3 percent of the purchase price while the other 2 percent comes from a family member, non-profit group, or a government agency in the form of a gift, grant, or unsecured loan.

To make the loan program more interesting, 3/2 financing offers these advantages.

- Although conventional loans usually require qualification ratios of 28/26, with 3/2 loans the allowable ratios are 33/38 or even 33/40 in certain cases. The result is that an individual or household with a given income has more borrowing power than they would have with a conventional loan.

- The qualification process has been eased. For instance, borrowers without a credit history—those who are young or have limited incomes—may substantiate good credit by providing such evidence as utility payment stubs and rent checks.

- A borrower can use gifts, grants or unsecured loans to pay closing costs. In effect, if the deal is properly set up, a borrower's total expense at closing need not be more than 3 percent of the property's purchase price.

- Although the 3/2 program is attractive, not everyone can participate. Those with incomes that exceed 115 percent of area median incomes (120 percent in California) are not eligible for 3/2 loans.

- The maximum amount that can be borrowed is limited to the conventional loan ceiling—$202,300 for a single-family home as of mid-1992.

Perhaps the most interesting feature of the 3/2 program is the requirement that a borrower must participate in a personal finance education program offered either by the lender or a community organization. Financial education is a concept which makes great sense, especially for borrowers who are young or unsophisticated.

Still another 3 percent program is Fannie Mae's "Magnet" plan. Here again the borrower puts down 3 percent while someone else puts down the remaining 2 percent. In the case of Magnet loans, that "someone else" is an employer.

Employer-assisted financing is designed to resolve a major problem in many expensive cities: attracting workers. To get workers to work in the big city (or the expensive suburbs) many companies are finding that relatively high salaries are not enough to attract qualified employees. The Magnet program, it is hoped, will help both employers and workers.

The Magnet program allows employers to assist workers with down payments, closing costs, and even monthly mortgage payments by using several strategies.

Direct Grants.   With a direct grant the employer provides an outright gift that can be used to pay a portion of the down payment, closing costs, or additional points up front. By paying additional points, the interest rate will be reduced and monthly costs over the life of the loan will be cut.

Forgivable Loans.   The probability is that few employers will elect to make direct grants because once a grant has been issued there is nothing to stop the employee from leaving the company. An alternative is to create a forgivable loan. As an example, Emory might receive a forgivable loan tied to the length of employment—if she works for the company for three years then the entire loan and all interest will be forgiven, if she quits or is fired before the three-year term ends then some or all of the loan may be due and payable as well as accrued interest.

Loans.   In this case the firm simply makes a loan to the employee. In practice it might be possible to repay the loan over time with a payroll deduction.

Monthly Payment Assistance.   The employer provides a monthly supplement paid directly to the lender. The idea is to reduce the employee's monthly housing cost (principal, interest, taxes, and insurance) to the point where it is less than 28 percent of gross monthly income. Payment assistance can also be in the form of a loan, money that is repaid to the employer once employee housing costs fall below 28 percent of gross monthly income.

Loan Guarantees.   Under this Magnet option the employer guarantees that the mortgage will be repaid. Given a sufficiently strong employer, it seems probable that such a guarantee could produce a somewhat lower interest rate and thus a smaller monthly housing cost.

3/2 Funding.   A company, working in concert with a local government agency or non-profit group, can help arrange 3/2 financing for an employee. Note that the 3/2 income limitations would apply under this option.

The Magnet program (except for the 3/2 plan) has no income limitation, so it can be used for both entry-level employees and high-ranking executives. There is, however, a limit on how much can be borrowed, not more than the amount allowed for conventional financing.

Questions to Ask:

What is the current interest rate for conventional financing?

What is the interest rate for a 3/2 loan?

What assistance can you get—down payment help, closing assistance, monthly supplements, or all three?

What is the income limitation in your area? (A lender, non-profit group, or governmental agency that uses 3/2 financing will have this information.)

How do you apply for a 3/2 loan?

Will an employer offer Magnet loan assistance?

If so, what type of assistance is available?

If the employer's Magnet program requires you to repay a loan, what rates and terms are required?

If a Magnet loan from an employer is forgivable, under what conditions is forgiveness available?

What happens if you get a Magnet loan and then leave your employer at an early date?

UNEMPLOYMENT INSURANCE

Headlines can have a chilling effect on real estate. When you read that 50,000 people have been laid off on Wall Street, that 100,000 people lost their jobs in Massachusetts during an 18-month stretch, or that a major corporation is firing 10,000 people in the next few months, the thought of buying a new home can be frightening.

To calm buyer fears a new form of assistance has emerged, what can be called "unemployment insurance" or "UI."

One form of UI is not insurance at all, merely a promise to help if unemployment should strike. In this situation a seller or builder might say, "Buy this property and if you become unemployed within the first year of ownership, I'll pay your mortgage for the next six months."

A second type of UI is insurance. You pay a premium—say $2 to $3 per $100 of coverage—and if you become unemployed an insurer will then step in to pay your mortgage for up to 12 months. "Coverage" in this case means your potential insurance benefit. For example, if you are eligible to receive $1,000 per month for 12 months the coverage is worth $12,000. If the premium rate is 2.5 percent, then the annual premium is $300. ($12,000 x 2.5 percent).

At first glance UI seems like a simple concept, but there are complications which should concern would-be beneficiaries.

Let us start with the issue of employment. The opposite of "employed" is "unemployed" but UI protection does not apply to those who merely elect to leave their jobs. Instead, "unemployment" in the world of UI means "involuntary unemployment." In effect, to collect you must be canned.

The trouble is that some people cannot be fired. If you are an independent, self-employed professional—a doctor, lawyer, real estate broker or whatever—you cannot qualify for state unemployment insurance because there is no employer who can fire you. In a similar fashion, it seems unlikely that UI would offer much help to the self-employed individual whose business fails.

When coverage begins is an important issue. Some plans do not kick in until a month after termination, others start after only three months. But when does coverage really begin?

For instance, if Hudson is fired March 5th does the first UI check arrive April 5th? Or, is April the month after termination and thus a UI check is not due until April 30th or May 1st? These are not minor questions if you are the one who is unemployed.

What is covered should also concern homebuyers. If unemployment insurance covers 12 monthly payments, then what is in a payment? Are only principal and interest covered, or does the insurance also include payments for taxes and insurance? Broader coverage is clearly an advantage.

A last issue involves the term "unemployment insurance." Some unemployment insurance really is insurance in the traditional sense. But other UI programs are merely promises by sellers, builders, or a third party to step in if unemployment hits. Non-insurers are not regulated, have no required reserves, and may not be in business at the very moment they are needed most.

Builders, for example, often create corporations to complete a particular project and then fold the corporation once the project is completed. If the "Whalebone Construction Corporation" is formed to build houses on West Street and provides a promise of UI that's great. If Whalebone shuts down after the last home is built, then what protection remains for buyers?

One solution to unemployment insurance from a private seller or builder can work this way: as a condition of the sale have the seller or builder create a trust account with enough money to cover mortgage payments for the entire protection period, say the first 12 months after purchase. Money from the fund can then be released to the seller or builder after each month expires because coverage is no longer required.

In rocky times, UI is a concept that will provide peace of mind to some prospective real estate buyers. Whether many people will actually collect is an open question because at the time a home is purchased buyers should be in peak financial condition. If they're not, they can't get a loan and thus they have no need for unemployment insurance.

Questions to Ask:

Who is providing unemployment insurance? An insurance company or an unregulated individual or entity?

If coverage is provided by a seller or builder, what happens if they go bankrupt, move overseas or close the corporate shell?

When does coverage begin? Ask for an example in writing.

How long are you covered? One year after purchase? Two years?

How much does coverage cost?

What is covered? Principal and interest? Taxes? Insurance? Other expenses?

If a payment is due, is the payment made to you or directly to a lender?

EQUITY-SHARING

It is not always so easy to classify mortgages, and equity-sharing agreements are not mortgages in the sense of FHA or conventional loans; yet they can be regarded as a form of assisted financing. Regardless of how they're defined, they're great for families who want to buy property together, and investors may use them also. Here's how they work.

Equity-sharing is an arrangement in which at least two people hold title to a given property. One, the "equity" or "money" investor, puts up part of the cash or credit needed for acquisition but does not live on the property. The second person uses the property as his or her principal residence and also pays in capital to participate in the investment.

Because equity-sharing arrangements are often made within families or between friends one is tempted to classify such financing solely as an assisted loan, something akin to a gift. However, while equity-sharing agreements can be structured so they are extremely favorable to one party or the other, they clearly involve an ownership interest and offer the possibility of profit based on economic appreciation, tax advantages and equity accumulation—benefits not enjoyed by true lenders or by the FHA, VA or private mortgage insurers.

Also, at first glance, it may seem as though there is little which makes equity-sharing arrangements new or different from earlier investment ideas but this is not the case.

For example, equity-sharing deals differ from an earlier concept, the *shared appreciation mortgage* (SAM). With a SAM loan, the lender traded an interest discount for an ownership interest in the property. Suppose interest rates are at 8.5 percent. A lender under a SAM loan might cut the rate by 40 percent to 5.1 percent, a level which would be a positive bargain. In exchange, the lender gets a 40 percent interest and shares in the profits when the property is sold.

SAM loans, however, are rare today for several reasons.

First, lenders must pay interest on the money they loan. If you pay 5.1 percent on funds that a lender can lend at 8.5 percent, the lender has to make up the difference somewhere or lose out on the deal.

Second, there is no guarantee that the value of the property will rise and therefore no guarantee of any appreciation to share. If the value of the property remains level or drops the lender will get back his principal but not interest at a market rate.

Third, oddly enough, if the value of the property skyrockets upward a lender can have usury problems. After all, regulated lenders may be prohibited from receiving returns above a certain level and a really profitable deal may be viewed as "unconscionable."

Equity-sharing arrangements are feasible today because of a change in tax regulations. In the past, when two or more people owned property and one resided at the site, no owner could claim a tax loss even if costs greatly exceeded income. With equity-sharing, the non-resident owner can claim a loss and thus reduce taxable income generally.

As an example, imagine that the Franklins and their son, Franklin Junior, agree to purchase an $85,000 house. A $10,000 down payment is required, of which the Franklins contribute $8,000 and their son pays the remainder. The son also agrees to reside at the property and pay a fair market rental. The ownership of the property is then divided equally in this case.

The property has a fair market rental of $1,000 per month. The cash costs of the property are also $1,000 for mortgage payments, taxes, etc. Here's how the deal works:

- Franklin Junior pays $500 per month to his parents as rent, since they own 50 percent of the property. He also pays $500 per month directly to the lender for the mortgage and taxes.
- The Franklins receive $500 per month from their son. They then pay the lender $500 per month.
- At the end of the year the Franklins report a taxable rental income of $6,000 (12 × $500). They also deduct 50 percent of all costs for which they are liable and that they actually pay, including mortgage interest, taxes, repairs, condo and co-op fees. In addition, they get a depreciation credit. The result is a significant tax loss.
- Franklin Junior claims deductions for the mortgage interest and taxes he actually pays and for which he is liable. However, because he resides on the property he cannot claim depreciation, repair, condo or co-op deductions.
- The investors' equity in the property increases as they make monthly mortgage payments. Hopefully, their equity also increases as a result of rising values.
- When the property is sold the profits will be divided according to the ownership interest of each party.

The equity-sharing rules, according to IRS spokesman Wilson Fadely, were devised to help families buy property together. However, it is not too difficult to envision a situation in which potential residential investors such as young families, retirees, college students and others will seek equity investors to assist in a real estate purchase.

Indeed, one can see real estate brokers putting equity and resident investors together and then selling them suitable properties. Not only are the tax shelter possibilities attractive, but the problem of rental management is neatly resolved since there is no need to search for a tenant.

In considering the issue of financing for equity-sharing deals, borrowers should be aware that many lenders will not make equity-sharing loans. Others will make such loans, but only with conditions. For example, lenders are likely to require that the resident owner must put up some cash to make the deal work, perhaps 5 percent or 10 percent; the equity-sharing arrangement must be between people and not corporations, partnerships or trusts; the property seller cannot retain a property interest as an equity-sharing owner; and there can be no agreement to sell the property in less than seven years.

Equity sharing arrangements should be seen as more complex than simple partnerships. For instance, in addition to requiring a resident-owner and a fair market value, regulations also mention that equity-sharing co-owners should *intend* to own their properties for at least 50 years. The 50-year requirement apparently conflicts with the seven-year buy-out clause found in many equity sharing deals, but a knowledgeable real estate attorney can explain how to resolve the problem.

Whether an equity-sharing arrangement is a family affair or a pure investment it is clear that a written understanding between the parties should be developed by a knowledgeable attorney. In addition, because equity-sharing arrangements can represent complex tax issues, the services of a CPA should be used.

Questions to Ask:

How much cash down is required from each party?

What is the percentage of ownership of each party? Note that the percentage of ownership does not have to be related to the cash contribution of the equity investor.

What are the responsibilities of the resident partner in terms of maintenance and upkeep?

How much notice must the resident investor give before moving out?

How will a fair market rental be established? How will rent increases, if any, be determined?

How are disputes to be resolved? Many business agreements contain a binding arbitration clause so that in the event of conflict a neutral party can resolve the issue without going to court.

What rights will each party have to buy out the other?

In addition to having a written agreement prepared by a lawyer, investors should also speak with a CPA or tax attorney to assure that all tax rules and requirements have been addressed. Also, of all things, each investor will need an appropriate will so that potential probate problems are avoided.

11
Alternative Mortgages from A to Z

Hardly a day passes without the introduction of a "new" loan format, yet the reality is that very few loan ideas represent a quantum leap beyond the current frontiers of finance. Instead most "new" loans are variations of older, core ideas.

While it is not practical to examine the endless variety of possible loan alternatives, it is feasible to review the central concepts of given loan formats. For instance, there may be 500 slightly different ARM loan variations built around a single financing concept. One can look at that concept and have a basic idea of how each variation works.

To fully understand the variation, however, it is necessary to know something more than the core idea. Rather than having a guide which will be quickly dated and forever incomplete, we have instead chosen to first describe central lending concepts and then provide checklists which can be used to understand and compare individual plans.

ARM LOANS

Tea leaves, tarot cards and a crystal ball may not seem to have much in common with something as mundane as a fixed-rate mortgage but in a sense they are all used to predict the future. If you get a 30-year loan at 10 percent interest a lender is betting that his cost of funds will stay far enough below 10 percent so that he can profit for the next three decades.

What makes the lender's calculations tricky is that while you have a 30-year debt at a known rate, he doesn't. Instead the lender borrows money on a short-term basis and at short-term rates from such sources as savings accounts and certificates of deposit to underwrite long-term mortgages.

Since the future has a way of being unpredictable, many lenders are trying to get out of the prophecy business by offering adjustable rate mortgages (ARMs), loans where interest rates, monthly payments and principal balances can vary. These loans now represent an important alternative to fixed-rate financing, an alternative which can be the best available choice for certain borrowers.

What is an ARM? If ARMs are good for lenders can they also be good for borrowers? Here's how they work:

Start Rate.   The initial rate of interest is generally below conventional financing levels because borrowers who use ARMs, and not lenders, are now penalized by inflation. Lower initial interest rates allow buyers to qualify more easily for ARM financing, a major advantage. The initial interest rate can be in effect for as long as several years or as little time as a month.

Interest Rate.   Once the initial rate lapses, interest is then computed with a two-part formula. First, the rate is determined by an index which may move up or down. Common indexes include:

- Treasury securities such as those with 6-month, 1-year, 3-year, and 5-year terms. Lenders use a floating average to obtain rates, an approach which tends to moderate interest levels.
- The Federal COFI, or federal costs of funds index, adds the monthly average interest rate for marketable treasury bills and treasury notes and then divides the total by two to establish a rate. Promoted by some lenders as an alternative to the 11th District COFI.
- The London Interbank Offer Rate (LIBOR) is used as an index for some ARMs. The LIBOR reflects Eurodollar borrowing costs for five British lenders.
- The Federal Home Loan Bank of San Francisco publishes the 11th District Cost of Funds Index, or the 11th District COFI. This index reflects the borrowing costs of approximately 200 sav-

ings and loan associations in California, Nevada and Arizona. Used nationwide, this index is widely regarded as the most stable index, the one least likely to rise rapidly, but also the one least likely to fall quickly.

In addition to an index the lender adds a *margin,* anywhere from 2.25 to 3 percent. The margin remains unchanged throughout the loan's life.

Suppose, then, that we have an index at 6 percent and a 2.5 percent margin. The interest rate will be equal to 8.5 percent (6 percent plus 2.5 percent). If the index falls to 5 percent, the interest rate will drop to 7.5 percent (5 percent plus 2.5 percent).

- Qualifying Rate. When borrowers apply for fixed-rate financing, they're qualified according to the loan's interest rate. With an ARM, lenders have different policies for different loans. Some use the low start rate to qualify borrowers. Others use the rate for the loan's second year. Still other lenders add 1 percent to the start rate to determine a qualifying rate.
- Rate Changes. Depending how the loan is written a lender may have the right to change the interest rate as often as every month. This is highly unusual, however, and it is more likely that the lender will be allowed to change the rate only once every several months or once a year. The fact that the interest rate changes does not necessarily mean that monthly *payments* will rise, how-

---

Indexes Move, Margins Stay Put

Here's how an ARM with a 2.5 percent margin can move from 8.5 percent interest to 7.5 percent interest.

Index Level, Year 1	6%
Margin	2.5%
Total Rate	8.5%
Index Level, Year 2	5%
Margin	2.5%
Total Rate	7.5%

ever, since payment changes may be restricted to once a year, once every six months or whatever.

- Rate Caps. An ARM may provide for an absolute cap on the maximum interest rate that can be charged. Conversely, there is likely to be an interest rate minimum.
- Payment Caps. Many ARMs have payment caps which limit monthly cost increases or decreases. For example, if a loan has a 7.5 percent annual payment cap and the monthly cost is $500, then if interest rates go up, monthly payments can only rise to $537.50 ($500 plus 7.5 percent of $500 equals $537.50).
- Principal Cap. If there is a payment cap that holds down monthly costs it is possible that the mortgage balance can grow regularly over a period of years. A lender does not want to have an endlessly rising mortgage on the books, so a principal cap is usually established, perhaps 125 percent of the original loan balance. If the original loan amount was $90,000 and the balance rose to $112,500 over many years because of negative amortization, the borrower will have to make a lump-sum payment to keep below the cap, refinance the property with another loan or sell.
- Negative Amortization. Some ARMs allow negative amortization, a concept that works this way: Suppose monthly payments are set at $600, but suppose also that interest rates rise to a point where to pay off the loan monthly payments of $625 are required. With negative amortization, the borrower will only be required to pay $600 a month, but an additional $25 per month will be added to the loan balance. Loans that permit negative amortization typically allow borrowers to make larger payments to eliminate negative amortization.
- Loan Term. Because it is possible that the size of the loan balance may increase, many ARM loans have a built-in extension provision. With the lender's approval, it is usually possible to extend the loan term from 30 to 40 years. The advantage of a loan extension is that it may eliminate the need to refinance the property.
- Prepayment. Since ARM loans reflect current interest costs, a lender will not lose money if a loan is repaid early. For this reason, ARMs may commonly be repaid in whole or in part without penalty.

Willoughby's ARM versus 9-Percent Financing		
	ARM	Conventional
Loan amount	$100,000	$100,000
Loan term	30 to 40 years	30 years
Initial interest rate	6 percent	9 percent
Initial monthly payments	$599.33	$804.62
Regular monthly payments	Variable	$804.62
Frequency of payment changes	1 year	None
Maximum interest rate	12 percent	9 percent
Minimum interest rate	6 percent	9 percent
Possible negative amortization	Yes	No
Self-amortization guaranteed	No	Yes

- **Assumptions.** Since ARM rates reflect current market trends a lender is not in the position of having a long-term, 9 percent loan underwritten with 12 percent, short-term financing. For this reason, ARMs are generally assumable by qualified buyers.

With all its specialized provisions and clauses an ARM may seem unusually complex. In practice, however, such loans are not hard to follow. Here's an example:

Willoughby is looking for a $100,000 mortgage. A local lender offers either a 9 percent, 30-year conventional mortgage or an ARM with the following terms:

- An initial interest level of 6 percent for six months, the so-called "teaser" rate.
- The loan will use an index based on the average weekly yield for one-year U.S. Treasury bills, an index published in most major newspapers.
- The margin will be 2.5 points above the index.
- The lender can change the interest rate and monthly payment schedule once a year. The maximum payment increase *after the teaser period* will be limited to 7.5 percent per year. In other words if the monthly payment is $600 today, it cannot rise to

more than $645 ($600 × 7.5 percent) when the payments are changed.

- If the true interest cost is greater than the required monthly payments, then Willoughby can pay additional money each month or the loan balance will increase through negative amortization. For example, if the monthly payment is $600 but the interest cost is $626 per month, then Willoughby must either pay the additional $26 or allow her mortgage debt to rise.

- In the event of negative amortization, the loan term may be extended to 40 years. With a longer loan term the borrower has more time to repay the debt and the lender can obtain far more interest.

- The maximum lifetime interest rate will be 12 percent and the minimum will be 6 percent.

What happens with this loan? In the first six months Willoughby has regular mortgage payments for principal and interest of $599.33. Once the teaser period is finished, payments rise to $767.10 per month for a year because the index is at 8.50 percent (the interest rate is created by adding a then-current 6 percent index to a 2.5 percent margin).

The next year inflation raises the index to 8 percent which means Willoughby must pay 10.5 percent interest (8 percent + 2.5 percent). Her monthly payments should go up to $916.27 but the payment cap is 7.5 percent. Her monthly bill instead rises to $824.63 ($767.10 + 7.5 percent) so she has negative amortization each month equalling $149.17 ($916.27 − $767.10). The sum of $149.17 will be added to her debt each month unless she elects to make additional payments.

A year later the world is a better place, inflation has been conquered (at least for the moment) and the index plummets to 4 percent. That rate, plus the 2.5 percent margin, means that Willoughby's ARM has a 6.5 percent interest rate and regular payments of just $646.44 per month.

Willoughby, if she is smart, will make larger payments at this point (more than $646.44 per month) to reduce her mortgage balance and effectively invest in her own mortgage. (See table, p. 170)

In the same way that the cobra and the mongoose are natural enemies, so too are inflation and fixed-rate loans. When the buying power of paper money drops—when it takes three dollars to buy groceries worth two dollars—the value of fixed-rate mortgages also drops.

Adjustable rate mortgages effectively shift the burden of inflation from the lender to the borrower. With an ARM, the interest rate of a loan will rise with inflation, thus preserving the lender's buying power.

ARMs are generally enticing to borrowers because they feature low initial interest rates: say 6 percent at a time when conventional loans are available at 9 percent interest. In particular, during periods when interest rates are high, ARMs may well be the best available financing for two reasons: First, with a low initial interest rate an ARM will represent below-market financing at a time when most buyers may not qualify for conventional loans; second, ARM borrowers are not eternally committed to the high interest rates in place at the time they make their loans. ARM costs can fall once high market rates pass.

Consider the example of an astute buyer who gets 7.5 percent ARM financing for an $85,000 loan when 30-year conventional loans are not available for less than 10 percent. The 7.5 percent rate is guaranteed for one year, and, after that, interest levels can rise only 2 percent per year. There is a 12.5 percent interest cap on the loan and a 6 percent interest minimum.

One year later conventional loans are still at 10 percent while the ARM rate has risen to 9.5 percent. Even though the cost of the loan has increased, the ARM borrower is still far ahead of the buyer with a fixed-rate loan. Despite the increased monthly expense, here's where the buyer benefited:

- At 7.5 percent interest computed on a 30-year basis, the ARM borrower paid $594.33 per month in the first year or a total of $7,131.96. In the second year, with the interest cost at 9.5 percent, the borrower paid $714.73 per month or $8,576.71. In comparison, a 10 percent fixed-rate loan cost $745.94 per month or a total of $17,902.46 over two years. The ARM buyer paid a total of $15,708.67 ($7,131.96 + $8,576.71). The difference: a savings of $2,193.79.
- The purchaser was able to acquire property in a high-interest, buyer's market—a time when few people qualify for financing because mortgage rates are steep. This means the buyer had a substantial negotiating advantage which potentially translated into

a lower selling price and thus a smaller mortgage than might otherwise have been possible.

- Only when ARM rates go above 10 percent does the purchaser suffer when compared to others who bought with fixed-rate loans at the same time.
- The ARM borrower had far lower initial monthly mortgage costs and thus qualified for a larger loan than his income would otherwise have allowed.
- If ARM rates drop, ARM borrowers may actually see a decrease in monthly costs.
- The people who got conventional loans at 10 percent did not benefit when rates dropped a year later. To pay less interest they will have to refinance their property—an expensive proposition with new settlement costs, title fees, etc. Conversely, conventional borrowers will not be hurt if interest rates go above 10 percent. Indeed, relative to then-current borrowers, folks with 10 percent fixed-rate financing will look both wise and prosperous while people with ARM loans may face far higher monthly costs than were anticipated.

THE TWO-STEP AND OTHER LONG-TERM ARMs

In the ongoing search to make ARMs more attractive, the world has now been introduced to the "two-step" mortgage, a financial instrument backed by Fannie Mae that reflects national home ownership

Two-Step Financing vs. Fixed-Rate Loans		
	Conventional	Combo
Loan Amount	$50,000	$50,000
Loan Term	30 years	30 years
Initial Interest Rate	9 percent	9 percent
Initial Monthly Cost, Years 1–7	$402.31	$402.31
Highest Possible Rate, Years 8–30	9 percent	15 percent
Highest Possible Cost, Years 8–30	$402.31	$596.61
Negative Amortization Allowed	No	No

patterns: There is a seven-year first stage with an interest rate marginally below fixed levels and then, if necessary, a 23-year second stage with interest set at then-current market rates.

The initial interest level may be as much as 3/8ths of a point below fixed-rate loans, and while less than half a point may not seem significant, Fannie Mae estimates that a lower start rate will allow as many as 110,000 additional households to qualify for a typical mortgage.

The two-step mortgage has its attractions in addition to a marginally lower rate up front. It has a higher loan limit than FHA loans and fewer restrictions than the VA program. And although the two-step is actually an adjustable product, having only one interest adjustment gives the loan a stability normally associated with fixed-rate financing. No less important, the two-step mortgage is a 30-year commitment, not a short-term balloon product with all the hazards and costs rollover financing normally presents.

Under the two-step program, the interest rate cannot increase more than 6 points over the mortgage term, but since there is only one rate adjustment, that adjustment can be a whopper in the worst possible case. If the rate for a $50,000 loan goes from 9 percent to 15 percent, then the monthly cost for principal and interest alone will rise from $402.30 to $596.61 for the remaining loan term.

The 6-point cap is not based on a "teaser" rate because, in the usual sense of the term, there is none. An up-front break equal to 3/8ths of a point—or less—simply cannot complete with the introductory rates associated with many available ARM products.

Perhaps the most interesting aspect of the two-step loan is the relationship between rates and buyers. Drop interest levels by a measly 3/8ths of a percent and suddenly another 110,000 buyers can enter the marketplace. This equation suggests that if expanding the housing market is an important national goal, then the way to find more buyers is through the simple expedient of lower rates.

The two-step loan, with its 10-percent down payment, will not replace FHA, VA or bond-backed mortgages as the financing most sought by first-time borrowers. Conversely, the two-step is a very attractive loan product, a form of financing that all buyers should consider.

OTHER LONG-TERM ARMs

The two-step mortgage is perhaps the best illustration of an idea that has become increasingly common in the world of ARM lending, the use of lengthy adjustment periods.

One of the major misgivings that ARMs create is the possibility that tomorrow's monthly payment can spiral out beyond the realm of affordability. Lenders have tried to reassure borrowers with such devices as payment and interest caps, but the steady monthly payments offered by fixed-rate loans remain enticing.

Visit a local lender and you may find a variety of long-term ARMs. Here are how several typical products work.

The 10 and 1 Loan. An ARM with an initial rate that lasts 10 years and then adjusts annually.

The 7 and 1 Loan. An ARM with an initial rate that lasts seven years and then adjusts annually.

The 5 and 1 Loan. An ARM with an initial rate that lasts five years and then adjusts annually.

The 3 and 1 Loan. An ARM with an initial rate that lasts three years and then changes annually.

The 3/3 Loan. An ARM where there is a three-year rate initially, and then rates are re-set every three years thereafter.

The 5/5 Loan. An ARM that has an initial rate for five years and then a new rate every five years thereafter.

The 10/10/10 Loan. ARM financing with rates and payments that can change every five to ten years.

Long-term ARMs are attractive because many people will move before rates and terms change, especially with loans that have an initial term of seven to 10 years.

In the usual case long-term ARMs are also worth considering because they represent full 30-year commitments. However, if your credit or earnings must be satisfactory to the lender for the loan to continue after the initial rate term, then we have a conditional balloon note, so borrower beware! If the lender is not happy with your finances for any reason, then what looks like a long-term commitment may suddenly evolve into balloon financing.

Another edge taken by some lenders makes long-term ARMs less secure than they might seem. Through the use of a "bail out" clause, some long-term loans can become discomfortingly short.

With the two-step loan backed by Fannie Mae regardless of how much interest rates rise, borrowers are *always* certain that they have a 30-year commitment. With other combo ARMs that may not be the case. What lenders sometimes say is this: if interest rates rise above a certain level, say 5 percent, then the lender is not obligated to continue the loan.

Imagine that you have a 5/25 loan with an initial rate of 9.5 percent. Imagine also that five years later the time has come to adjust the interest level for the loan's remaining life and that rates are pegged at 15 percent. At this point a lender with a bail-out clause set at 5 percent can say, "look, the loan contract provides that if the interest rate rises 5 percent or more, we are simply not obligated to continue the loan. Either refinance with someone else within 30 days or we will foreclose."

Another not-so-cute trick is to have a combo mortgage where the borrower must qualify to continue the loan after the first five or seven years. In this case, the catch is that to "qualify" a borrower must meet standards established by a lender, regardless of whether those standards are appropriate, fair or reasonable. The lender, of course, is not a neutral party, but rather an entity with a great interest in the outcome of such qualification procedures.

ARMS with bail-out clauses should be seen for what they are: *potential time-bombs that can ruin a borrower*. In the situation above where interest rates have risen to 15 percent, a combo borrower with a weasel clause can be forced to refinance in a poor market or at a time when personal finances are weak. The result, at best, will be the loss of time, fees and energy; a great increase in monthly mortgage costs; and a vast amount of aggravation.

Warning: Do NOT accept any combo mortgage which is anything less than an absolute commitment to finance property for 30 years. The only reason a lender should be allowed to curtail a loan is in the event the borrower fails to make payments.

While one can construct situations in which ARMs represent favorable financing, there are many times when ARMs are simply inappropriate. For example, if ARM and fixed-rate financing are available at the same rates, the fixed-rate mortgage is the better deal because it places the burden of inflation on the lender. ARMs that permit monthly *payment* changes should be avoided, since they play havoc with personal budgets.

In addition, while ARMs clearly have a place in the mortgage market—especially when rates are steep—they raise serious issues with which borrowers—and lenders—should be concerned.

First, ARM borrowers cannot anticipate mortgage costs over the life of their loans. Not only are payments subject to change, but if negative amortization is allowed it is entirely possible that the loan will not be paid off in 30 years. ARMs thus make personal financial planning far more difficult than fixed-rate loans. With an ARM, one cannot count on having the mortgage paid off by the time Junior goes to college.

Second, ARMs do not guarantee lender profits. What ARMs do, at best, is shield lenders from the worst effects of inflation and limit losses. Since lender profits are based on the difference between all income and all expenses—how much it costs to borrow money on a short-term basis plus all other business charges such as rent, salaries, etc.—it is entirely possible that a lender's cost of funds can rise above mortgage portfolio returns and thus create losses.

Third, since the whole ARM structure is based on an index it is important to determine which measure is used to set interest rates. In general terms, the longer the span of events being measured the less volatile the index. Thus borrowers should greatly prefer an index based on the weekly average of five-year U.S. Treasury securities adjusted to a constant yield rather than daily stock averages.

Fourth, lenders may have less security with ARM financing than is now believed. If indexes rise substantially it is possible that many ARM borrowers will be unable to meet monthly payments and wholesale foreclosures can ensue. The ability to foreclose in such times may be of limited value, since few people will be able to buy housing. Lenders who do foreclose—in addition to having a considerable public relations problem—may find that they control properties that can be sold only at steep discounts. This is precisely what happened in Houston and other cities. Lenders foreclosed but then found that with a glutted market they either had to hold the properties they now owned, or sell at prices that were below original loan amounts.

Fifth, the opportunity to own a home is one of the most sensitive political matters existent. If ARMs result, or are perceived to result, in an excessive number of foreclosures one would expect to see immediate regulatory and statutory restrictions. Iowa, for example, enacted a 1985 law which gave farmers a 1-year grace period during which time lenders could not foreclose.

Sixth, ARMs are likely to supplement but not replace fixed-rate, conventional financing. Fixed-rate financing is important to pension fund managers, who need investments with predictable returns. Each year pensions buy mortgages worth billions of dollars through secondary lenders, so there is a continuing demand for fixed-rate loan products. That demand, in turn, means that fixed-rate financing will remain available in local communities.

When ARMs were first introduced every lender seemed to have a different loan product. Like snowflakes, no two were alike. The problem with thousands of different loan formats is that it is impossible to sell such loans to secondary lenders such as Fannie Mae. Standardized loan products are easy to evaluate and price whereas non-standard loans are not. Moreover, non-standard products are usually not produced in the quantities big buyers demand.

Now, with experience in hand, standardized ARM loans are available nationwide. These loans represent more of a compromise between the interests of borrowers and lenders than early ARMs, loans that completely favored lenders in most cases.

In addition to standardized ARM loans hybrid financing has begun to emerge. Already, for instance, a "convertible adjustable rate mortgage" allows the borrower to have a loan that initially acts like ARM financing. During the first three to five years the loan is outstanding, borrowers may convert to a fixed interest rate. The conversion cost is typically modest—say $250 to $500—but the fixed interest rate is likely to be .625 percent to .750 percent above then-prevailing interest levels for fixed-rate financing.

Convertible loans thus appear attractive, but the exact rates and terms associated with such financing may not be appealing. For borrowers who intend to own their property for many years, it may actually be cheaper to get new financing, even with all the closing costs involved, than to pay high rates over a long period of time.

Another approach is the *graduated payment adjustable rate mortgage,* or GPARM. A GPARM is essentially a loan with two phases. In the first phase, perhaps five years, monthly payments are initially set at a low figure. This low monthly payment, plus the initial below-market rates usually associated with ARMs, allows more buyers to qualify for financing.

Each year the payment level is raised by a set amount, say 7.5 percent. Also, while payments are rising but known in advance, interest costs are determined by an index. There is negative amortization during this first phase which is added to the loan balance.

In the second phase, a GPARM behaves like a regular ARM. Depending on how the loan is negotiated, the payments may remain steady for given intervals, one to five years, but interest costs will fluctuate with an index. When the monthly payments are scheduled to change they may be adjusted up or down.

Perhaps the least known yet most interesting ARM has been one developed by the FHA. While not widely accepted by lenders because of its 1 percent annual payment cap, the FHA ARM offers several interesting features:

- Interest costs can rise or fall 1 percent yearly.
- The maximum interest rate cannot rise or fall more than 5 percent over the initial rate.
- FHA ARM loan rates are based on an index selected by the government, most likely a floating weekly average for 1-year Treasury securities.
- Maximum loan limits are the same as those established under the basic 203(b) program.
- Negative amortization is not permitted.
- The loans can be prepaid in whole or in part without penalty.
- FHA ARMs are assumable under the same guidelines that cover other FHA financing. In other words, today's FHA ARM can only be assumed by qualified owner-occupants. Loans made earlier, however, may be assumable by investors and in some cases, it is

possible that older FHA ARMs are freely-assumable. See Chapter 9 for more details concerning assumptions.

- Under current rules, as much as one-third of all FHA loans can be adjustable, an allocation the FHA has yet to reach.

The FHA ARM is an attractive ARM, yet it is rarely promoted. Why? Perhaps because lenders prefer to offer conventional ARMs with larger adjustment caps, say 2 percent a year rather than 1 percent. There is some discussion in Washington to revamp the FHA program and make it more attractive to lenders. That, of course, will also make it less attractive to borrowers.

Because there are so many potential ARM formats borrowers should carefully compare programs offered by local lenders. With ARMs, it is not enough to know interest rates, down payment terms or initial monthly payment costs.

ARM ERRORS

ARMs are far more complex than fixed-rate financing and it follows that the administration of such loans can create major headaches for both borrowers and lenders.

The essential problem with ARMs is that calculations can vary with great frequency and therefore lenders must constantly update their records to assure that proper credit is given to borrowers.

- One study, by six state attorneys general, shows that 70 percent of all escrow funds have been incorrectly calculated and that consumers have been overcharged by as much as $3 billion.
- A major lender has agreed to compensate as many as 500,000 borrowers for escrow fund errors. More lenders are likely to follow suit, or be sued.
- Estimates of ARM errors range from 50 percent to 70 percent.

All of which raises a question: If you have an ARM how do you know the lender is treating you right?

First, check your property tax and insurance payments. If the lender is collecting money to make such payments and they have not been made, an automatic red flag should go up. If, because a tax or insurance payment is late, there is an effort to assess a late fee or charge a penalty or interest, those costs should be seen as the lender's responsibility.

Second, read your statement to assure that all payments have been properly credited. Look for incorrect charges such as improper late fees.

Third, make certain you receive credit for additional payments. For example, if you owe $700 a month but pay $750, then $50 should be used to reduce your loan balance. Some lenders will credit the excess payment to your escrow account unless it is clearly marked as a principal reduction.

Fourth, watch for your lender in the news. If you see that your lender or the firm that services your mortgage is making the front page of the real estate section (or the business pages or the paper generally) because of ARM problems, you can assume that your interests are potentially involved. Contact the lender for more information, or contact whoever is debating ARM matters with your lender—parties such as state attorneys general, consumer protection offices, mortgage banking regulators, and attorneys.

Questions to Ask:

What is the current interest level for fixed-rate, conventional financing?

How much cash down is required?

What is the initial interest rate for an ARM?

What is the initial monthly payment?

How long does the initial interest rate last?

How long does the initial monthly payment last?

Is your qualifying rate the same as your ARM start rate? If not, what is your qualifying rate?

What ratios are used when qualifying loan applicants?

How frequently can the lender change the monthly payment?

How often can the lender adjust the interest rate?

Is there a cap that limits the size of each payment change? Is there a limit on the dollar amount to which the monthly payment can be reduced at each change?

How much notice must the lender give before each payment change?

What index is used to adjust the interest level?

What is the margin above the index rate?

Is there a cap on the amount by which the interest charge can be raised at each change?

Is there a cap on the loan's maximum interest? Is there an interest minimum?

If the monthly mortgage payment is insufficient to reduce the mortgage principal balance, is negative amortization permitted?

Relative to the original mortgage principal, how much negative amortization is allowed? That is, can the mortgage balance grow to 105 percent of the original balance, 110 percent, 125 percent, etc.?

If you have negative amortization, can the loan term be extended? If so, to how many years?

Is a loan extension guaranteed or is any extension at the lender's option?

Are there extension fees that must be paid to the lender? If so, how much?

Is the lender obligated to continue the loan regardless how high interest levels may rise?

Will the lender refinance the property if you reach the negative amortization limit? If so, are any terms, such as maximum interest levels, guaranteed in advance?

Do you have the right to prepay the loan in whole or in part without penalty?

Is the loan assumable by a qualified buyer?

Do you offer FHA ARMs? What are the precise terms associated with this program currently, including such items as maximum loan amounts, payments caps, margins, and indexes? What ratios do you use to qualify borrowers?

BLEND LOANS: HOW TO FINANCE AND REFINANCE AT DISCOUNT

Many borrowers believe they are at the lender's mercy when it comes time to negotiate loan rates. While this may be true with marginal borrowers, it is surely not accurate in all cases.

If you've got a loan with an ancient interest rate you've got leverage. Lenders want to dump old financing, particularly low-rate mortgages that can be assumed, and that means they want your old loan off the books. In many instances lenders will encourage you to trade in your old, low-interest, low-balance mortgage for a new loan with higher interest and more principal. However, while the interest rate on the new financing may be higher than your current rate, it will be less than the going market rate.

What if Mr. Rivera has an assumable mortgage with a 6 percent interest rate and a $45,000 principal balance. The loan has 10 years to go. Current interest rates are 8.5 percent.

Rivera wants to add a $25,000 addition to his house and he can get the extra money with a new mortgage for $70,000 ($45,000 plus $25,000) or a $25,000 second trust. Another approach would be a $70,000 wraparound loan.

However, what Mr. Rivera would really like is a 30-year loan but at something less than 10 percent interest. So he makes the following agreement with the lender: Rivera will give up his old assumable loan if the lender will give him new, 30-year financing worth $70,000 at 7.75 percent interest—a "blended" rate below market interest levels but above the old rate on Rivera's current financing. Since the lender wants to purge his books of Rivera's loan, he agrees to the deal.

Note that a blend loan and a wraparound mortgage are essentially the same concept. The major difference is that with blend financing the original loan is wiped off the books, while with a wraparound agreement the old mortgage is retained—usually to the discomfort of the original lender.

Negotiating a blend loan is a contest between borrowers and lenders, and whoever has the better position wins. Sometimes the "better position" is a matter of perception rather than reality. Here are three advantages borrowers need to get the best refinancing deals:

First, the interest rate on old financing must be well below current mortgage levels.

Second, the original loan may or may not be assumable but you will have a much stronger position if the loan can be assumed.

Third, you cannot be dependent on the lender for financing. If you *need* money the lender will have little incentive to offer a bargain rate. You must have alternatives that do not require the current loan's repayment such as cash on hand, second trusts, wraparound loans or personal credit.

In those cases where borrowers want a blended rate to buy rather than refinance, the situation is somewhat different.

To start, the current financing must be freely assumable at its original rate and terms. If a loan is not freely assumable the lender has no incentive to bargain. Look for certain FHA, VA and older conventional loans to meet this requirement.

In addition, the purchaser must demonstrate to the lender that it is possible to acquire the property without disturbing the original loan. This might occur if the seller or third party takes back a second trust or wraparound loan or the buyer can pay cash above the current financing. In essence, if the old loan is assumable and the buyer is not dependent on the lender for financing, then blend loans may be a practical, and money-saving, home financing alternative.

Questions to Ask:

> What is the remaining loan balance?
> What is the interest rate on present financing?
> Is the current loan freely assumable?
> What are the current monthly payments?
> How much additional cash do you need?
> What is the current interest rate for conventional financing?
> Are local lenders making wraparound mortgages and second trusts? If so, how does a blend loan arrangement compare with a wraparound deal or a combination of the old financing plus a new second trust?
> What fees and points will the lender charge in a blend deal? Note that these costs, like interest, are negotiable.

BRIDGE LOANS CLOSE FINANCING GAP

While first-time buyers play an important role in the real estate marketplace, most buyers are seasoned vets who have bought before and own a home even as they look for a new one.

Many owners—if they sell their current property—will have more than enough capital to buy a new house. But what if house No. 1 does not sell and settle at the same time as house No. 2?

Although most move-up buyers sell and settle before buying home No. 2, sometimes home No. 1 does not sell on time. This situation is usually temporary, but it may mean that seller/buyers will need "bridge" financing.

Bridge financing is nothing more than a loan secured by the unsold property. The loan can last a few days, a few months, or longer and it is instantly repaid as soon as the property sells.

Although bridge financing can provide the cash needed to buy a new home, it is a form of financing that has a number of curiosities.

Some seller/buyers, for example, create their own bridge loans by taking money from an existing line-of-credit home equity loan and using that cash to buy a second house. This is generally okay with lenders, provided the borrowers are living in the house that secures the home-equity loan.

There is a catch, however, that should be addressed. When buyers borrow money to finance home No. 2, the lender generally asks if it is the intention of the buyers to move into the new property within 30 days. Since the seller/buyers cannot be in both homes at once, there is a potential conflict.

The solution is to work with both lenders and to properly complete all loan and closing materials. The assistance of an attorney is advised so that all issues are correctly disclosed.

Another choice is a true bridge loan, new financing that will remain in place until house No. 1 sells or for given time period, say six months.

Many lenders offer bridge financing, but to get the best deal borrowers should ask several questions.

- How much can you borrow? Generally lenders will not exceed a certain proportion of the property's value. If a home is worth $200,000 and there is an existing $110,000 mortgage, that means the owners have equity worth $90,000 before marketing costs. But if a lender will only provide bridge financing that does not exceed 75 percent of the property's value, then the largest possible bridge loan will be $40,000 ($110,000 + $40,000 = $150,000, or 75 percent of $200,000).
- What happens if the property does not sell by the end of the loan term? Lenders, perhaps for an additional fee, may extend the loan term. But what if they don't?
- How are monthly payments handled? With some bridge loans there are no monthly payments, while others require the payment of interest only.

- What are the fees and charges? Lenders will generally require a full-blown closing for a bridge loan. Relative to the amount borrowed, and relative to the amount of time the loan is expected to remain outstanding, such fees can be expensive.
- Are there points to pay? In the general case, borrowers are best off not paying points.

Suppose you have a $50,000 bridge loan and pay 10 percent interest at a time when first mortgages are available for 8 percent. You are paying a premium rate because the bridge loan is typically a second trust or second mortgage, and thus more risky than a first trust.

If you pay 1 point, $500 in this case, look what happens to the interest rate.

If the loan is outstanding three months, and if no payments are made until the home is sold, interest will amount to $1,250. Add $500 for a nonrefundable point and the total interest cost jumps to $1,750. That's an effective interest rate of 14 percent annually.

If the loan lasts a year, then the interest cost is $5,000. The interest cost, plus $500 for a point, gives an effective interest rate of 11 percent.

Another choice seller/buyers should consider are bridge loans offered by new-home builders and brokers. In this situation both builders and brokers are motived to complete the transaction, so terms are likely to be especially favorable.

BUY-DOWNS AND BUY-UPS

When interest rates soar, owners are often stuck with unsalable properties. Even though properties are not moving, however, interest costs accrue, taxes continue and owners want to sell as quickly as possible to preserve their profits.

With a buy-down, someone other than the borrower pays a portion of the mortgage, thus making properties more affordable. In effect, buy-downs are a subsidy. When times are tough and properties don't move it is the seller who pays for the buy-down.

Suppose prevailing interest rates are 12 percent and builder Thompson has unsold houses priced at $106,250. With interest rates so high, payments for a 30-year, $85,000 loan total $874.32 monthly. To qualify for such financing, assuming that insurance and taxes cost $150 per month, a buyer must earn at least $42,742 a year if a lender will allocate no more than 28 percent of the purchaser's income for principal, interest, taxes and insurance.

Thompson is paying interest on his construction loans, prime plus two points, 14 percent in this case. He figures it's better to sell the properties at discount than hold on and pay construction loan interest, so he offers this deal: he will pay $100 per month for the first 36 months of ownership to any buyer. (Alternatively, Thompson can pay points to a lender to bring monthly costs down. Whether he pays the buyer or lender directly is not important—the significant idea for borrowers is that their loan costs are being subsidized.)

With monthly payments for principal and interest down to $774.32, an income of $39,613 is now required for financing worth $85,000. The effective initial interest rate, at least to the buyer, is just above 10 percent. The lender, however, is being paid the full amount due for a 12 percent loan, $874.32 in this case ($774.32 from the buyer and $100 per month from Thompson).

With lower monthly costs Thompson soon sells one of the remaining

Buy-down Comparison Chart			
	Discounted Buy-Down	Conventional Sale	Loan
Sales price	$106,250	$102,650	$106,250
Loan size	$85,000	$82,120	$85,000
Down payment	$21,250	$20,530	$21,250
Monthly buy-down	$100	None	None
Effective interest rate			
Years 1–3	10 percent	12 percent	12 percent
Years 4–30	12 percent	12 percent	12 percent
Monthly principal and interest			
Years 1–3	$774.32	$844.70	$874.32
Years 4–30	$874.32	$844.70	$874.32
Projected interest cost	$226,155	$221,972	$229,755
Potential buyer savings	$3,600	$7,783	None
Qualifying income	$39,613	$42,630	$42,742

3-2-1 Buy Down		
Loan Amount		$100,000
Conventional Interest Rate		9.5 Percent
Loan Term		30 Years
Monthly Payment		$840.85
	Rate	Payment
First-Year Rate	7.5 Percent	$699.21
Second-Year Rate	8.5 Percent	$767.63
Third-Year Rate	9.5 Percent	$837.07
Years 4–30	10.5 Percent	$907.23

units but he must pay out $3,600 (36 × $100) for the buy-down but his actual cost is somewhat less. The reason: he doesn't pay all the money up front. Instead he deposits or invests the money and collects interest.

A Model Buy-Up			
Loan Amount	Rate	Lender Contribution	Monthly Payment
$112,500	10 Percent	0	$ 987.27
$112,500	11 Percent	$3,750	$1,071.36
$112,500	12 Percent	$7,500	$1,157.19

The second house is sold differently. The buyers, Mr. and Mrs. Poppin, want Thompson to apply the $3,600 buy-down as a credit against the purchase price, bringing the cost down to $102,650. The 20 percent down payment will drop from $21,250 to $20,530—a $720 saving. The mortgage will also drop, from $85,000 to $82,120. A 30-year, $82,120 mortgage at 12 percent interest will require monthly payments of $844.70 for principal and interest. If we estimate that taxes and insurance will cost $150 per month, a borrower will need a $42,630 income to qualify for this loan if 28 percent of the purchaser's income can be allocated to housing costs.

During the first three years of ownership the buy-down saves $70.38 per month ($844.70 less $774.32) or $2,533.68 over 36 months when compared to the lower-price arrangement negotiated by the Poppins. However, since the Poppins paid $720 less at closing, the buy-down's true benefit is just $1,813.68. Or is it?

After the first three years the numbers change rapidly. Now the Poppins' mortgage is lower by $29.62 per month, $844.70 versus $874.32. If they own their home another 62 months ($1,813.68 divided by $29.62 equals 61.23) the two deals will be equal—at least in the sense of total mortgage payments to date. After 62 months, the Poppins pull ahead by nearly $30 with each payment.

The Poppins, however, don't need to wait five years to benefit from their decision. By taking a price reduction rather than a buy-down, they've owed $2,880 less to the lender from the day they bought the house. (See table above.)

Buy-downs are not restricted to any term—one can have a buy-down for the entire length of the loan. However, if the numbers are right, even a short-term buy-down can be a good deal. For example, if you had a five-year buy-down but only intended to own the property three years because of a business relocation, then a buy-down can be attractive.

Although buy-downs can be attractive when sellers and builders agree to pay points, or at least more attractive than comparable loans available at the same time, a new generation of buy-downs has become available where there is no subsidy. Borrowers, rather than builders or sellers, pay extra fees up front in exchange for lower rates.

For instance, in a market where conventional financing is available at 9.5 percent, lenders may offer a "3-2-1 buy-down," a loan that works like this:

- In the first year, the interest rate is 3 percent lower than the base rate, or 7.5 percent
- In the second year, the interest rate is 2 percent lower than the base rate, or 8.5 percent.
- In the third year, the interest rate is 1 percent lower than the base rate, or 9.5 percent.
- In the fourth year and each year thereafter, the interest rate is set at 10.5 percent.

There are two catches to this loan. First, the base rate is likely to be set at 10.5 percent rather than the lower 9.5 percent rate which is otherwise available. Second, to get the buy-down borrowers must pay additional points up front.

Why would anyone want a 3-2-1 buy-down? With a lower start rate, it will be easier to qualify for financing. But while qualifying may be easier, paying additional points up front is hard, if not impossible, for most borrowers.

Worse yet, with a 3-2-1 buy-down, borrowers will reach the prevailing interest rate (9.5 percent in our example) in just three years. In the fourth year, the loan rate will be a full 1 percent higher than conventional loans.

Can borrowers come out ahead with a 3-2-1 buy-down? Not likely. Whatever advantages are gained up front will quickly be offset by more points and higher rates.

When considering a buy-down it always pays to review a sale to see if the deal will be better by simply discounting the purchase price. While a buy-down is certainly a better deal than conventional financing, it may be less attractive than a simple discount. When comparing discounts versus buy-downs you must gauge the size of the monthly payment you can afford and consider how long you expect to hold the property. In general, if you have the income, short-term buy-downs go well with short-term ownership; discounts go well with long-term ownership.

We saw with buy-downs that borrowers were able to get lower rates when money was paid to the lender up front. But what happens when buyers can afford monthly payments, but not closing costs?

Lenders typically allow sellers to make "contributions" to the buyer at closing. For sellers, the obvious reason to make contributions is to entice purchasers into buying the property. For lenders, contributions may convince borrowers to accept one loan rather than another.

The catch is that seller and lender contributions are limited. Depending on the amount down, contributions usually range from 3 to 6 percent of the sale price.

If we have a situation where loans are available at 10 percent, then a lender might trade a 1 percent interest hike for a closing credit equal to 3 percent of the sale price, or a 2 percent hike in exchange for a 6 percent credit.

Suppose a home sells for $125,000 and a buyer puts down $125,000. The lender will finance the deal with a $112,500 loan at 10 percent. Or the lender will finance the deal at 11 percent and make a $3,750 contribution at closing (3 percent × $125,000). If the borrower will pay 12 percent interest, the lender will pay $7,500 at settlement. (See table, p. 188.)

Is this a good deal?

To answer the question borrowers must consider that they are exchanging higher monthly costs for lower closing expenses. In areas where home values are rising and borrowers have little cash, buy-ups can be attractive if you only intend to hold the property for a relatively short time.

In our example, if there is a $112,500 loan at 10 percent interest, then over a 30-year term the monthly payments will be set at $987.27. If we borrow at 11 percent interest, the monthly cost for principal and interest will be $1,071.36.

The difference between the two loans is $84.09. If we divide $84.09 into the money contributed up front, $3,750, it will take 45 months before the lender's credit is eaten up in higher monthly costs.

The deal with 12 percent interest works the same way. Monthly payments rise from $987.27 to $1,157.19 and the payment difference is $169.92 per month. Since $7,500 was credited up front in exchange for a 2 percent interest rate increase, it will again take 45 months ($7,500 divided by $169.92) before the borrower loses ground.

Buy-ups can be attractive for borrowers who need additional cash to close a deal but who otherwise have stable incomes. However, since higher rates mean higher monthly costs, borrowers with limited incomes will not qualify for buy-up programs. In addition, borrowers who intend to own their property for many years will not be attracted to buy-ups because the initial advantages can be lost in less than four years—not a long time-frame for most owners.

Questions to Ask:

What is the current rate of interest for conventional financing?
What is the effective rate of a loan with a buy-down provision?
How much cash down is required?
How long will the buy-down remain in effect?
What is the buy-down total value?

If the buy-down is to be a monthly mortgage supplement, what happens if the builder or owner goes bankrupt? Is there any requirement to set aside buy-down funds in an escrow account?

If buy-down funds are to be held in escrow who gets the interest? If you are the purchaser you should certainly argue that it belongs to you.

If the buy-down's value is applied to the sales price of the property, how will down payment, mortgage size, monthly payments and income qualification standards change?

How long do you expect to own the property?

Is the loan assumable by a qualified buyer at its original rate and terms?

Can the loan be prepaid in whole or in part without penalty?

Do you offer buy-up financing? If so, what credit is available up front? How much will interest rates rise?

CREDIT CARD FINANCING: PLASTIC MORTGAGES FOR EVERYONE?

Borrow money to finance a car, boat, vacation, pool table, or refrigerator and Uncle Sam will say thanks for boosting the national economy, but forget about deducting that personal interest at tax time.

But if you borrow money with a credit card and use it to buy a car, boat, or whatever, and then secure that credit card with your home, the rules change. You now have "real estate" debt, and for most of us the interest is entirely deductible.

Given that a car is a car and a vacation is a vacation, by playing the definition game one can quickly and easily cut financing costs merely by placing debt in the right column. Pay for that trip to Bora Bora with "secured real estate" debt rather than "personal" debt and your interest costs suddenly become deductible.

If you're in the 15 percent federal bracket, writing off interest worth $1,000 will effectively place $150 in your pocket. If you're among the rich and famous and suffer with a 39.6 percent rate, then you're ahead by $396 dollars. No less interesting, if you also pay state income taxes, that too makes deducting interest attractive.

The catch to all of this—and you knew there would be one—is that using credit cards secured by real estate is risky, costly, and generally not advised. To see why, consider the nature of home-equity credit cards.

To create a home-equity credit card we first need a home-equity loan, generally a second trust with a revolving line of credit. Such financing is commonly available with little cost up front and rates that are marginally higher than traditional first mortgages. Money from a typical home-equity line of credit can usually be obtained by just writing a check. As the loan is repaid, the line of credit is restored so that continued borrowing power is assured.

With typical credit cards there is also a revolving line of credit. However, credit cards routinely represent high rates of interest—14 to 21 percent—annual fees, low monthly payments, and special charges in the event cash is withdrawn.

Combine home-equity loans with credit cards and suddenly one has two forms of borrowing which do not mix particularly well.

A typical credit card may have a credit limit of $500 or $1,000, but with a home-equity card huge volumes of credit may be available, perhaps $25,000 to $50,000—or more.

The very size of such credit lines coupled with the easy and instant access represented by credit cards may create the illusion of vast wealth, at least until the credit limit is reached.

Borrow $1,000 with a credit card and the monthly payments can be as little as $25 or $30. Borrow $25,000 and suddenly the monthly bill can total $625—enough to sink many households. In comparison, a $25,000 mortgage at 8.75 percent will cost $249.86 per month over 15 years, or $196.67 monthly over 30 years.

Fail to repay a credit card with $1,000 outstanding and the credit card lender is apt to be fairly peeved. You will surely receive a steady stream of letters and calls to resolve the matter, and perhaps a court date as well.

But if the credit card is secured by your home the lender has enormous leverage. Unpaid real estate debt, even $1, can lead to foreclosure, the loss of years of equity, a woefully flawed credit history, and financial ruin.

If your mailbox is like mine there is no shortage of credit card companies that would like your business. And as long as that business is not secured by your home, then fine; have as much plastic as makes sense.

But when it comes to credit cards secured with real estate, beware. Big numbers can produce big problems, easy access to credit cannot continue indefinitely, and if complications arise they are unlikely to be either minor or marginal.

So while writing off credit card interest seems appealing and logical, there can be enormous costs for the unwary, the unsophisticated, and the irresponsible.

If you want a line of credit secured by real estate, stop by any mortgage source and look into a plain and simple home-equity loan with a revolving line of credit. Compare deals in terms of closing costs, interest levels, repayment terms, and annual fees.

And if someone suggests a home-equity credit card, offer a hearty "no thanks" and go elsewhere before you lose your shirt—or worse.

ECOLOGY LOANS

It was Jimmy Carter who said that the use of oil pricing and the withholding of energy to further political aims were the "moral equivalent of war," a comment we ignore at our peril.

With America dependent on foreign oil (but not coal, natural gas or nuclear power), and with a growing interest in conservation and ecology, the mortgage industry now offers loans to encourage the construction of energy-efficient housing and the use of appliances which hold down energy consumption. Such loans, known as energy-efficiency mortgages (EEMs), can save more than kilowatts.

Although the programs vary somewhat, EEMs are available with conventional financing as well as FHA and VA backing. Here's how they work.

Suppose the Shermans can afford to borrow $100,000 at 9 percent interest. With a typical conventional loan, and with conventional loan standards, the Shermans will pay $804.62 per month for principal and interest.

The Shermans can make a conventional loan because lenders will allow up to 28 percent of their income to be used for principal, interest, taxes and insurance. With an EEM, however, up to 30 percent of a borrower's income can be used for home expenses.

The addition of a 2-percent qualification allowance may not seem important, but with an EEM it represents three significant values.

First, a family such as the Sherman's can borrow more. In this case, $108,918 rather than $100,000.

Second, several EEM programs allow buyers to purchase properties and to then make the homes more energy-efficient with improvements made after closing. For example, the Shermans might borrow roughly $109,000 plus some additional amount to make approved, energy-related improvements. The money for improvements will be held in an escrow account by the lender and disbursed as the repairs are completed.

The amount available for repairs will depend on how the property is financed. With FHA as much as $3,500 in additional funds can be borrowed while the VA program allows up to $5,000 in extra funding for energy improvements. For conventional loans the situation is somewhat more complex: there is no formal limit on the financing of approved upgrades, however, at the time a lender sells a mortgage in the secondary market, the rules change somewhat.

Freddie Mac and Fannie Mae—the two big secondary lenders—will buy energy efficient mortgages but only if the escrow fund does not exceed 10 (Freddie Mac) to 15 (Fannie Mae) percent of the amount borrowed. Since lenders may look for a quick sale in the secondary market, it is possible that some will simply limit the funds available for improvements to 10 or 15 percent of the basic mortgage to assure that the loan can be sold immediately.

Third, to qualify for an EEM, the Shermans must buy an energy-efficient house. Such a home will consume less energy per month and cost less to operate. Not only will the borrowers benefit, but so will everyone in town.

To see how the Shermans help themselves and the rest of us, look at the way we fund generating stations, gas lines, and other big energy projects.

To assure there are no shortages, utilities must always have excess capacity to account for energy surges (such as peak use on the hottest days) and future growth. But, if energy consumption declines, there is less need to fund generating stations and other fixed-cost facilities. The result is that the utilities borrow less, pay less interest, buy less fuel, and have less idle equipment. The benefit for consumers is that utility rates need not go up so quickly.

Questions to Ask:

Does the lender handle EEM financing? If so, are there any additional charges? More points? (With an EEM loan where an escrow account is established for improvements and upgrades the lender has additional work when compared to a traditional loan arrangement.)

What, specifically, will qualify a property for energy-efficient financing?

What improvements can you make with EEM loans? How much time is available to make improvements? (Figure 120 days after closing, unless a lender says otherwise.)

How much additional money can you borrow with an EEM mortgage? What improvements and upgrades can be funded with additional EEM funds?

How much will you save each year on fuel when you buy an energy-efficient home?

ESCROW SOLUTIONS

Mortgages are complex arrangements and if you miss a payment there is little doubt that problems will arise. But what happens if your lender misses a payment or otherwise errs?

At first it may seem implausible that a lender owes anything. You're in debt, not the lender, but in fact lenders are commonly obligated to make payments on your behalf.

If you bought a home with less than 20 percent down, the lender undoubtedly had two basic requirements: first, that you obtained insurance or a guarantee from the VA, FHA or a private mortgage insurer. Second, that you established an escrow (or trust) account with the lender to assure that all property tax and insurance payments would be made.

If your property tax is $1,000, then a lender will want to collect $85 a month—plus as much as a two-month cushion to guard against sudden tax increases. In addition, the lender will want money to pay property insurance costs for fire, theft, and liability coverage.

The money you pay to the lender not only assures that property taxes and insurance bills are paid, the money also provides a steady income for the lender. While the money must be placed in escrow, separate and apart from the lender's funds, it can earn interest—

money which traditionally goes right into lender accounts rather than your pocket. To understand how much money is involved, consider that one lender recently settled escrow overcharge claims in 12 states that will require the firm to pay roughly $100 million to more than 350,000 borrowers.

Escrow accounts require minimal management and administration but when there are problems, they can severely impact homeowners. For instance, if a lender fails to pay a property tax bill, **you** are still obligated to pay the debt and it is a lien against your property. Or suppose that local taxes go up by $500. The money isn't in the escrow account, so the lender says pay up now or you'll be in default. If you don't happen to have $500 immediately available then you've got troubles.

A more subtle problem works like this: You owe $750 a month to the mortgage company and you pay $800. Rather than reducing your debt and thus lowering interest costs, the lender instead credits the pre-payment money to the escrow account where it draws interest for the lender.

An escrow account should be seen as an asset for borrowers, one that requires careful supervision. To assure that no problems arise, or to deal with a lender if problems develop, take the following steps.

- Check your escrow balance yearly to assure that all payments and credits are shown. Under 1990 legislation, lenders must provide an annual statement showing your monthly payments, the amount held in escrow, total escrow payments during the past year, and the money paid out for taxes, insurance, or any other approved purposes.
- If you prepay your mortgage, clearly show that the prepayment is to be credited against the loan's principal balance and not simply added to the escrow account or held in escrow for 30 days.
- Watch the cushion rules. Federal regulations generally allow lenders to maintain a two-month cushion, but not all lenders are federally regulated. Also, FHA and VA loans only permit a one-month cushion.
- If you find an error, keep up all payments otherwise you can set-off a chain reaction of late charges and default notices. Work with the lender by phone and letter to resolve the problem, most will

be helpful. If the lender is uncooperative, contact the state attorney general in the jurisdiction where the property is located.

- If you have a choice, and if you have the discipline, forget escrow accounts and pay your own taxes and insurance. The money set aside can then earn money for you.
- When you refinance or pay off a loan, be certain the lender returns or credits all escrow funds as quickly as possible. The money in an escrow account is yours and lenders have no justification for holding it once the debt has been retired.

FANNIENEIGHBORS

For many years the question of financing entry-level properties has been one of the most difficult to resolve, especially in urban areas historically underserved by traditional lenders.

The issues involved with financing low-income neighborhoods are complex and often controversial, but the bottom line is that many potential homebuyers rent because mortgage money has not been readily available in the past.

While it is true that FHA, VA, MCC, and municipal (bond-backed) financing programs are open to qualifying low-income homebuyers, each program has significant limitations when compared with conventional financing.

- FHA rules limit the amount of money available to borrowers, a substantial problem in high-cost metropolitan areas.
- VA loans are available only to individuals with qualifying federal service. Since most people do not qualify for VA financing, such loans are effectively off-limits to the majority of all buyers.
- Mortgage certificate programs as well as loans underwritten through the sale of tax-exempt bonds work well, but such programs are simply unavailable in many situations because of excess demand and limited funding.

What is needed is a different approach, one that opens up the conventional mortgage system to low income purchasers while at the same time assuring that lender funds are not unduly at risk, the very benefits offered through the FannieNeighbors, a program developed by Fannie Mae.

FannieNeighbors is available in any designated "central city," a description so broad that it includes 544 communities. In addition, the program can also be used in low-income and minority census tracts as well as specific areas targeted for neighborhood revitalization by local housing agencies.

Under FannieNeighbors, borrowers obtain conventional mortgages, which means conventional loan limits apply—a top loan in late 1994 of $203,150 versus $152,362 with FHA financing.

To qualify, an individual must live within a designated area and have enough cash for a 5 percent downpayment. The usual requirement that borrowers have two months cash reserves is waived and more liberal qualification standards are used.

To see how FannieNeighbors works, imagine that the Stapletons live in a central city and want to buy a $125,000 property. They have 5 percent down, a total of $6,250 in this example, and they also have the cash required for closing.

The Stapletons have a good credit record by traditional standards, but if necessary they could turn to utility bills and other alternative credit references under the FannieNeighbors program.

To qualify for a conventional loan, the Stapletons would normally be allowed to use 28 percent of their gross income for principal, interest, taxes, and insurance (PITI). As much as 36 percent of their income could be used for PITI plus credit card debt and other monthly obligations.

While the ratios for a conventional loan are generally pegged at 28/36, more liberal guidelines are available under the FannieNeighbors program, ratios of 33/38.

To see how more generous ratios work, imagine that the Stapletons have a gross household income of $33,600 a year or $2,800 a month. Imagine also that mortgages are now available at 7.5 percent interest.

- With a sale price of $125,000 and $6,250 down, the Stapletons will need a mortgage of $118,750.
- A $118,750 mortgage at 7.5 percent interest will require monthly payments of $830.32 for principal and interest. Annual property

Loan Choices for the Stapletons

	Conventional Loan	FannieNeighbors
Home Price	125,000	125,000
Amount Down	6,250	6,250
Mortgage Amount	118,750	118,750
Interest Rate	7.5 percent	7.5 percent
Monthly Principal and Interest	830.32	830.32
Monthly Taxes	50.00	50.00
Monthly Insurance	20.00	20.00
Monthly Housing Costs	900.32	900.32
Annual Income	33,600	33,600
Monthly Income	2,800	2,800
Front Ratio	28 percent	33 percent
Allowable PITI	784.00	924.00
Home Purchase Possible	No	Yes

taxes are $600 ($50 a month) while insurance costs $240 ($20 per month). Total housing cost: $900.32.

- The Stapletons earn $33,600 a year, or $2,800 a month. With conventional underwriting standards they can devote up to 28 percent of their monthly income to principal, interest, taxes, and insurance. In the case of the Stapletons, 28 percent of their monthly income is $784—not enough to buy the property.
- Under the FannieNeighbors program, as much as 33 percent of a borrower's income can be devoted to PITI. For the Stapletons this means $924 can be used for housing costs, enough in this case to buy their home.

FannieNeighbors combines conventional loan amounts, liberal qualification standards, and geographic targeting to produce a program that can have a significant community development impact. In addition, the program reduces risks for local lenders, which means they have a substantial incentive to bring additional financing into targeted areas.

Community housing programs traditionally include wage limitations that effectively dampen the development of mixed-income neighborhoods. The FannieNeighbors program is different because it's open to everyone, regardless of earnings, with an interest in living in particular areas. The net result is that FannieNeighbors can do much to encourage the economic diversity local communities need if they are to successfully support a wide array of local stores and services.

FARM AND RURAL LOANS

While much of the United States is defined by huge cities and endless suburbs, a trip to the Cheyenne rodeo shows another side of the domestic realty market: farms and ranches as far as the eye can see, as well as future home sites for a growing number of urban refugees.

Cheyenne, the capital of Wyoming, is an immaculate micro-city (population 50,000) that symbolizes a different way of life—a place without subways, two-hour commutes, or soaring office towers. And the rodeo—the biggest outdoor event of its kind in the world— reminds everyone that in a high-tech society there is still no substitute for farms, fields, and the people who work them.

In the not-too-distant future we may well find that a steady stream of city folks (and suburban ones) will be heading to places like Cheyenne in search of a quieter lifestyle. That migration can occur today in large part because jobs are no longer localized—a growing army of people can live on the prairie, in the mountains, or by the sea and still connect with big-city employment centers via faxes, modems, and e-mail.

In addition to a new lifestyle, urban migrants may also discover a new world of mortgage financing. While such common financing choices as FHA, VA, and conventional mortgages are available, there are restrictions in country settings that may be unfamiliar to city dwellers.

Fannie Mae, for instance, owns one out of every four mortgages nationwide. Such loans are bought from local lenders, but when it comes to rural properties Fannie Mae (and other secondary lenders) have several special concerns.

For example, Fannie Mae will not buy a mortgage secured by a property that is not habitable year-round. There must be road access 12 months a year—even if the roads are unpaved. Barns, silos, and stables are okay, but the property must be a residence rather than a working farm, ranch, or orchard.

Low- to moderate-income buyers with an interest in rural property should get in touch with the local office of the Farmers Home Administration (FmHA), a part of the Agriculture Department.

The 502 Direct Lending Program—which is available only through FmHA offices—allows buyers to purchase homes with no money down. However a qualifying property is likely to have 1,050 square feet of interior space and be located in communities with not more than 25,000 people. Interestingly enough, a direct loan for less than $2,500 need not be secured with a mortgage. Instead, it can be a personal loan to a rural property owner.

The 502 Guaranteed Rural Housing Loan Program is more liberal. It allows purchasers to buy with 100 percent financing and with qualification standards that match those used for FHA loans—as much as 29 percent of gross monthly income can be used for principal, interest, taxes, and insurance (PITI). In addition, as much as 41 percent of gross monthly income can be used for all monthly debt such as credit cards, student loans, and PITI. Loan limits parallel local FHA maximums, $77,197 to $152,362 at this time, depending on location. A one-time mortgage insurance fee of .9 percent is required, but the insurance fee may be financed over the life of the loan.

For those who want not just a residence but a working farm, ranch, or orchard, the deal is different. While such properties may seem like real estate, they are regarded (not unreasonably) as businesses and require business financing.

FmHA-guaranteed financing for as much as $300,000 is available for those who want to buy farms, are U.S. citizens or legal resident aliens, and are unable to obtain financing from commercial mortgage sources. In addition, up to $400,000 is available for "production" financing; that is, money to operate the property.

When you finance a home no one asks if you know how to adjust the furnace or seed the yard. With a farm, the situation is different. Loan applicants first meet with a local eligibility committee, three area residents familiar with farming and credit, to discuss the loan. After passing muster, one then meets with the local FmHA county supervisor.

FmHA also operates a "limited-resource" farm-loan program. This program makes available as much as $200,000 to beginning farmers with agricultural training and skills but limited capital. An interesting aspect of this program is that before a loan is granted the borrower and local FmHA officers work out a "farm and home" plan, essentially a budget and management feasibility study, before the first seed is planted.

Lastly, those who are VA-qualified and are Native Americans, Pacific Islanders, or Alaskan Natives can obtain loans (not just loan guarantees) directly from the Department of Veterans Affairs to purchase or refinance homes on government trust lands, such as reservations. Such financing is extremely important because commercial mortgages cannot be secured by government property, and thus financing on trust lands has long been in short supply.

GRADUATED PAYMENT MORTGAGES (GPMs)

Most of us enter the work force with the thought that our incomes will rise over time. Unfortunately we often buy real estate long before we enter our peak earning years, a situation that creates two problems:

First, because our incomes are limited we can only afford smaller mortgages and less expensive homes.

Second, what mortgage payments we do make are difficult to afford because we are also buying furniture, cars and first trying to support families.

GPMs are designed for people with rising incomes. They feature fixed interest rates plus low initial monthly payments that rise annually during the loan's first years. Here's how a GPM will work:

The Hunts were married last July and are now looking for their first home. They have a combined income of $27,500. If 28 percent of their income can be devoted to the payment of mortgage interest and principal, they can pay $633 a month for principal, interest, taxes and insurance (PITI). If taxes and insurance in the Hunts' price range cost $150 per month, then the Hunts have $483 available each month for principal and interest. At 9 percent interest, a monthly payment of $483 will support a 30-year mortgage worth $60,000.

GPM versus Conventional Financing		
	GPM°	Conventional
Loan size	$79,450	$60,000
Loan term	30 years	30 years
Interest rate	9 percent	9 percent
Monthly payment		
Year 1	$482.77	$482.77
Year 2	519.23	482.77
Year 3	588.15	482.77
Year 4	600.01	482.77
Year 5	645.01	482.77
Year 6-30	693.39	482.77
Year-End Loan Balance		
Year 1	$80,864.67	$59,590.13
Year 2	81,956.02	59,141.80
Year 3	82,287.73	58,651.43
Year 4	82,502.20	58,115.05
Year 5	82,173.96	57,528.35
Year 6	81,209.01	56,868.62
Year 7	80,155.21	56,184.69
Year 8	79,001.69	55,416.91
Year 29.5	0.00	n.a.
Year 30	n.a.	0.00
Yearly negative amortization		
Year 1	$1,414.67	——
Year 2	1,091.35	——
Year 3	331.70	——
Year 4	214.48	——
Year 5	——	——

°GPM loan with 7.5 percent payment increase annually for five years.

Source: GPM figures based on HUD Transmittal Document No. 4, Appendix 1, Page 3 (Jan. 21, 1978).

But suppose the Hunts consider a GPM mortgage. Assuming that the Hunts are qualified on the basis of first-year payments, they can borrow $79,450.

Their lender tells the Hunts that with a GPM loan the first monthly payments are lower than those for a self-amortizing, conventional mortgage, while later payments are higher. The size of the monthly payments is determined by a schedule. For example, the Hunts can arrange to have monthly payments rise 7.5 percent annually for the first 5 years of their loan. In years 6 through 30 the payments will be level. Since the Hunts expect their incomes to rise they take the GPM financing.

Since payments in the first 5 years of the Hunts' loan are not high enough to produce a self-amortizing loan, negative amortization is occurring. This problem can be resolved by making an extra-large down payment at settlement or by having higher payments in the loan's last 25 years. Since the Hunts do not have the dollars to make a big down payment they opt for larger monthly costs in future years. They make this decision because they assume they will have the income to carry such costs easily.

It should be said that when negative amortization occurs 100 percent of any monthly payment is being used to pay interest and is usually tax deductible. Speak to a CPA or tax attorney to find out if money paid at settlement to forestall negative amortization can be deducted.

Because GPMs have small monthly costs up front, there are lenders who will qualify borrowers on the basis of these low initial payments.

Borrowers considering GPMs should be aware, however, of several potential hurdles.

First, some lenders who qualify borrowers on the basis of initial GPM payments also charge a "lock-in" fee to assure that the rate they've quoted will actually be available at settlement.

Second, some lenders who offer very attractive GPM rates also require borrowers to pay an up-front "subsidy" account. In effect, the money paid up front offsets the low initial payments.

Third, some lenders only offer GPMs with a 15-year payment schedule, a schedule which produces higher monthly costs than 30-year GPM loans. Higher monthly costs, of course, translate into less ability to qualify for financing.

Fourth, GPMs commonly produce negative amortization in their early years. This means if a borrower has to refinance after just a few years, the loan balance is likely to be greater than the amount originally borrowed.

Fifth, while a GPM may allow individuals to increase their borrowing ability, the cost of such borrowing is not extravagantly more expensive on an overall basis. A $79,450 loan at 9 percent interest would have a potential interest cost of $150,688 over 30 years. A GPM for the same amount would have a potential interest expense of $158,340.96.

Sixth, a GPM is a woefully bad idea for those with declining incomes. Conversely, a GPM is great for individuals with growing salaries.

In addition to *conventional* GPM mortgages, such financing is also available under FHA Sec. 245(a) for owner-occupied, single-family homes and condos. This program features low down payments—usually less than 5 percent plus the value of deferred interest (negative amortization) and has five repayment plans:

Plan I. Monthly payments increase 2.5 percent each year during the loan's first 5 years.

Plan II. Monthly payments increase 5 percent each year during the loan's first 5 years.

Plan III. Monthly payments increase 7.5 percent each year during the loan's first 5 years.

Plan IV. Monthly payments increase 2 percent each year during the loan's first 10 years.

Plan V. Monthly payments increase 3 percent each year during the loan's first 10 years.

Certain buyers may also be interested in a somewhat different FHA program known as Sec. 245(b). This is a graduated mortgage program intended for first-time home buyers or for those who have not owned a home in the past three years and who do not otherwise qualify for other FHA programs. It can be used to purchase new or "substantially rehabilitated" housing. The attraction of this program is that it requires somewhat less money down than the Sec. 245(a) program and offers an additional repayment schedule: monthly payments increase 4.9 percent each year over a period of ten years.

The GPM concept can be combined with an adjustable rate to produce a GPARM, or graduated payment adjustable rate mortgage. With a GPARM, there will be set—but rising—monthly payments in the loan's first few years. Since payments are set but the interest rate is not it is possible that negative interest will occur in the first years of the loan. After the initial period when monthly payments are set, a GPARM will behave just like a regular ARM with payments and interest rates that can vary throughout the loan's life.

A GPARM is probably a better financing choice than an ARM, especially for young property buyers. Individuals first entering the work force are the people least able to cope with rapidly rising housing costs because they have relatively little disposable income. By fixing initial costs, a GPARM gives buyers the below-market interest levels that ARMs often feature at first plus some time in which incomes can rise.

GPM loans in general represent one of the best forms of first-time financing, because they are fixed-rate mortgages attuned to the needs of entry-level purchasers. Be aware, however, that because they feature negative amortization in their first few years, buyers who intend to move in less than five years may find that they owe more with GPM financing at settlement than they borrowed.

Questions to Ask:

What is the GPM interest rate?

How many points, if any, are being charged for conventional financing and for GPM loans?

When points are considered, what is the true annual percent rate (APR) for a GPM loan?

What GPM formats are available from local lenders?

How much money down will you need for a conventional GPM? How much for an FHA-backed GPM?

How is negative amortization handled? By an enlarged down payment? By higher monthly payments through most of the loan term? By a balloon payment? By extending the loan term?

If you are selling a home with a GPM where you have paid additional money up front to account for negative amortization, have you received any credit from the purchaser?

If you are assuming a GPM loan, is a balloon payment scheduled?

GROWING EQUITY MORTGAGES (GEMs)

For 50 years the fixed-rate conventional loan has been the standard against which "creative" financing has been measured. But in the early 1980s the *growing equity mortgage,* or GEM, loan was developed. Radically different from conventional mortgages, the GEM loan has a unique payment concept that can readily cut interest costs by 50 percent and sometimes more.

With GEM financing monthly payments for the mortgage are figured on a 25- or 30-year amortization schedule, depending on the plan. However, the mortgage term is nowhere near 25 or 30 years because GEM loans have a rapid repayment feature.

Instead of paying a set amount each month, GEM loans have graduated payment increases that can be calculated two ways:

First, the monthly payments can be increased 2, 3, 4 or 5 percent annually during the loan's first years. Thereafter monthly loan payments are flat.

Second, one can tie monthly payment increases to an index. For example, if the Commerce Department cost-of-living index rises 4 percent, monthly mortgage payments in the coming year will rise by some portion of that figure, say 60 percent of the increase, or 2.4 percent. The idea of indexing GEM loans to an inflation barometer was imported from nations where triple-digit inflation rates are common. Without indexing, loans of any type in such countries would be impossible.

So far it sounds as though a GEM loan is nothing more than a graduated payment mortgage but there is one significant difference: As monthly GEM payments rise, additional dollars paid by the borrower are only used to reduce the mortgage's principal balance. The result is that GEM loans with fixed monthly increases can often be repaid in less than 15 years.

Rapid repayments create substantial advantages for borrowers. Even though GEM monthly payments are increased annually, the sum total of those payments is nowhere near the aggregate cost of 360 monthly payments. Look how interest costs between a 30-year, $75,000 conventional mortgage at 9 percent interest compare with two $75,000 GEM loans.

The 30-year conventional loan will have 360 monthly payments of $603.47. The total value of all payments will be $217,248. Subtracting

	Conventional and GEM Financing Compared		
	$75,000 Loans 9 Percent Interest		
Year	Conventional ($)	2 Percent GEM ($)	5 Percent GEM ($)
1	603.47	603.47	603.47
2	603.47	615.54	633.64
3	603.47	627.05	665.32
4	603.47	640.41	698.59
5	603.47	653.22	733.52
6	603.47	666.28	770.19
7	603.47	679.61	808.70
8	603.47	693.20	849.14
9	603.47	707.06	891.60
10	603.47	721.20	936.18
11	603.47	735.63	982.98
12	603.47	750.34	1,083.74
13	603.47	765.35	1,083.74
14	603.47	780.65	0.00
15	603.47	796.27	0.00
16	603.47	812.20	0.00
17	603.47	828.44	0.00
18	603.47	845.01	0.00
19	603.47	861.91	0.00
20–30	603.47	0.00	0.00

Note: Final year payments for GEM financing require less than 12 full installments.

the original principal of $75,000 will leave a potential interest cost of $144,248.

A $75,000 GEM loan will start with payments of $603.47. If monthly payments rose by 5 percent each year the entire loan will be repaid in 168 months—a little less than 14 years—and the total interest cost will be $66,653. If monthly payments were raised by 2 percent annually, the loan will have 240 payments (20 years) and a total interest cost of $89,617.

It doesn't take an electronic calculator or a strong familiarity with the new math to see that GEM loans substantially cut interest costs. With the first GEM format, potential interest expenses drop by $77,595, while the second format creates interest savings of $54,631.

Short repayment schedules are extremely attractive to lenders, since they represent less risk than long-term financing. Less risk means lower interest rates and that is another important GEM feature.

Lower interest rates allow buyers who do not qualify for financing at market rates to get GEM mortgages, or—seen another way—to get larger mortgages at any income level. Lower rates also speed the amortization process, since less interest is required to pay back the loan.

One can refine the GEM concept even further for buyers with limited incomes. Suppose, for example, our purchasers can afford initial monthly payments of just $550.00 a month rather than $603.47 as in the previous examples. Can we formulate a loan that will accommodate such purchasers, one that allows them to qualify for a mortgage? Sure. Assuming that the buyers will have rising incomes, we can have a loan that's a 5 percent GEM in its first seven years and then a level-payment mortgage thereafter. The table on page 205 illustrates how the monthly payments will look.

The attractions of this loan format are that initial monthly payments are far below current market rates, and overall payments never reach the steep upper limits found with traditional GEM financing. Indeed, this loan even offers a "bonus" of sorts: monthly payments *drop* in the final 23 years.

The problem with this mortgage, however, is that while monthly payments are low, interest costs are high. Interest fees over the life of a 30-year "bonus" GEM total $156,605 in this example—almost $14,360 more than one would pay with a 30-year conventional loan. Also, because the loan has negative amortization in its first year, a buyer who sold during that time will owe more money to the lender than was originally borrowed.

Are there cases when a "bonus" GEM is attractive? Such loans can be useful with investment property when low monthly costs are important. But for home owners generally, a "bonus" GEM is not a bargain.

From the borrower's viewpoint there are three negative aspects of a GEM loan:

Bonus GEM Mortgage		
Year	Loan Payment ($)	Balance ($)
1	550.00	75,156.34
2	577.50	74,983.40
3	606.38	74,433.01
4	636.69	73,451.88
5	668.53	71,980.48
6	701.95	69,953.04
7	737.05	67,296.40
8–30	644.45	0.00

First, there is the monthly payment, which rises each year. Not everyone will be able to afford such payments but for those who can it is comforting to know that since the entire amount of the increase is going toward amortization rather than interest, such increases represent nothing more than a form of forced savings.

Second, because less interest is being paid, the mortgage interest tax deduction is reduced. While it is true that GEMs offer less tax shelter, it is also true that they require far fewer payment dollars. With less to spend on the mortgage a borrower has more dollars to place elsewhere, including, perhaps, alternative investments that produce significant tax advantages. (If a home interest tax shelter is important, a borrower can always refinance in the loan's last years.)

Third, a GEM is not a good financing vehicle for those who anticipate declining incomes. GEMs require an increasing proportion of available income at a time when there are fewer dollars to spend. For this reason, GEMs should be avoided by those who expect to retire within the next ten to fifteen years.

In addition to conventional GEM mortgages there is also an FHA-backed GEM program. Yearly payment increases from 1 to 5 percent are allowed, but the maximum size of such loans is limited according to the same terms as the FHA 203(b) program. FHA GEMs offer the low down payments normally associated with FHA financing and may be prepaid in whole or in part without penalty. This is an attractive GEM program because it offers flexibility in the event plans change, the property is sold or a borrower elects to make a prepayment.

Borrowers may want to consider an alternative GEM program, their own. Take any loan which allows prepayments in whole or in part without penalty and simply add an additional amount each month. Since prepayments are not required by the lender, the borrower can make— or not make—additional payments at will.

Because of their inherent advantages—below-market interest rates, predictable payment increases and rapid amortization—GEMs should be regarded as one of the best mortgage formats. Because they neatly balance the needs of both lenders and borrowers and because they offer the potential to substantially reduce homeownership costs, GEM financing is well within the definition of a common-sense mortgage. Simply stated, GEM financing is a mortgage concept that should not be overlooked.

Questions to Ask:

What is the initial GEM interest rate? How does that rate compare with conventional financing costs?

How much money down is required?

How much will the monthly payments increase each year? For how many years will the increases continue? Does the rate of interest change during the loan term?

How long will it take to pay off the loan?

Is the loan assumable?

Can GEM financing be prepaid in whole or in part without penalty?

Are FHA-guaranteed GEMs available? If so, under what terms?

HOME EQUITY MORTGAGES

Real estate has traditionally been considered a non-liquid asset, property that can be converted to cash only by selling or refinancing—two very expensive and time-consuming ways to raise capital. But the old image of real estate is now changing. Today property can be converted to cash immediately through the use of a home equity loan secured by real estate.

Credit is the great wonder of American society. You can be born on credit, live on credit and probably die on credit. Like gravity, credit is silent, invisible and with us every moment.

While credit is all around us all forms of credit are not identical. Consumer credit differs from traditional real estate financing, another form of credit, in three ways:

First, the credit represented by hundreds of millions of flat plastic cards is unsecured debt. When you make a credit purchase the card company advances money to a gas station or department store on the theory that you will repay. Real estate debt, in contrast, is secured by the value of your property. If you don't pay the property will be sold to pay off what you owe.

Second, real estate debt traditionally has been advanced at one time. Consumer debt is usually a revolving line of credit. You may have the right to borrow $5,000 from a single credit card company but you don't have to. If you borrow only $150 you pay interest only on the outstanding debt. Moreover, once you pay back the $150 you can again borrow up to $5,000. With most real estate loans, it's understood that once you pay back any portion of the principal the lender is not obligated to loan to you again.

Third, there are few if any charges to get consumer credit. Companies will gladly send you credit cards with the fervent hope you really do buy now and pay later. Real estate lenders will not only charge a fee to apply for financing but they also have a variety of closing costs which the borrower must pay.

Home equity mortgages are hybrid loan products that take features both from traditional mortgages and consumer credit practices. A real estate loan with a line of credit can work like this:

The Taylor house is worth $125,000 in today's market and has a $40,000 mortgage balance. The Taylors feel they may need some ready cash in the next two years to start a small business and send Junior to college, so their lender suggests a credit line arrangement.

The lender says the Taylors can borrow up to 70 percent of the equity in their home and values their equity like this: 70 percent of $125,000 equals $87,500 less the remaining mortgage balance, $40,000, equals $47,500.

The lender tells the Taylors that the minimum home equity loan is $5,000 and the minimum loan advance is $1,000. Since they have equity worth $47,500, the Taylors elect to get a $25,000 line of credit.

To get this loan the Taylors pay for a credit report, title search and other closing expenses. Their application costs are figured on the basis of a $25,000 loan but they do not, however, pay any points. While interest rates for second trusts at the time of their application average 8 percent, the Taylors pay 1.5 percent over the prime rate charged by a major bank, or 7.5 percent in this case. The lender has the right to change the rate of interest every three months. In contrast, it should be noted that the cost of consumer credit ranges from 16 to 24 percent.

The lender explains that the Taylors may select any loan term they choose, from 1 to 30 years. They select 15 years and make their first draw, $12,000, eighteen months after their application is approved so they have a maximum of 13.5 years to repay the $12,000 debt. The Taylors can repay the loan in advance, however, without penalty.

How do the Taylors withdraw their money? The lender offers four choices: a check mailed to their home or business; a deposit in a savings or checking account maintained with the lender or at another financial institution; a telephone transfer or, most interestingly, a book of blank drafts which the Taylors can use up to their credit limit.

After 6 years the Taylors have paid down their debt to $7,000. Because of the revolving nature of the credit line system, the Taylors can still borrow $18,000 ($25,000 less $7,000). In effect, by making their monthly payments they have raised their available credit line from a low of $13,000 ($25,000 less $12,000) at the time they made their first draw.

Home equity loans are attractive to lenders because they can collect processing fees up front even though actual monies may not be advanced for months or years—or at all. Also, such loans are commonly adjustable rate mortgages so lenders are largely protected against inflation.

Borrowers like credit lines because they have the ability to instantly convert bricks and pipes to cash with relatively little cost up front and far lower interest than they would normally pay for unsecured consumer credit. The access to such credit may prove extremely valuable. For instance, when they wish to buy a new home the Taylors in our example need not wait to sell their house before placing a down payment on a new property. Instead they can just advance the money from their credit line as long as they are able to make the proper payments. As soon as the property is sold the debt will be paid in full from the sale proceeds.

Home equity loans also have several features that should concern potential borrowers.

Since a home equity loan is a second trust a borrower who defaults can be foreclosed. The difficult issue here is this: Suppose a homeowner has a $10,000 credit line, becomes unemployed and for some reason borrows $500 on a credit line mortgage which is not repaid. Can a lender foreclose if only $500 is outstanding? Absolutely. Will a lender necessarily foreclose? The answer depends on the fact and circumstances in each case and the lender's policies. As a matter of good public relations it seems likely that most lenders would try to work out some arrangement before seeking foreclosure.

Another potential problem may seem somewhat contradictory. Home equity loans may be too accessible for certain borrowers. Many otherwise responsible people overextend themselves with unsecured credit card loans and it is probable that some homeowners will do the same with credit lines secured by real estate.

As this is written, for example, lenders often permit the withdrawal of relatively small sums, say $300, $400 or $500. To prevent frivolous expenditures that can result in foreclosure, lenders may set higher minimum draws, say $1,000, as they gain more experience with this type of financing.

HOME EQUITY LOANS AND SPECIAL RULES

On November 7, 1989 the federal government issued rules that significantly changed the home-equity lending game.

One rule that clearly benefits borrowers is that so-called "call" clauses are no longer permitted. With a call clause, a lender had the unilateral right at any time to seek full and immediate repayment of the entire loan—even if loan payments were up-to-date and the borrower had fully honored all terms.

A second pro-borrower rule eliminates the use of internal indexes. For instance, under the old rules a lender could raise its prime rate thereby causing home equity costs to go up—even if interest rates generally were falling.

A third provision of the new rules says that lenders cannot reserve the right to change fixed rates. It may seem as though a fixed rate should be, well, fixed, but in the wonderful world of lending some institutions created home equity loans with a fixed rate, but then reserved the right to change that rate later.

Along with three pro-borrower rules, the government also created new regulations that make home equity loans less certain than they were under the old guidelines.

Under the new guidelines lenders *may* unilaterally prohibit additional withdrawals under several conditions:

- If the value of a principal residence used to secure a loan is "significantly less than the original appraisal value of the dwelling" then lenders can freeze withdrawals. In areas where home values have dropped, this rule can cover large numbers of homeowners.
- If the lender has "any reason to believe that the consumer will be unable to comply with the repayment requirements of the account due to a material change in the consumer's financial circumstances" lenders can stop further home equity withdrawals. Surely if someone has filed for bankruptcy this rule makes sense, but what happens if borrower Langston is hit by a bus, the accident is reported in the local paper, and a lender stops home-equity withdrawals because one can "reasonably believe" that Langston's financial circumstances have changed. This scenario seems possible under the new rules, though not fair or equitable.

  The "financial circumstances" regulation raises an important question: How can a lender know when a borrower has financial problems? The answer is that many home equity agreements now permit lenders to make regular credit checks.

  Not only can lenders make credit checks, but other lending regulations virtually insure that such checks will be made. New rules require lenders to reserve relatively large amounts of capital for home-equity loans, but reserve requirements drop substantially if lenders have the right to limit withdrawals and if they make annual credit checks.

- If a home equity interest cap is less than prevailing interest rates, then lenders can freeze withdrawals. Since home equity loans often have caps set at state usury rates—more than 20 percent in many cases—the possibility of hitting this cap is remote. Conversely, if a cap is hit, not too many people will want to make withdrawals anyway.

- If the value of a principal residence used to secure a loan "declines significantly below the property's appraised value" then lenders can freeze withdrawals. In areas where real estate values have dropped, this rule can cover large numbers of homes.

In addition to federal legislation, individual state regulations may also apply to home equity financing. Matters such as interest rate limitations, prepayment regulations, and rights in the event of foreclosure are generally covered. In Texas, home equity loan regulations are even more straight-forward: home equity loans are not permitted.

Questions to Ask:

What is the interest rate for conventional financing?

What is the interest rate for unsecured consumer credit?

What is the market value of your home?

What portion of your equity can be used to calculate a maximum credit line? Various lenders are likely to have different standards, so speak to several loan officers in your community.

Is the home equity loan structured as an adjustable rate mortgage? If so, how often is the rate adjusted? Which index is used? How frequently can payments be adjusted? Is there an interest cap? Is there a payment cap? Can there be negative amortization?

What is the lender's policy on late or missed payments?

What is the minimum and maximum credit line?

What is the minimum and maximum draw?

How long is the loan term?

What is the full, up-front cost of establishing a home equity mortgage?

Do you have the right to repay in whole or in part without penalty?

LISTING IMPROVEMENT LOANS

At first glance it sounds like a very simple idea: you want to sell your home, the home is likely to sell more quickly and for a better price if it is in tip-top condition, so a lender offers to finance up to $20,000 in home improvements.

With a listing-improvement loan (LIL) you'll pay second-trust interest levels as long as the money is outstanding. As to points, with a LIL you may pay 2 or 3 points, or maybe you won't pay anything. To keep your business, a lender may waive all points for a LIL providing your next home is financed through the LIL lender.

What are the costs and risks of a LIL?

The interest level is not an issue, or much an issue, since a LIL is likely to be a second trust and therefore it should carry a higher rate than a first mortgage.

And since a relatively small amount is outstanding, it doesn't sound as though points are particularly expensive. After all, 1 percent of $20,000 is just $200, not much in the context of a real estate deal.

However, the points associated with a LIL can be very costly. If the LIL interest rate is set at 12 percent and the loan is repaid within three months, then a borrower who pays 3 points has an effective interest rate of 24 percent.

Moreover, a borrower who wishes to evade points and stick with the lender may find that financing for a new home is only available at a marginally higher rate, say an additional half point or an interest level that is .25 percent higher than competitors. For someone borrowing $120,000, the extra half point is worth $600 while the marginally-higher interest rate will cost roughly $300 the first year the loan is outstanding and not much less for the next few years thereafter.

What happens if the home doesn't sell? Then a LIL either evolves into a second trust or it becomes a balloon note that is quickly due and payable.

As an alternative to a LIL, plan ahead and have a home equity loan in place before you sell. Then, if you need repairs, you can just write a check.

Questions to Ask:

What is the cost of conventional financing?
What is the LIL interest level?
How many points will you pay for a LIL?
Can the points be waived if you finance a property with the lender? If so, at what rates and terms?
What happens if the property does not sell within a given period?
If the LIL converts into a second-trust, what are the rates and terms?

If the LIL converts into a balloon note, when must it be repaid and under what conditions?

What is the cost of a home-equity loan?

THE LOWDOWN ON LOW CASH LOANS

Americans are cutting back consumer debt as fast as paychecks allow, a sensible idea when many credit cards continue to charge anywhere from a "modest" 20 percent to rates best associated with large, well-armed personal lenders who are willing to hold a borrower's knees as collateral.

But a dilemma arises when it comes time to deal with the biggest debt of all: the household mortgage. Mortgage rates have declined in the past two years and there is no doubt that 8 percent, more or less, is far better than the 10 percent rates which were common in the recent past.

The trouble is that mortgage financing generally costs big bucks up front, money that might otherwise be used to pay off high-rate credit cards. Borrowers can find several financing alternatives that cost little up front, but a careful look at such programs produces a surprising result: in some cases credit card interest is **lower** than the marginal cost of low-cash loans.

If Preston wants $100,000 to refinance his home, a traditional deal might look like this: say 8 percent interest as this is written with two points worth $2,000, a 1-percent origination fee ($1,000), plus closing costs in Preston's community worth $2,000—a total of $5,000.

Alternatively, Preston might consider a variety of low-cash options, including the following choices:

Par Pricing.   Preston was quoted 8 percent plus 2 points, so he can probably get financing at 8.385 percent and no points. The par-pricing strategy saves 2 points, or $2,000 in this example.

Buy-Up.   In this case Preston trades a .25 percent interest increase in exchange for a lender contribution at closing equal to 1 percent of the loan amount. Preston "saves" $3,000 at closing with a buy-up by raising his rate to 8.75 percent. His monthly cost increases from $733.76 a month for principal and interest to $786.70 for the entire loan term, a hike of $52.94 per month.

Combined.   If Preston combines par pricing with a buy-up, he pays nothing at settlement but accepts a 9-percent interest rate. His monthly cost rises from $733.76 to $804.62, but he saves $5,000 in cash outlays.

Which of the choices above is best? If the goal is to save cash and repay high-interest credit card debt, then the analysis works like this:

The 8 percent deal where Preston pays $5,000 is the benchmark arrangement. If Preston goes to par pricing, he saves $2,000 in cash, his interest rises by .375 percent, and his monthly cost for principal and interest rises from $733.76 per month to $760.07. Ignoring amortization, to save $2,000 Preston pays an additional $315.75 per year, or 15.8 percent on his "savings," an interest rate higher than some credit cards, but not all.

With the buy-up, Preston cuts up-front costs by $3,000 but pays an additional $750 a year. The effective interest rate to save $3,000 is 25 percent, an interest level which is higher than any credit card.

The combined arrangement costs Preston an additional $1,000 in extra interest per year (9 percent versus 8 percent on a $100,000 loan), but saves $5,000 at closing. In effect, Preston pays 20 percent per year to save $5,000, another sky-high rate that tops many credit cards.

Preston the refinancer effectively pays premium interest rates to save cash up-front. But what if Preston is buying?

Suppose Preston can extract a $2,000 seller "contribution." Preston's cash needs decline by $2,000 and he is still able to obtain 8-percent financing. In this case, seller contributions cover the cost of points and lower Preston's true interest level to 7.79 percent.

Or, what if Preston gets the seller to front all points ($2,000) while the lender pays closing expenses and the origination fee ($3,000)? In this low-cash arrangement, Preston will pay 8.75 percent interest on his loan, a rate that would have totaled 9.125 percent (8.750 + .375) had it not been for the seller's generous assistance.

In considering the alternatives above, borrowers should be aware that interest payments secured by real estate are generally tax deductible, while personal interest is not.

Also, time is important. If Preston pays little or nothing up front and stays in the property a short time, he wins with higher rates and less cash up front. If he is a short-term owner, paying excess cash at closing is very expensive.

And if Preston refinances, he needs to check his costs with care. It's hard to believe, but in some cases credit card interest may be a bargain.

MUNICIPAL (BOND-BACKED) MORTGAGES AND MORTGAGE CREDIT CERTIFICATES

Bond-Backed Mortgages at a Glance

Q. Who buys bonds?

A. Investors, pension funds, etc.

Q. Why are bond returns so low?

A. Interest on bonds issued by governmental agencies is generally exempt from federal taxation.

Q. Are bond-backed mortgage rates lower than conventional financing?

A. Yes, in virtually all cases.

Q. Are bond-backed mortgages always available?

A. No. Occasionally Congress has made an effort to stop or curtail bond-backed mortgages nationwide. In addition, bond-backed mortgages are not available in every jurisdiction at every moment, in part because funding is usually limited. If you're interested in bond-backed financing, be certain to keep up with the latest developments in your community.

Q. Who qualifies for financing with bond-backed mortgages?

A. Standards vary but low-to-moderate-income individuals buying a first home generally qualify.

Q. Are bond-backed mortgages available to investors?

A. Usually not for single-unit purchases such as an individual home or condo.

Q. If I qualify for a bond-backed mortgage are there any restrictions?

A. In some programs there may be restrictions on renting property and assuming loans.

There is no limit to the artful ways in which tax policies can be written. At this time we have a system that provides subsidies for some industries but not for others, a tax break for those over 65 but not over 61 and a deduction for the blind but not the lame.

In this maze of exemptions, deductions, exceptions, interpretations, rulings, codes and court cases are benefits which greatly favor property ownership. Without tax exemptions for mortgage interest and real estate taxes the number of residential property owners would be greatly reduced—as would the number of construction workers, real estate brokers, mortgage loan officers, appliance manufacturers, lumberjacks, etc.

One tax exemption of some interest is the right of governmental bodies such as cities, counties and states to issue tax-exempt bonds which can be used to build dams, roads, industrial parks or whatever.

Issuers like tax-exempt bonds because they can cheaply fund projects that produce local employment and other benefits. Investors like such bonds because they often produce a higher after-tax income than alternative investments.

Suppose a tax-exempt bond pays 4 percent interest. A bond buyer in the 28-percent tax bracket will have to earn 5.56 percent from a taxable investment to have the same net return after taxes. Since not all investments pay 5.56 percent, and since private securities are not backed by a governmental entity, tax-exempt bonds are attractive to investors looking for good yields with little risk.

Tax-exempt bonds can be used to build factories and roads, and they can also be used to underwrite home mortgages, the theory being that cheap mortgages create more real estate sales and more sales produce additional local employment. Here's an illustration:

South County sells bonds worth $75 million and paying 4 percent interest to investors. The money from the bonds is then used to underwrite 6 percent mortgages for local homebuyers at a time when conventional rates are 7 percent. The principal and interest home buyers pay is used to pay off the bond holders, and so South County will not raise taxes to repay the debt—a politician's dream. In some cases, as in this example, the issuing jurisdiction actually profits by charging homeowners more interest than bond holders receive.

Although tax-exempt bonds can bring millions of mortgage dollars into an area, that money is not available to everyone. Instead, only individuals with a certain income, family size, and length of residency within the jurisdiction can apply for financing in most cases. Also, many programs will not issue mortgages to otherwise-qualified individuals who have owned property within the past three years.

Tax-exempt mortgage revenue bonds have stirred considerable controversy. Critics argue that tax-exempt bonds unnecessarily shift billions of dollars from the federal treasury to well-heeled investors. Worse, they say, bonds are not an efficient way to stimulate home ownership.

Supporters believe that bonds are necessary and that without such funds home ownership is not possible for most participating borrowers. Also, bond backers believe that comparing the benefits of bonds with other housing programs, such as Sec. 8 subsidized housing, is not realistic because of what they see as the inherently different nature of each program.

The politics and economics of tax-exempt mortgage revenue bonds are simply irrelevant if you are the one looking for mortgage money. If you qualify, such financing may represent the cheapest money source in town and that fact by itself may make bond-backed financing the common-sense mortgage for many first-time and moderate-income buyers.

Because bond-backed mortgages are a good deal, there is considerable demand for these loans when they become available. Waiting lists, lotteries and all-night vigils outside banks have been known to occur. In a sense, part of the qualification process for these loans may include luck and physical stamina as well as how many dollars you earned last year.

When considering bond-backed mortgages potential borrowers should be aware that such financing often contains specialized restrictions. For example, bond-backed mortgages are usually not available to investors; there may be renting limitations; individuals may be required to live in the property for a certain number of years; and loans may be assumable only by individuals who are qualified to participate in the program.

Information about mortgages backed from tax-exempt bonds is available from real estate brokers, local lenders (who often service such loans), home builders, community groups and governmental officials. Because this type of financing is often snapped up the day it becomes available, borrowers should obtain program information as much in advance as possible. With advance information plus prepared applications and supporting documents in hand you'll have the best shot at bond-backed mortgages when they are announced.

MORTGAGE CREDIT CERTIFICATES (MCCs)

Bond-backed mortgages may be a great financing tool for borrowers, but they present problems for Uncle Sam.

One concern is the reduction of federal tax revenues. When states issue bond-backed mortgage bonds, there is no tax on the interest paid to investors—and thus the federal government collects fewer tax dollars. The result is that while bond-backed mortgages are great for individual states, they are not so great for the federal government.

A second issue involves fairness. The federal government limits the amount of bond-back mortgages each state can issue. Bigger states with more people can sell more bond-backed mortgages then small states with tiny populations. This is fair because if there was no limit, then states would issue as many bonds as possible to raise capital. The loser would be Uncle Sam's dwindling treasury.

Since the purpose of bond-backed mortgages is to help entry-level homebuyers, and since the thought of tax-exempt income for investors bothers many people, perhaps it might be possible to use tax benefits in a different way to encourage homeownership, a thought that brings us to mortgage credit certificates, or MCCs.

Imagine that the federal government allows states to issue tax-exempt bonds for mortgages *and* MCCs worth a total of $1 billion. Suppose as well that Montana has the right to issue tax-exempt bonds worth $50 million this year. But rather than issuing bonds, the state instead creates MCCs worth $12.5 million. In other words, once states have an allocation of tax credits from the federal government, they can issue either tax-exempt bonds, MCCs, or a combination of bonds and MCCs.

With bond-backed mortgages we have securities sold in the financial markets to investors, thus netting something less than face value for local mortgages because fees for an assortment of brokers and middlemen must be subtracted. With MCCs there are no bonds and no middlemen, just a straight deal between the government and those who need assistance.

MCCs create a tax shelter for qualifying homebuyers. For example, if Rogers has a $50,000 MCC mortgage at 7 percent interest with a 20-percent tax credit, he will have a first-year interest expense of roughly $3,500. Twenty percent of this amount, $700, can be used as a tax credit while the balance, $2,800, is a regular itemized deduction.

It may seem that $700 is not much money in the context of a home purchase, but those who buy with MCC assistance typically have entry-level incomes which means a tax rate of 15 percent or less. If the tax rate is zero, then the benefit of the tax credit is also zero.

If taxes are owed, however, an MCC tax credit can be very important.

Suppose there are four people in the Rogers household and suppose as well that there is a deduction of $2,350 per person. Rogers is thus able to shelter $9,400.

In addition, since he now owns a home, Rogers has itemized deductions, perhaps $2,800 in mortgage interest, $500 in property taxes, and $300 in state income taxes, a total of $3,600. In effect, Rogers can earn up to $13,000 ($9,400 + $3,600) before paying federal income taxes.

Because he has a $700 credit, however, Rogers' taxable income does not begin at $13,000. Instead we take $700 (the amount of Rogers' tax credit), divide by 15 (as in the 15 percent tax bracket), and the result is $46.66. Multiply by 100 and the result is an additional $4,667 that can be sheltered from taxes. Add $13,000 and $4,667, and the result is untaxed income worth $17,667 to Mr. Rogers.

Under the MCC program, states are allowed to vary the tax credit for individual loans, however the annual tax credit is limited to 20 percent for loans where the annual tax credit exceeds $2,000.

MCCs are available only to those who meet the standards established for mortgages funded with tax-exempt bonds. The standards—outlined in Sections 25 and 143 of the Internal Revenue Code—include

---

Mr. Rogers' MCC

Amount Borrowed	$50,000
Interest Rate	7 Percent
Interest in Year 1 (Approx.)	$3,500
MCC Tax Credit	20 percent
Mr. Rogers' MCC Tax Benefit	$700
Amount Available as an Itemized Deduction	$2,800

---

income limitations, purchase price requirements, non-ownership status for a three-year period prior to buying, and the purchase of property in targeted areas in some cases.

While MCCs are a very attractive program, it may not be easy to obtain MCC financing.

One problem is that MCC financing is tied to federal budgetmaking. This may be less of a problem than in the past because under the 1993 budget reform plan, MCC financing was made permanent for the first time. While some financing is now assured, exact amounts may vary from year to year.

A second issue is that because MCC loans are in demand, they may not be available when you need them. Try to find out as much as possible about MCC financing in your state before looking at houses.

Third, within some state programs is a "recapture" provision. A recapture provision says that MCC borrowers who sell their property within a given time, say 10 years, and for a profit, must pay back some or all of the taxes they saved by using the MCC program.

The purpose of this provision is to prevent low and moderate income families from profiteering through the use of governmental programs—a concept which obviously does not apply to the wealthy and well-connected.

Fourth, under current regulations, those with MCC mortgages cannot refinance their property and retain their tax credits. Thus if someone has an MCC deal at 9 percent and they can now get a loan at 7 percent, their MCC tax benefit stops the moment they refinance.

While it can make financial sense for an MCC owner to refinance, the program does not encourage refinancing and thus the reduction of tax write-offs.

The bottom line with MCCs is that they are an attractive, valuable program for those who can obtain such loans. They offer low cost, low rate financing with substantial tax benefits—but only for a limited number of borrowers in each state.

Questions to Ask:

What is the current rate of interest for conventional financing?

Are bond-backed mortgages available in the jurisdiction where the property is located?

What is the current interest rate of bond-backed mortgages?

What are the income, family size and residency requirements, if any, associated with bond-backed mortgages?

How much cash down is required?

When will bond-backed mortgages next be available? Is there a waiting list? If so, how do you get on it?

Can you get a bond-backed mortgage from a local lender? If so, what are the proper application procedures? Are you part of a group such as a union that is buying a large quantity of bond-backed mortgages? If so, you may be able to get preferential treatment.

Are you required to live in the property for a certain period, say 5 years?

Are you allowed to rent all or part of the property once you have obtained bond-backed financing?

Is the mortgage assumable? If it is assumable must the buyer be qualified to participate in the program?

Can the loan be prepaid in whole or in part without penalty?

Is MCC financing now available in your state?

What percentage of your loan interest can be claimed as a credit if you obtain an MCC loan?

What interest rate will you pay with MCC financing?

Is there a recapture provision if you sell the property? If there is a recapture provision, how long must you hold the property to avoid recapture rules?

Can you avoid recapture rules if you sell to an MCC-qualified buyer?

Does MCC financing restrict your right to rent the property?

NEIGHBORWORKS: $1,000 DOWN FOR A HOME—OR LESS

Some of the largest players in real estate have teamed up to offer new financing for entry-level buyers, mortgages with as little as $1,000 down.

Under the NeighborWorks program, a purchaser can buy a home costing as much as $80,000 with either $1,000 down or 2 percent of the purchase price—whichever is less. If the home costs more than $80,000, then a 2 percent down payment is required.

In addition to a tiny down payment, the NeighborWorks program also features liberal qualification standards. As much as 35 percent of an individual's income can be devoted to housing costs, such as mortgage principal, mortgage interest, taxes, and insurance. For example, if a household has an annual income of $36,000, as much as $1,050 can be spent on housing costs under the NeighborWorks guidelines. In comparison, a conventional loan would only allow $840 for housing expenses.

The program—which kicked off in Baltimore, Chattanooga, Chicago, Los Angeles, Milwaukee, Minneapolis, and New York—is expected to include 20 cities in the short term, with more likely added if the initial program is a success.

There is little doubt that NeighborWorks will succeed, if only because it is supported by an alliance of major players. Freddie Mac and Fannie Mae, two financial giants that buy loans from local lenders, are backing the plan. The Mortgage Guaranty Insurance Corporation (MGIC), which insures loans when people cannot buy with 20 percent down, supports the program. And the Neighborhood Reinvestment Corporation, an organization that seeks to increase home-ownership options for low- and moderate-income borrowers, is also a backer.

How will the program work? Here are the key points.

- Loans under the program can be used to buy or refinance residential property. Homes with one to four units are eligible, as are homes in need of rehabilitation.
- Borrowers under the NeighborWorks plan must attend educational seminars before they buy or refinance.
- If a property is refinanced, no cash can be taken out by the owner. In other words, owners may refinance to get a better rate and term, or to upgrade the property.

- Single-family homes, condominiums, and properties with one to four units can be financed with NeighborWorks mortgages. Co-op units are excluded from the program.
- There is no minimum loan amount. The maximum loan amount is the same as conventional financing today—$203,150 at this time for a single-family home.
- There are income limitations, but they do not apply if the property is located in an area targeted for revitalization.
- The loans may not be assumed.
- Reserve requirements are dropped for single-family home buyers. Instead of being compelled to have enough cash on hand to cover two mortgage payments, single-family borrowers under NeighborWorks have no reserve requirements.

What does it all mean?

Freddie Mac and Fannie Mae are under orders from Congress to increase their commitment to low- and moderate-income households. One way to increase loans to target groups is to modify standards so that more people can participate. But because both Freddie Mac and Fannie Mae must operate on a sound financial basis, they cannot simply give out money without some assurance of repayment.

Appropriate guarantees come from MGIC. It insures the loans. If a borrower defaults, MGIC steps in and pays off Freddie Mac and Fannie Mae.

MGIC, however, does not want unlimited risk. Under the NeighborWorks program, MGIC will insure loans, but its risk is offset by a reserve fund created by the Neighborhood Reinvestment organization. The reserve fund will be maintained for eight years to protect MGIC against losses. After eight years, any money remaining in the reserve fund will be returned to the Neighborhood Reinvestment Corporation.

In effect, we have risk sharing all around. Local lenders make mortgages under NeighborWorks and then sell the loans to Freddie Mac and Fannie Mae. Freddie Mac and Fannie Mae are insured by MGIC, and MGIC has a reserve fund to cushion any losses. Those with low and moderate incomes are the obvious winners under the NeighborWorks program.

For more information regarding one of the better loan programs now available, speak with local neighborhood organizations, brokers, and lenders.

And if the NeighborWorks program is not yet available in your community, speak with neighborhood organizations and alert them to the new program. The probability is that NeighborWorks will rapidly expand once the pilot stage is completed.

PLEDGED AND RESERVE ACCOUNT MORTGAGES

The idea of "no money down" financing should mean that no cash is required to purchase a property. Yet it is possible to have a sale with "no money down" that is offset by cash elsewhere in the deal. Such loans are called pledged account mortgages (PAM) and reserve account mortgages (RAM).

For example, with a PAM loan, Mrs. Tilton, the borrower, gets 100 percent financing under the best available rates and terms. Rather than making a down payment, money is instead deposited by Tilton or a seller with a lender in a pledged, interest-bearing account.

The lender then takes a certain sum from the account, say $150 or so a month, to offset Tilton's regular mortgage payments until the account is drawn down. If Tilton defaults, the lender can claim the entire account immediately and foreclose on the property. In effect, the pledged account money offsets the lender's risk, since it is a substitute for the security of a down payment.

As an illustration, if Mrs. Tilton buys property for $100,000 a seller can set up a $10,000 pledged account with a lender. Tilton will get a $100,000 mortgage but her monthly payment will be reduced by $150. The $150 comes from the interest-bearing pledged account. Once the money in the pledged account, including interest, is used up, Tilton will then have to make the entire monthly payment.

In most instances PAM accounts are established by sellers as a form of buy-down financing to aid purchasers with limited incomes and little capital. Since they are not getting their money out of the property in cash, however, it follows that sellers will want higher prices when they sell. If higher prices are not possible because of depressed market conditions, PAMs may represent a genuine discount.

Pledged accounts are not necessarily buy-downs, however. When a pledged account is established by a friend or relative, that individual can withdraw a specified sum from the account each month. The money taken out coincides with the reduced mortgage balance and growing equity in the property.

The attraction of this arrangement is that it enables individuals to help buyers without making a direct cash contribution toward the property's purchase price or acting as a co-signer or co-owner. If the buyer defaults, however, the money remaining in the pledged account will go immediately to the lender.

A RAM is a specialized type of loan that can offer 100 percent financing at conventional rates to buyers with limited capital but good incomes.

PAM versus RAM			
	PAM	RAM	Conventional
Down payment	None	None	20 percent
Account size	5 percent minimum	5 percent minimum	None
Monthly withdrawal	Regular sum, say $100 or $150	None	None
Term held	Until paid out	Until sufficient equity is established in property	None
Account money returned	None	Deposit plus accrued interest	None
Can account be taken in foreclosure?	Yes	Yes	Not appropriate

Suppose RAM financing was used by Robertson to buy a home valued at $85,000. Robertson will get an $85,000 loan at conventional rates and no money down except closing costs. The lender will also get something: security worth at least 5 percent of the property's value in the form of a pledged asset such as a certificate of deposit or funds in a passbook savings account. Interest on the security deposit will be paid to whoever puts up the deposit.

The question is: Who put up the deposit? One choice is the borrower. Rather than using money for a down payment Robertson can deposit money with a lender under a RAM arrangement.

The idea from Robertson's viewpoint is to get interest income from money that would otherwise be used for a down payment. The problem is this: If mortgage money costs, say, 8 percent, and reserve accounts pay 4 percent interest, it is better to have a larger down payment. The interest earned in the reserve account in this case is offset by higher mortgage costs.

Another possibility, and one that is far more sensible, is that a friend or relative of Robertson places money in a reserve account. Essentially this is an assisted loan in a situation where someone wants to help Robertson, again without becoming either a co-signer, co-owner or actually contributing cash to the purchase.

A third deposit source can be a seller. To get the most money out of a deal, a seller (possibly a builder or developer) might offer to deposit cash in a reserve account to assure the purchase of his property. The problem here is one of economics: sellers are looking for maximum profits and one way to justify a reserve account is to charge premium prices when possible.

The purpose of the reserve account is to protect the lender in the event of a loan default. This means a lender will want access to the reserve account until a certain point, say until the loan's value is less than 90 or 95 percent of the overall property value. This sounds fine until one realizes that no down payment has been made. If property values remain stagnant or decline the lender may not be obligated to release reserved funds for many years.

If you haven't got the capital or the income, PAMs and RAMs are better than rental stubs. However, these programs raise four issues:

First, with both loans 100 percent financing means bigger mortgages and larger interest payments.

Second, with PAMs set up by sellers one has to ask if the borrower would be better off with a simple price discount. (See section on buy-down and buy-up financing.)

Third, if you are the party putting up money for an account with a lender, where is your security, if any? Is your account considered a second trust secured by the property or is it merely a personal loan? In the event of foreclosure how do you get your money back?

Fourth, if the return of reserve account money is dependent on a certain loan-to-value ratio there is no specific time when this ratio will be achieved and therefore there is no absolute time when the money will be returned. This can be a problem if the donor needs funds by a certain date.

While alert buyers can benefit from PAM and RAM financing, particularly when friends and relatives are involved in the purchase, such loans are often outside the definition of a common-sense mortgage when it is a seller, developer or builder who underwrites such accounts. If you've got the cash you're probably better off bargaining for a lower sales price and a loan format that requires little or nothing down, such as mortgages backed by the VA, FHA or private mortgage insurance.

Questions to Ask:

What is the prevailing interest rate for conventional financing?

How much money is required to set up either a PAM or RAM account?

How much is withdrawn monthly from a PAM account?

If you set up a reserve account for a friend or relative who defaults on the mortgage, do you have any recourse to get your money back? In other words, if a reserve account is not intended to be a gift is it a lien against the property?

With either PAM or RAM financing, does the donor have a choice of accounts in which the money can be deposited, such as certificates of deposit, money market accounts, etc.?

With either PAM or RAM financing, does the donor have any liability beyond the money originally placed in an account with the lender?

In the case of a PAM loan set up by a seller, will the buyer be better off with a direct price reduction instead?

REVERSE MORTGAGES

American homes include not only bedrooms and baths, but also untapped equity worth at least $2 trillion. Such a vast storehouse of wealth interests not only homeowners, but also lenders of every type.

In many cases the owners of mortgage-free properties are age 60 and above and find that while they have property with a substantial economic value, they cannot transform that value into cash without selling the property or having it refinanced. Selling is not a good choice because it merely substitutes the problem of a house and no cash for cash and no house. Refinancing is not a good choice either, because it means making monthly payments at a time when income may be limited.

Reverse mortgages, in contrast, are designed for people with real estate equity but limited cash flow. They allow individuals to retain home ownership while providing needed cash.

Mr. and Mrs. Nelson are each 65 years old and about to retire. Their house, worth $150,000, is mortgage free. They want more cash once they retire and so they speak to a lender who suggests reverse financing.

A reverse mortgage, says the lender, works like this: Each month we give you $500. That money earns 9 percent interest for us. The Nelsons are told that with their projected income they can get a $100,000 reverse mortgage.

Unlike other mortgage formats where the sum of $100,000 represents only principal, with a reverse mortgage $100,000 is equal to the combined total of all principal and interest. The final term of this loan is 10 years and 3 months, and at the end the borrower actually owes $100,461.82. Of this total, $61,500 represents principal and the balance of $38,961.82 is interest.

To control interest costs it's best to have a reverse mortgage with set monthly payments rather than payments designed to last a given number of years. For example, if the loan was structured so that the total obligation was simply $100,000 paid out over 15 years, a borrower will receive only $265 per month. The principal payoff will be $47,700, while interest totals $52,577.53. (To be precise, the final principal balance of this loan will be $100,277.53.)

	Reverse Mortgage at a Glance		
	A $100,000 Loan at 9 Percent Interest		
Month Number	Deferred Cost ($)	Principal ($)	Balance ($)
1	500.00	500.00	500.00
2	503.75	500.00	1,003.75
3	507.63	500.00	1,511.38
4	511.33	500.00	2,022.71
5	515.17	500.00	2,537.88
123	744.13	500.00	101,461.82

A second way to control interest costs is to have larger payments. If the $100,000 loan illustrated here was arranged so that the borrowers received $600 a month, the loan will run 9 years and one month. However, interest payments will roughly total $34,600 while principal amounts to $65,400.

The loan above will end if the Nelsons sell, lease, or refinance the property, if they fail to maintain the property, or if they do not pay property taxes. In addition, the loan will terminate when both die. If the Nelsons die before the entire $100,000 is paid out, their estate will simply owe less money to the lender. If it should happen that the Nelsons outlive the loan term the lender, in this case, will refinance the property at then-current rates.

As an alternative to a reverse mortgage the Nelsons consider several other strategies. They can get a regular $100,000 mortgage and invest that money. However, it may not be possible to get a return above the loan's rate of interest. They can also finance the house and purchase an annuity. Annuity income, however, may be taxable.

Another alternative is to get a $100,000 mortgage and then invest the money in a tax-free annuity. The problem here is that the mortgage interest may not be deductible, since the purpose of the mortgage loan is to generate tax-exempt income.

Since money received under a reverse mortgage is principal rather than income, such advances are not taxable. The issue of interest deductions is more complex, however.

The Nelsons owe interest but they have not actually made payments to a lender. According to IRS spokesman Roy Young, if the borrowers use a cash-based system of accounting they are not entitled to a deduction until payments have been made. If they have an accrual-based system, a form of accounting often used by businesses, then deductions may be possible. When the loan is paid off, by the Nelsons or their estate, it is then that payments have actually been made and a deduction may be in order. For specific advice speak to a tax attorney or CPA.

It is usually estimated that fewer than 7,500 reverse mortgages have been issued, a tiny number considering that millions of real estate loans are outstanding. In the future, the number of reverse loans is expected to increase, though again the totals are so small as to be almost invisible.

If marketplace success is one test of a product or service, then reverse mortgages are the Edsels of home finance. They're out there, but nobody is buying. They can provide cash to people who need more money, but somehow lines are not forming at lender offices.

As logical and reasonable as reverse mortgages may seem, they contradict the traditional American desire to be mortgage free. People may burn mortgage papers but nobody holds a party to celebrate more debt. (Please, if you must burn, *only burn copies* since original loan documents can have important financial and legal values).

Not only is additional debt unattractive, the particular manner in which reverse mortgages have been developed is particularly distasteful.

Some lenders have concocted reverse mortgage schemes which allow them to share in such appreciation as a property may generate. Under such programs a lender is effectively a partner, not a lender, and most people have demonstrated that they do not want to own their home with anyone else, much less a lender.

Worse, reverse loans that simply transfer ownership to a lender after a given period—say ten years—have been reported. Under this scenario, the hapless homeowner borrows money for a number of years and then title to the property reverts to the lender.

Reverse mortgages raise questions with fees and charges that also require careful scrutiny. Reverse loan repayments are commonly triggered by death, and—not to be ghoulish—lenders with steep charges up front benefit from the quick and early demise of their borrowers.

Suppose Norwhich obtains a reverse mortgage and pays $3,000 in points and charges up front. Suppose as well that Norwhich receives $500 a month from his loan.

If Norwhich dies in a year, he has borrowed $6,000 ($500 x 12) on which he has paid interest, say 11 percent, or roughly $660 in this example. He has also paid $3,000 to make the deal, thus his cost is $3,660—61 percent of all the money he collected.

But if Norwhich lives for 20 years the deal is different. He obtains $120,000 in payments, pays 11 percent interest, and has a $3,000 cost up front. Now his up-front cost averages out to $150 a year ($3,000 divided by 20 years), or 2.5 percent of the $6,000 he receives annually. Add his 11 percent interest rate with a 2.5 percent annual cost and Norwhich is paying 13.5 percent a year—not great, but better than 61 percent.

Lenders, too, have not flocked to the reverse mortgage concept because this form of financing hides several flaws.

First, interest from the loan accumulates until the entire mortgage is due. Rather than cash, lenders are getting a credit for income not actually received but which may be subject to taxation. Lenders may charge more points or higher interest to offset this problem.

Second, security for the loan—the house—can be tied up in probate court for years as relatives argue over who is entitled to the property.

Third, because the loan can be terminated by death or other reasons, reverse loans do not produce an assured income over time and are thus not attractive to pension funds and others who buy mortgages. Given this situation, local lenders will have difficulty selling a reverse loan to bring new funds into the community.

Fourth, if a reverse mortgage sours, a lender can have an unseemly public relations problem. One can just picture the headline, "Local Lender Forecloses on 94-Year-Old Widow of Town Minister."

Additional Information. To find out more regarding reverse mortgage options, consider these sources:

- The American Association of Retired People (AARP). Contact your local chapter.
- The National Center for Home Equity Conversion, Apple Valley, MN (612-953-4474).
- Fannie Mae, at 800-732-6643.

Questions to Ask:

Are local lenders making reverse loans? Groups such as the American Association of Retired Persons (AARP) may be able to suggest lenders who offer reverse mortgages.

What is the value of your property? A lender will want an appraisal.

What reverse mortgage terms are best for you? Have a lender provide you with amortization statements to show which alternative monthly payments and terms will work best.

How will a reverse mortgage affect your income tax obligations? Speak to a tax consultant.

How will a reverse mortgage affect your pension and Social Security benefits? Speak to appropriate professionals and administrators.

Does the loan include a written guarantee to refinance the property at then-current rates in the event you reach the reverse loan limit?

Is a will required as part of a reverse mortgage? Even if it isn't, do you have an adequate will? Speak to an attorney for more information.

Would a life insurance policy equal to the value of the reverse mortgage be a good purchase? In the event of death the policy's proceeds can be used to retire the reverse mortgage debt. Would your heirs want to pay for such a policy on your behalf? If so, what are your obligations to them, if any?

SECOND HOME FINANCING

If you're reached that point in life and finance where a vacation home looks more and more interesting, congratulations. But before venturing into the wondrous world of ski chalets and beach-front cottages, consider some of the issues represented by second homes.

The first question is whether you're buying a second home, an investment property, or a little bit of both. In the eyes of Uncle Sam, a second home is still a residence if you rent it 14 days or less per year, or less than 10 percent of the days the unit is in use. The good news here is that if the property is a "residence" that also produces rental income within the guidelines, then the rental income need not be declared. Because of details involving "fair market" rental rates and other issues, be certain to consult with a tax professional for the latest rules before you buy.

If you have a second "residence," then you may deduct mortgage interest and property taxes. The amount of deductible mortgage interest, however, is limited—but only if you are among the landed gentry. Interest on first and second home loans totaling $1 million or less is generally deductible, as is the interest on home-equity debt of up to $100,000.

If the second property is rented 15 days a year, or more than 10 percent of the time the property is in use, you then have an investment property, which means that mortgage interest, property taxes, repairs, management fees, and depreciation may be deductible. Note that deductions may be limited or deferred if your adjusted gross income exceeds $100,000.

Whether the second home is something you use in addition to your principal residence or is an outright investment makes a big difference to lenders. It will be easier to get financing for a second home than for something that falls into the investment category.

There are several interesting concepts buyers should consider for a second home that will be used for personal purposes.

- A two-, three-, or four-unit property cannot be classified as a second residence for conventional mortgage purposes. That is, you can get residential financing for a single-family second home or a vacation condo, but not for a vacation four-plex.
- Rental income from a second residence cannot be used to boost buyer qualifications. The logic here, apparently, is that such income is likely to be spotty and inconsistent.
- Do not expect a big check at closing if you refinance a vacation home. Cash-out conventional refinancing is not available. Refinancing to obtain better rates and terms is allowed.
- Conventional second mortgages are not available on vacation homes.

Those buying second homes should certainly consider both conventional financing with 20 percent down (or less, with private mortgage insurance) as well as nonconventional financing, which is likely to have more liberal qualification standards.

Alternatively, if you have a large amount of equity in your current home, it may make sense to refinance your principal residence and pay cash for a second home.

Since lenders are most liberal with loans secured by personal residences, you are likely to encounter the fewest hassles by refinancing your home. As well, interest on as much as $100,000 in new financing may be deductible. See a tax professional before considering this approach.

Whether a second home can be both a personal retreat and a good investment is a complex question. Clearly, where you buy and what you buy makes a difference. If it happens that rent covers expenses and you can still get some personal use out of the property, so much the better.

Moreover, one cannot overlook the fact that what may well have been a remote retreat 10 or 20 years ago is now "nearer" to metro living. With fax machines, e-mail, and modems, physical proximity is no longer required to maintain a given income level. What may have been a second-home location in the past may emerge as a prime residence for those with the skills, training, and transferable talents to make location irrelevant. Indeed, it may well make sense to have a second home and to gradually move from an urban location to something more scenic and calm.

If your intent is to buy now and retire later, then purchasing a second home can make great sense. If, in the preretirement years, the property produces income to offset ownership costs then such income can be seen as a retirement subsidy—sort of an IRA contribution without the paperwork. And if values rise, then the property will effectively have been bought at discount.

TITLE I: IS THIS THE BEST SMALL LOAN IN TOWN?

There are many people who simply don't like the idea of refinancing their homes. When they need extra dollars they use checking account overdraft credit, credit cards, and signature loans—anything but the equity in their homes. For these people, and for many others, the FHA has devised a unique form of financing that straddles both real estate and personal finance.

If you need $25,000 or less for home improvement purposes, it may pay to look at the FHA Title I program. If the amount sought is less than $5,000, the loan is regarded as a personal debt and not recorded as a lien against property. From $5,000 to $25,000 the loan is recorded as a lien but one subordinate to other loans, so you can get Title I financing even with other loans on your property. Since 90 percent of the loan is guaranteed by FHA, the risk to your lender is minimal and there should be little resistance to giving a loan that can be regarded as a personal loan or as a first, second or even third trust, depending on such other loans as may be in place on the property and the size of the debt.

The FHA loan program provides for a maximum term of 15 years and an interest rate usually not much higher than conventional loans and lower than credit card financing.

Not all lenders handle FHA Title I home improvement financing, so you may have to call your local FHA office (it's part of the U.S. Department of Housing and Urban Development) to get the name of area lenders who are active in the program.

Because personal interest is not deductible, borrowers will have to weigh their Title I strategy. It is comforting to borrow money without placing a lien on your property. Conversely, if you borrow more than $5,000 under the Title I program, a lien is created, the money is being used to improve the property and therefore the interest *should* be deductible.

If your need for cash is at or about $5,000 it can make sense to check with your lender to see what additional costs you might face if you breech the $5,000 plateau. It will also make sense to speak with a CPA, tax attorney or enrolled agent to assure that if the loan is recorded your interest payments will be fully deductible.

Questions to Ask:

> What is the Title I interest rate?
> What is the maximum Title I loan?
> How much Title I money can you borrow as a personal loan?

WRAPAROUND LOANS

One of the most innovative forms of creative financing is the wraparound mortgage, a type of loan which in the best of circumstances provides below-market financing for purchasers and above-market yields for lenders. While high yields and low rates sound like the defin-

Wraparound Loan versus Conventional Financing		
	Conventional Loan	Wraparound Loan
Cash down	$30,000	$30,000
Assumable financing	None	$50,000
Interest rate	10 percent	9 percent
New Financing	$120,000	$70,000
Term	30 years	20 years
Monthly payment	$1,053.09	$1,017.46 (on total debt of $120,000 [$50,000 old loan + $70,000 new financing])
Potential interest cost	$259,119.92	$124,190.40
Extra potential interest	$134,920.52	None
First trust liability of wraparound lender	None	$50,000
Net buyer liability	$120,000	$120,000
Recorded debt	$120,000	$170,000
Recorded price	$150,000	$150,000

ition of the ideal loan there are potential complications that make wraparound financing difficult, if not unacceptable, to large numbers of borrowers and lenders.

A wraparound loan consists of two parts: First, there is the original financing on the property. This loan remains in place at its original rate and terms. Second, there is the wraparound loan, financing in addition to the original mortgage.

Imagine that a home is sold for $150,000. There is a freely assumable loan on the property with a remaining balance of $50,000. The assumable loan has a 7 percent interest rate and 20 years left on a 30-year term. This loan requires a monthly payment of $387.65.

To buy this property a purchaser, Mr. Morton, knows that with $100,000 in cash he can merely assume the original loan. Few people, however, have $100,000 in ready cash, so Morton looks into assuming the original loan and having a lender or the seller take back a second trust. As good as it sounds, this approach has problems too. Second trusts tend to have short terms, high rates and balloon payments. Add up the first and second trust payments and the monthly mortgage bill is far more than Morton can afford.

As an alternative, Morton can put $30,000 down and qualify for conventional financing at the market interest rate, perhaps 10 percent in this case. The problem here is that 10 percent interest will leave Morton with few dollars for anything other than mortgage payments.

To get a better rate—and to reduce monthly payments—Morton suggests a wraparound deal under which the seller will take back a $120,000 mortgage at 9 percent interest from the purchaser. The loan term will be the remaining length of the assumable loan, 20 years in this case. The seller, however, remains responsible for the original $50,000 first trust.

The effect of this deal is to provide Morton with 9 percent financing in a 10 percent market. Not only does Morton get a good rate, but he saves extra interest payments worth $166,434.41. In addition, if it is the seller who takes back the loan many settlement expenses can be avoided.

For the seller or wraparound lender the deal looks like this: the loan appears to generate 9 percent interest. However, the original 7 percent loan must be repaid and thus the seller receives 9 percent interest on $70,000 ($120,000 less $50,000) and 2 percent on $50,000 (9 percent interest from the buyer less 7 percent which must be paid on the assumable loan).

If yield is defined as the return on money actually loaned, the seller is taking in far more than 10 percent interest. Since the seller is not actually lending the first $50,000, the yield in this illustration is 10.35 percent.

The Wraparound Note Holder

1. Gets a monthly income of $1,017.46.
2. Makes a monthly first trust payment of $387.65.
3. Has a net monthly return on $70,000 of $629.81.
4. Earns an annual return of 10.35 percent on $70,000.

The interest earned by a wraparound note will be taxed as regular income, while the principal payments are likely to be treated as installment payments if a seller is providing the wraparound loan. For borrowers, the interest paid is deductible in the same sense as any mortgage interest payment.

As good as this deal looks, and in practice properly structured wraparounds can work well, it does raise a number of concerns which need to be carefully reviewed. There are several issues that both borrowers and seller/lenders should discuss with a knowledgeable attorney before making a wraparound commitment.

- Is wraparound financing a first trust or a second trust? It is sometimes argued that a wraparound has the effect of a first trust, while others maintain that it is nothing more than a glorified second trust. The difference can be important for two reasons:

    First, many states have different usury limits for first mortgages and second trusts. How a wraparound mortgage is defined can determine whether or not usury statutes are being violated.

    Second, what is the order of repayment in the event of default? In the example above, there are liens on the property for both the original first trust and the wraparound financing, a total of $170,000. What if the buyer gets still another loan secured by the property? Is it a second claim? A third claim?
- What happens if the buyer wants to prepay the first trust?
- What happens if the buyer wants to get additional financing above

the value of the wraparound loan? How does this affect the wrap-around lender's security?

- What if a payment is missed? If the wraparound lender fails to make a payment on the first trust it is possible that the original lender can foreclose, in which case the borrower can lose his home and the wraparound lender can lose his equity.

  One way to resolve the missed payment problem is to have the buyer issue separate checks each month, one to the first trust holder and a second to the wraparound lender for the balance due. Another approach is to deposit payments with a local lender who then pays the original lender and the holder of the wrap-around note. This approach assures that a precise record of all payments will be made and avoids the potential problem of payments lost or delayed in the mail.

- What about property taxes? Both the original financing and the wraparound note will be recorded liens against the property for $170,000 in our illustration even though the actual sales value was only $150,000. An unsympathetic assessor can read those numbers and assign a higher value to the property for tax purposes than might otherwise be warranted. Check with local assessors to find out how such matters are handled.

- Is a wraparound a good deal? To analyze this question one must consider alternative monthly costs and potential interest expenses.

Also, if a buyer intends to occupy a property for only a few years and a seller is willing to hold either a wraparound or a second trust, then consideration must be given to the fact that up-front, one-time financing charges are being avoided—a significant cost reduction in the short run.

For sellers, holding a wraparound becomes attractive if such financing provides an equal or better rate of return than alternative investments of similar risk. Also, wraparounds may be extremely attractive in those situations where market interest levels are high and few buyers qualify for financing. In such circumstances, no financing means few sales and so a seller who can hold financing has a decided marketing advantage. The fact that interest rates are high generally also insures a good rate of return on a wraparound.

Questions to Ask:

What is the current interest rate for conventional financing?

What is the remaining loan balance on the property?

Is the current loan freely assumable?

How many years remain on the original loan?

Will the seller hold wraparound financing?

How much cash down is required if a wraparound is to be used to buy property?

Do commercial lenders in the jurisdiction where the property is located make wraparounds?

What are the precise terms of the proposed wraparound? How much are the monthly payments, what is the interest rate, how long will the loan last?

How does a wraparound deal compare with assuming the first trust and getting a second mortgage to acquire or refinance a property?

For purpose of defining usury limits, is a wraparound regarded in your jurisdiction as a first trust or as a second trust?

ZERO-INTEREST (ZIP) MORTGAGES

By definition, the idea of a no-interest mortgage seems to be a contradiction in terms. Is a loan without interest a gift? How can a lender profit if there is no interest? Who will make an interest-free loan?

With an $85,000 zero-interest (ZIP) loan the payments for a $127,500 house look like this: one-third down ($42,500) plus 60 monthly installments of $1,417. That's it.

In comparison, with 20 percent down ($25,500), a 30-year, $85,000 conventional mortgage at 10 percent interest will have 360 payments of $745.94 and a total interest cost over 30 years of $183,536.40 (360 × $745.94 equals $268,538.40 less $85,000 equals $183,538.40). (See table, p. 241.)

Why no interest? The answer lies elsewhere. Buried in the deal is a higher price for the property, a bigger down payment and the world of discounted loans.

Suppose a property is marketed for $106,250. With 20 percent down there will be an $85,000 mortgage. The builder, paying some closing fees, will net in the area of $100,000.

If the same property were sold with a ZIP loan, the price will be higher, say $127,500. Here the buyer will put down $42,500 and get an $85,000 zero-interest mortgage for the balance.

In many cases, it is the builder who first holds the zero-rate mortgage. Since the builder wants cash from the loan, he'll sell the note to an investor. The investor will see that the note has a term of five years, a $1,416.67 monthly payment and an $85,000 face value. If the investor wanted a 12 percent return he will buy the $85,000 mortgage at discount and pay $63,686.45 in cash to the builder. (Alternatively, a lender can make a zero-rate loan if a builder pays points up front. This arrangement has the same effect as an investor buying the loan at discount.)

The builder has now collected $42,500 from the buyer and $63,686.45 from the investor, or a total of $106,186.45 for his property.

The note holder—whether builder, lender or investor—will view zero-rate mortgages as low-risk loans. They have short terms, usually five to seven years, and represent only a fraction of the property's market value, 80 percent or less.

Because ZIP loans have limited risk, qualification standards for such mortgages are generally far more liberal than the guidelines used for conventional financing. With a ZIP loan perhaps one-third of an individual's gross income can be applied to principal and interest payments, up from 25 to 28 percent with conventional mortgages.

It should be said that even with easier qualification standards a ZIP borrower will not get a larger loan than a conventional borrower. For example, a person earning $35,000 a year can afford monthly mortgage payments of $972.22 per month for a ZIP loan with a total value of $58,333 (60 × $972.22). At 28 percent, the maximum allowable monthly mortgage payment for principal and interest will drop to $816.67. This smaller monthly figure, however, will support a 30-year, $93,060.22 conventional mortgage at 10 percent interest.

ZIP loans, as good as they seem, raise four issues for borrowers.

First, is it worth paying a premium purchase price to obtain zero-rate financing? In this example, the buyer has paid $42,500 up front to save as much as $183,536.90 in future interest payments. If you've got the cash there are few investments of equal risk (very small) or economic potential (savings are not income and are therefore not taxed). However, it should be noted that the borrower does pay a premium up front and loses potential income that the premium payment may have earned.

Second, some borrowers will be bothered by the apparent lack of interest payments. With no interest payment there can be no tax deduction. However, the IRS may allow an "imputed" rate of interest as a tax deduction. To find the latest IRS rulings with regard to zero-interest loans and to determine the size of any possible imputed interest claim, check with a CPA or tax attorney before buying property with a zero-interest mortgage format. Of course, if borrowers can deduct imputed interest, then lenders must *receive* imputed interest, money on which they should pay taxes even though they have not actually received spendable cash. The concept of paying tax on theoretical interest is not one which thrills many lenders.

Third, resale profits over a short period of time may be hindered by ZIP financing. Prices for properties of equal size, location and quality will have to rise before the market value of your property exceeds its purchase price.

Fourth, because ZIP financing is generally associated with premium prices borrowers might pay higher taxes when local assessors check selling prices.

While zero-interest loans are generally available only through new home builders, a seller can conceivably take back a zero-interest loan directly from a purchaser. This can be an attractive sales tool, particularly if combined with a premium price and down payment. However, be aware that there may be income tax to pay on the imputed interest credited to the seller but not actually received. Again, see a tax specialist for current advice in this area before making commitments.

Although premium prices are associated with ZIP financing there is no rule which requires owners to raise asking values. In a "buyer's market" or where property is not selling well, it may be possible to get both ZIP financing and a normal price—a deal that effectively offers a steep discount. In any case buyers would be well advised to negotiate.

ZIP loans are clearly designed for people who can afford to put a significant sum of money down and pay large monthly costs for a few years thereafter. Even with premium property prices ZIP loans deserve careful consideration by qualified borrowers, particularly if an imputed tax benefit is available. If you are a buyer without sufficient dollars to afford ZIP financing on your own, a shared-equity arrangement can help get the cash you need.

ZIP versus Conventional Purchases		
	ZIP	Conventional
Sales price	$127,500	$106,250
Down payment	$42,500	$25,500
Loan size	$85,000	$85,000
Interest rate	0 percent	10 percent
Monthly payment	$1,416.67	$745.94
Income required	$60,714	$31,968
Number of payments	60	360
Total payments	$85,000	$268,538.40
Total interest	None	$183,536.40

Questions to Ask:

What is the interest rate for conventional financing?

What is the price of comparable properties financed conventionally?

How much cash down is required for a ZIP loan?

What are the monthly payments?

Can you claim a tax deduction for imputed interest? If so, at what rate?

If you hold ZIP financing, will you pay a tax on interest not actually received? If so, what portion of the loan is regarded as taxable income?

12
Loans to Avoid

There is a vast array of loan choices available to the public at any time and yet borrowers are frequently lured into transactions that are implausible if not unworkable. Often these arrangements are described in glowing terms as "too good to be true," a literally correct phrase in too many instances.

Different arrangements work for different borrowers, so with the exception of fraudulent transactions there are few strategies not right for someone. The problem is that a given strategy that is "right" for one person may be "wrong" for virtually everyone else. Three such mortgages are land contracts, roll-over loans and 40-year mortgages.

LAND CONTRACTS

If one were to concoct the worst possible consumer mortgage it would be difficult to construct a concept less appealing than the land contract, an arrangement in which borrowers have debt without title.

With a land contract a borrower makes payments on a loan but *title* (ownership) is not conveyed until a certain number of payments, or all payments, have been made. Since ownership has not officially changed hands a buyer has only an "equitable" interest in the property. In the event a single payment is missed the borrower can lose the property, down payment, and all accumulated equity because title is in the lender's name.

This arrangement, also called an *installment contract, contract for deed* or a *conditional sales agreement,* is commonly used in recreational land sales and timesharing purchases because the developer has many, many small units to sell and the cost of foreclosing on tiny loans is prohibitive. By using land contracts the developer is assured of either getting paid or being able to re-sell the property quickly since he has not given up title.

Since recreational land sales and timeshare purchases tend to be relatively small real estate deals, buyers should consider personal loans as an alternative to land contracts. With homes, where far more money and much deeper personal concerns are at stake, land contracts should be avoided. Indeed, the suggestion of land contract financing for a private home should cause buyers to look at the entire deal with caution.

Although title does not change hands immediately when land contracts are employed, borrowers should ask if the deal will at least be filed in public records, a requirement in a growing number of jurisdictions. Recordation alerts the public to the title holder's claims and the existence of any rights a borrower may have with a land contract.

In most instances land contracts involve either newly developed properties or sales with freely assumable financing. However, when interest rates are high it sometimes happens that a home is sold with a loan that cannot be assumed. To get around the assumption ban, buyer and seller may try to use a land contract which is not recorded in public records.

The seller in such cases continues to make monthly mortgage payments to the original lender, while the buyer, in turn, pays the seller on a monthly basis. The buyer gets to record title when interest rates drop and the property can be refinanced or when the debt to the seller is paid off.

This is an area of great controversy, since some attorneys argue that a land contract does not violate assumption bans, so-called due-on-sale clauses. Other lawyers strenuously disagree because, they contend, the seller has no intention of regaining occupancy and has therefore effectively given up possession.

In those situations where the loan is assumable, it makes far more sense for the buyer to assume the loan, get a second trust or wraparound note from the seller and record the entire transaction to assure that all legal and equitable rights have been fully protected. If the original loan is not assumable, then one has to ask if the purpose of an unrecorded transaction, where the original mortgage is not paid off, is to deny the rights of a lender. If there is a question about whether or not the loan is assumable, then one should consult with a knowledgeable real estate attorney before making a commitment.

In discussing land contracts there has, as yet, been no mention of interest rates or terms. The reason is that any loan format can be the basis of a land-contract arrangement as long as title does not pass to the borrower when the loan starts.

Note that a *land contract* is entirely different from a *land lease* or a *ground lease.* A land lease is an arrangement in which ground and improvements are owned separately. For instance, Mr. Hubbard can erect an apartment building on ground owned by Mrs. Thornton. Thornton can rent the use of the land for a given period, say 75 years, at which point Hubbard's rights as a renter will end and Thornton or, more likely, Mrs. Thornton's heirs, will then own the building.

From the questions that follow, it should be clear that land contracts raise a variety of basic issues not found in other financing arrangements. If, for some reason, a land contract seems enticing at least have a knowledgeable real estate attorney review the deal before getting involved.

Questions to Ask:

If a payment is late is there a grace period?

What are the borrower's rights if a payment is missed entirely?

Who pays the property taxes?

What are the rights and credits, if any, of the borrower if a single payment is missed?

Since he or she is not an owner of record, what right does the borrower have to modify the property? Must the title holder give permission before the property is painted or the hot water heater is updated?

What right, if any, does the buyer have to raise capital by getting a second trust? What lender will make such loans to someone without actual title?

Is the installment contract assumable? Can it be prepaid?

What right does the borrower have to sell the property?

In those jurisdictions that have rent control, is the borrower a tenant under such regulations? If so, what rights and obligations are created?

What are the buyer's rights if the seller fails to pay the original lender?

Who pays for fire, theft and liability insurance, the borrower or the seller? (Lenders often find out about unrecorded land contracts when they receive annual renewal notices from insurers. When the names of the owner of record and the insured don't match, lenders will ask why.)

If the property burns down, who gets the insurance money? The owner of record (the seller)? The borrower? Neither? Both? If both, who gets what portion?

Who pays property taxes? If you are not an owner can you get a tax deduction? Speak to a CPA or tax attorney for advice.

ROLL-OVER LOANS

Outside of a land contract there is no loan with less innate appeal than a roll-over mortgage. Roll-overs feature interest at or near conventional rates, conventional down payments, short terms and mammoth balloon payments—a foul recipe for virtually all borrowers. (See table on p. 257.)

When self-amortizing, long-term conventional loans were first popularized in the 1930s they largely replaced the "term" mortgage. A term mortgage was short, say 5 years, which usually required only payments for interest. When the term finished the borrower repaid the entire principal.

Since borrowers did not normally have enough cash to pay off the loan at the end of each term, they would merely go out and get new financing. This process meant that loan balances were forever outstanding and that new fees and interest rates could be charged every few years.

Today the term loan with minor modifications is back, only now it is called a *roll-over* or *Canadian roll-over* mortgage. (Roll-overs are used more widely in Canada than in the United States.) With a roll-over loan, a borrower gets a mortgage for a stipulated amount and with payments figured on a 25- or 30-year term. The loan, however, lasts only 5 years.

At the end of five years there's a gargantuan balloon payment that may not be very much smaller than the original principal balance. For example, at the end of five years, a fixed-rate $70,000 loan at 9 percent interest will have a remaining balance of $67,115.78.

What does a buyer do now? In many cases, roll-over loans have a provision through which the lender "guarantees" to provide another 5-year note. However, unless there is a cap the interest rate in the second term may be any number selected by the lender.

When the loan term ends the lender is in a marvelous position to get a premium rate, since the borrower's alternative, other than selling or being foreclosed, is to refinance with someone else. Refinancing is likely to involve costly loan origination fees, points, and settlement charges—new title searches, appraisals, etc. A premium interest rate in such circumstances may be the best of several poor choices. (See table below.)

Even if a second 5-year term is guaranteed, a third term usually is not. At this point a borrower must find new financing if the property is to be retained.

The lack of a long-term loan commitment raises all the problems associated with balloon financing generally: There is no guarantee that funds will be available to refinance the roll-over note and there is no promise that if such funds are available the borrower will qualify for financing. Even if money is available, interest rates may be so high that new financing is ludicrously expensive anyway. Finally, a roll-over loan is nothing more than a short-term balloon note—a terrible arrangement from the borrower's standpoint.

It is difficult to imagine a situation in which roll-over financing is advantageous to borrowers. If interest rates are abnormally high, the time when roll-over loans are more likely to be in style, one is better off with ARM financing. The ARM interest rate is likely to be at or below current market levels. Moreover, an ARM is a long-term commitment by a lender. While borrowers may worry about rising monthly

Roll-Over Amortization	
Loan size	$70,000
Interest rate	9 percent
Monthly payment	$563.24
Loan balance at the end of	
Year 1	$69,521.71
Year 2	$68,998.55
Year 3	$68,426.32
Year 4	$67,800.41
Year 5	$67,115.78
Balloon payment	$67,115.78

Roll-Over versus Conventional Financing		
	Roll-Over	Conventional
Interest rate	At or marginally below market	Market
Down payment	20 percent	20 percent
Initial term	Usually 5 years	30 years
Balloon payment	Yes	No

payments with an ARM, at least they are not faced with the certainty of a giant balloon payment in a few years.

If interest rates are low the need for a roll-over loan approaches zero. Why get a loan that is essentially term financing when plenty of money is available in more attractive formats?

Questions to Ask:

What is the interest rate for conventional financing?

What is the interest rate for a roll-over loan?

How much cash is required for a down payment?

What is the term of the roll-over loan?

Does the lender guarantee to continue the loan for an additional term?

Must you be "financially qualified" to continue roll-over financing for a second term?

Will the lender continue the loan for a third term? A fourth?

Will the lender allow you to convert to conventional financing if interest rates decline to a certain point? What point?

If the lender does guarantee to renew the loan, how much notice will you receive regarding any new interest rate?

Is there a cap on the interest level for a second term?

Is the roll-over loan assumable?

Can the roll-over loan be prepaid in whole or in part without penalty at any time?

THE 40-YEAR MORTGAGE

Whenever money is tight some bright person comes up with this thought: Monthly mortgage payments will be lower if loan terms are stretched from 30 to 40 years. If monthly payments are lower more people can qualify for financing. Therefore, why not have more 40-year loans? Here's why:

Suppose you want to borrow $85,000 at 9 percent. A 30-year note for this sum will require monthly payments of $683.93, while a 40-year loan will have monthly installments of $655.66. However, for the monthly saving of $28.27, a figure positively minute in the context of this loan, the 40-year note will require 120 additional monthly payments. (See table above.)

If paid out over their respective terms, the ultimate difference between the two loans will be $68,500.97 ($683.93 for 360 payments vs. $655.66 for 480 payments). Thus by making 360 additional monthly payments of $28.27–or $10,177.20 over 30 years—a borrower can potentially save over $58,323.77.

Huge potential interest costs plus marginal monthly savings suggest that longer loans are simply unfavorable to most buyers. If in the context of an $85,000 mortgage it's important to save $28.27 per month, both buyer and lender will be better off if the purchaser bought a smaller, more affordable property.

Conventional Loan Comparison by Term			
Loan size	$85,000	$85,000	$85,000
Loan term	15 years	30 years	40 years
Interest rate	9 percent	9 percent	9 percent
Number of payments	180	360	480
Monthly payment	$862.13	$683.93	$655.66
Monthly cost differential	+178.20	None	−28.27
Balloon payment	None	None	None
Total potential interest	$70,182.79	$161,214.52	$229,715.49

Questions to Ask:

What is the monthly cost of a 30-year mortgage?

What is the monthly cost of a 40-year loan?

How much cash is required for a down payment with 40-year financing?

What is the possible interest cost for a 30-year loan? (To find the total potential interest cost of a 30-year mortgage, multiply 360 times the value of the monthly payment and subtract the loan's original face value.)

What is the potential interest cost of a 40-year mortgage? (Multiply 480 times the monthly payment and subtract the loan's original face value.)

13
Refinancing: Four Profit Strategies Produce Big Mortgage Interest Cuts

Many people believe that once a mortgage has been made its terms are set in stone. Year after year they make regular payments without a thought to restructuring their loans and as a result they fail to quickly and easily cut interest costs by thousands of dollars.

As attractive as refinancing may be, it has become a more complex process under tax reform. Prior to tax reform, if you refinanced a house the interest on your new loan was fully deductible. Under tax reform, however, interest costs may be deductible, not deductible or possibly deductible only in part.

In basic terms, married couples can deduct interest payments on loans worth up to $1 million, providing such financing is used to acquire or improve a prime residence or a second home. They can also deduct up to $100,000 for a second trust, home equity loan or for a refinanced loan which exceeds the current mortgage amount by up to $100,000. In total, under the rules interest on loans worth as much as $1.1 million can be fully deductible by homeowners.

The catch comes with refinancing. Suppose a home was purchased 10 years ago for $100,000 and has a $75,000 balance. Suppose also that the property value has risen and that the owners, Mr. and Mrs. Connors, decide to obtain a $120,000 second trust.

At this point the Connors have a $75,000 first trust balance plus a second trust worth $120,000, a total debt of $195,000. Interest on the $75,000 current loan balance is deductible because it represents original acquisition debt—money used to acquire the property. As to the $120,000 second trust, interest on $100,000 is deductible while interest on the $20,000 balance may be treated as personal interest, interest which is not deductible at all.

To make matters more complex, it's possible that a home mortgage may be deductible regardless of its size. For instance, suppose Mr. Carlson pays off his mortgage and refinances three years later with a $400,000 loan. Of this amount, interest on $100,000 is deductible. As for the rest, if Carlson uses the money for a commercial purpose, perhaps to expand a business or buy investment property, then interest on the entire debt may be fully deductible.

Since deductibility can be based on the current loan balance, capital improvement costs, plus $100,000, those who buy property for cash or who pay off their loans may find that future deductibility is limited.

Points are another tax issue to consider when refinancing. In general terms, points used to acquire real estate are deductible in the year paid while points paid to refinance must be deducted over the loan term.

Now, however, those who buy with interim financing—say a short-term balloon note—have some glimmer of hope that if they buy today, finance temporarily, and refinance tomorrow then the points paid to refinance may be immediately deductible. That was the gist of a decision made by the U.S. Court of Appeals in the Eighth Circuit which said that since the refinancing was "in connection" with the original purchase of the property the points could be deducted immediately. Note that although this decision raises an interesting perspective, it has no direct effect except inside the Eighth District, an area that includes Arkansas, Iowa, Missouri, Minnesota, Nebraska, North Dakota, and South Dakota.

Interest deductions and points are two major issues which should concern property owners who refinance. Before you obtain or restructure a loan, be certain to *first* check with a CPA or tax attorney for the latest rules, regulations and interpretations.

In addition to revised tax rules, borrowers should also be aware that lenders have begun to make refinancing easier. Old, and unbelievably picky, application requirements are giving way to new and more rational standards. Your efforts to refinance should be greatly simplified if:

- You have made timely mortgage payments for the past year.
- Your old loan was a conforming mortgage.
- Your new payments are not more than 15 percent larger than the old ones.
- Your income is at least equal to the income used to qualify for the old loan.
- You refinance with your current lender—that is, the lender who now services your mortgage.
- You simply want a rate-and-term refinancing for the same amount of money but at a lower interest rate.
- If you use the same lender, it may be possible to refinance without a new appraisal.
- You have equity in the property. The old standard—at least 10 percent equity—has been replaced with a new and better guideline: home owners must have at least a 5 percent stake in their property.

The new and simplified guidelines should make refinancing quicker and easier. However, to find the best possible deal, borrowers should check with many lenders when refinancing. If a lender who wants more paperwork offers better rates and terms, sharpen your pencil, fill out the forms, and perhaps you can save thousands of dollars.

THE 2 PERCENT MYTH: REFINANCING REFIGURED

The public is forever told that refinancing makes sense only when the difference between today's interest rate and the old rate is at least two percent. Such advice is quick, convenient and commonly wrong.

Imagine an owner with 10 percent financing and a five-year-old, $100,000 mortgage balance. Monthly payments for principal and interest total $908.70. If the owner refinances the outstanding balance at 8 percent, the monthly payments over 25 years will be $771.82, a savings of $136.88 per month.

Let us also imagine that to close this loan the owner will pay 2 points plus $1,500 in taxes, fees, and other expenses. All told, our owner must shell out $3,500 to refinance. If the owner keeps the property for at least 26 months, he or she will come out ahead ($3,500/$136.88).

Alternatively, our owner can fold the refinancing costs back into the loan and borrow $103,500. Now the monthly payment is $798.83 for principal and interest and the cost of ownership is reduced by $109.87 per month.

Folding back refinancing costs is an attractive strategy for those who wish to cut monthly expenses. However, in areas where real estate values are stable or declining, owners should be aware that when they sell they will owe more to the lender, money which may not be available in the form of increased equity.

So far it looks as though the 2 percent rule makes sense, at least for those who intend to own their property for at least 26 months or who live in regions where property values are rising.

But suppose interest rates only fall 1 percent? In such circumstances, can refinancing be a good deal?

If our owner refinances $100,000 at 9 percent, then regular mortgage expenses will drop to $839.19 for principal and interest, a savings of $69.50 per month. If it still costs $3,500 to close the deal, then it will take another 51 months of ownership—a little more than four years—before refinancing makes economic sense.

Again, of course, we need not pay closing costs in cash, we can simply fold such expenses into a larger mortgage amount. If we borrow $103,500 over 25 years at 9 percent interest, the monthly expense will be $868.57 and an owner will save $40.13 with each payment.

Clearly saving 2 percent is better than saving 1 percent, but the oft-forgotten point is this: Saving 1 percent is not shabby. For those who intend to hold their property for a sufficient term—a little more than two years in this example—refinancing with even a 1-percent differential can make sense.

Rather than relying on the mystical 2 percent solution, owners should refinance when visible economic returns are available over a reasonable term. A basic formulation would work like this:

- First, what is the cost for principal and interest today?
- Second, what is the cost for principal and interest at new and lower rates if all closing costs are paid up front?
- Third, how many months does the owner intend to hold the property?

- Fourth, divide the monthly savings created by a new and lower monthly payment into the cost of refinancing.
- Fifth, if the number found in item four is larger than the number of months shown in item three, refinance.

For those who elect to fold refinancing costs into a slightly larger loan, the issues are somewhat different. If property values are rising, then refinancing can be an attractive way to reduce monthly housing costs.

If housing values are falling, then monthly savings can be seen as a hedge against declining values. At the same time, monthly savings in a continuing weak market also imply a contest of sorts: Which is greater, savings through refinancing or monthly equity losses? If property values are declining 3 percent a year, and if a home has a $100,000 market value in January, then a year later the owner has lost $3,000 or $250 per month. The monthly savings gained through refinancing place real dollars in the owner's pocket, while lost equity is an accounting item, at least until an owner wants to sell.

It should also be said that folding closing costs into a loan may be advantageous in the face of inflation. As inflation eats away at buying power, as it always does, then paying for closing costs sometime in the future may well be a bargain when considered in the context of today's buying power.

A RESTRUCTURING QUARTET

Restructuring a loan means nothing more than changing the terms of repayment on an existing mortgage with few if any fees to the lender. For example, Mr. Conrad has a 30-year, $85,000 mortgage at 10 percent interest. After 5 years the principal balance is down to $82,088.17.

Rather than make 300 more payments (25 years) of $745.94, Conrad decides to pay off the loan in 20 years. He does this by merely increasing his monthly payments $46.23 a month to $792.17. The result is that over 20 years he makes additional payments of $11,095.20 (240 months × $46.23). He saves $44,756 (60 months × $745.94). His net benefit is $33,660.80 ($44,756 less $11,095.20).

Before mortgages can be revised a borrower must first find out about prepayment rules and penalties.

Mr. Conrad's Restructured Loan		
	Original Terms	New Terms
Loan amount	$82,088.17	$82,088.17
Remaining term	25 years	20 years
Monthly payment	$745.94	$792.17
Extra monthly cost	None	$46.23
Total extra cost	None	$11,095.20
Total payment	$223,782	$190,120.80
Cash saved	None	$33,660.80

Prepayment penalties are fees and charges designed to stop or discourage borrowers from making early repayments. Lenders, however, cannot always charge prepayment fees, since they are regulated in many jurisdictions and with certain types of loans.

For example, there is no prepayment penalty with FHA loans, provided the prepayment is not less than the monthly installment. In some jurisdictions there is no prepayment penalty if a loan is over three years old or if the prepayment is above a certain size, say $10,000 in the first year. Moreover, it should be said that in many cases lenders will wave penalties to rid their books of an unwanted (read "low yield") mortgage.

Conceivably, if a loan is silent on the matter of prepayments or permits the borrower to repay the note at any time in whole or in part without penalty, a borrower has the right to restructure a loan at will as long as monthly payments do not drop.

To restructure a loan one must first examine the lowly amortization statement, a table showing monthly mortgage payments, payment allocations for interest and principal and the mortgage balance.

Except for adjustable rate loans, where future monthly payments, interest rates and principal balances cannot be guaranteed, amortization schedules demonstrate how various mortgage formats compare. They also illustrate how rapid repayment strategies can produce tremendous mortgage savings.

With a 30-year, $85,000 conventional mortgage at 10 percent interest the monthly payments will be $745.94 per month for 360 months. Yet while the payments are equal, the pace of amortization is not.

- In the first month only $37.60 of the $745.94 payment goes to reduce the principal balance. In fact, in the first year the total principal reduction is just $472.50, while interest payments amount to $8,951.23.
- At the end of the tenth year, payment #120, the mortgage balance is $77,297.32—despite total payments of $89,512.80 (120 × $745.94).
- At the end of the fifteenth year, payment #180, the mortgage balance drops to $69,414.88—after total payments of $134,269.20 (180 × $745.94).
- In the twenty-ninth year, the principal reduction is $8,484.65, while interest amounts to only $466.58. (The last month's payment is $745.95, or $0.01 more than the previous 359 installments.)

The nature of mortgage amortization shows that prepayments at the beginning of the mortgage term have greater financial impact than those made as the loan matures. The reason is that prepayments made up front provide a longer stream of benefits than additional payments made later in the loan term.

RESTRUCTURING VS. REFINANCING

Is it better to refinance or restructure?

There is no universal rule, but here are the major factors to consider.

What is the interest-rate differential? The bigger the interest rate decline, the more likely that refinancing will be preferred.

How long will you own the property? Refinancing, with its up-front costs, becomes more attractive as the term of ownership increases. Conversely, if you expect to own just a few years, restructuring can be the best approach.

What about up-front costs? If refinancing is expensive it can make sense to restructure even though the interest rate remains high. With restructuring, there are no appraisals, credit reports, points, surveys, settlement fees, title searches, title insurance, taxes based on a new loan, etc. In some cases the value of these up-front costs is best used to reduce the outstanding loan balance.

With the factors above in mind, here are four rapid repayment programs for a 30-year, $85,000 mortgage at 10 percent interest.

Amortization Schedule		
	30-Year Loan	15-Year Loan
Loan amount	$85,000	$85,000
Interest rate	10 percent	10 percent
Number of payments	360	180
Payment size	$745.94	$913.41
Extra monthly payment	None	$167.47
Potential interest cost	$183,538.40	$79,413.80
Potential saving	None	$104,124.60

Program 1: The Steady Payment Approach.   Prior to settlement you see that your $85,000 mortgage requires monthly payments of $745.94. However, if the same loan were repaid over a 15-year period, the payments increase to $913.41—a difference of $167.47 per month. Since you anticipate a rising income, you elect to spend a week of vacation at home in the coming year to raise the additional $2,009.69 needed for the first 12 monthly payments. Future pay raises will cover the additional cost in the following years.

You tell the lender of your plan and the lender agrees, in writing, to waive any prepayment penalties. Why? Because most loans are outstanding less than 15 years anyway and by making regular monthly payments at a set rate the lender has few bookkeeping problems. (See table above.)

Potential Savings: You pay an additional $167.47 for 180 months, or $30,144.60 over 15 years. You save $104,124.60 (180 payments × $745.94 equals $134,269.20 less $30,144.60).

Program 2: The Double-up Plan.   You check the amortization schedule and see that in the first month the payment is $745.94, but only $37.60 goes to reduce principal. In the second month you see that the same payment is made but the principal balance drops by the munificent sum of only $37.92. You decide to go from payment #1 to payment #3. When it comes time to make your first payment you write out a check for $783.86 ($745.94 plus $37.92). The principal balance has now been reduced by both $37.60 and $37.92.

Potential Savings: You effectively move down the amortization schedule from month 1 to month 3 and therefore do not pay $708.02 in interest for month 2. However, you do make your regular payment

	Interest	Principal	Balance
Month 1	$708.33	$37.60	$84,962.40
Month 2	$708.02	$37.92	$84,924.48
Month 3	$707.70	$38.23	$84,886.25

in the second month and in all following months. If you hold the loan to maturity there will be one less payment to make.

Note that by paying ahead your interest deduction for the year has hardly dropped at all. Instead of paying interest on months 1 through 12, a total of $8,478.73, you pay interest on month 1 ($708.33) and months 3 through 13 ($7,766.78), a total of $8,474.80. For tax purposes, then, the amount of interest you deduct for the year is reduced $3.93.

Program 3: The Lump-Sum Rapid Reduction.   Lenders are not normally too pleased about an advance payment of $37.92, and your lender requires prepayments of at least a full month's usual payment, or $745.94 in this case. At the end of the first year you have made 12 payments and the mortgage balance is reduced to $84,527.50. By making an additional payment of $745.94 you reduce the loan balance to $83,781.56. Had you followed the usual amortization program you would not have reached this level until payment 37, when the principal balance was scheduled to total $83,378.20.

Potential Savings: You have skipped ahead 25 payments worth $18,648.50. To achieve this advantage you spent $745.94.

Your maximum potential net benefit is $17,902.56 ($18,648.50 less $745.94).

Program 4: Large Lump-Sum Rapid Repayment.   You see from the amortization statement that the principal balance of the loan will be $69,414.88 after 15 years of payments—a drop of only $15,585.12. The first year you get the mortgage you decide to postpone the purchase of a new car and instead get a $16,000 personal loan from a local lender at 13 percent interest. The loan must be repaid over 4 years with monthly payments of $429.24, or a total cost of $20,603.52. (Alternatively, you receive a gift of $16,000 from a relative, sell stock or whatever.) You take the $16,000 and eliminate 182 mortgage payments.

Potential Savings: You spend $20,603.52 but save $136,104.21

	Interest	Principal	Balance
Payment 12	$704.74	$41.20	$84,527.50
Payment 37	$695.24	$50.70	$83,378.20

(182.46 × $745.94). The maximum net benefit is $115,500.69 ($136,104.21 less $20,603.52). At the beginning of the loan, you have effectively created a self-amortizing loan with an initial principal of $69,000 that can be paid off with 177.54 monthly installments of $745.94. (See table, p. 261.)

The benefits of these strategies can be measured within two boundaries. If you hold a mortgage through its full term you will get the total benefit cited in each example. If, however, you sell a property before the mortgage is paid off your minimum benefit will be interest not paid, taxes not assessed on interest "savings" and a smaller loan balance to pay off when you sell.

In addition to saving money, each of these mortgage-reduction strategies offers a series of important advantages:

First, each program is at the option of the borrower. You don't have to develop an interest-reduction program but it is good to know that you can.

Second, in each case 100 percent of the principal is being repaid. Since there is no discount there is no income to tax.

Third, all property owners should periodically review the mortgage market to see if an interest-reduction program is appropriate. Deals which may not have been possible at the time property was acquired may arise in later years.

Fourth, many people view a home mortgage as a discomforting burden which should be repaid even if rapid repayments are not the best financial choice. Interest-reduction programs are especially valuable for such individuals.

Questions to Ask:

Can you repay present financing in whole or in part at any time without penalty?

If there is a penalty what is it?

Will the lender waive the penalty if you agree to higher but steady payments?

Large Lump-Sum Repayment Plan	
Car loan principal	$16,000
Monthly payments	$429.24
Number of payments	48
Total cost	$20,603.52
House loan principal	$85,000
Monthly payments	$745.94
Number of payments	360
House loan less money from car loan	$69,000
Monthly payments	$745.94
Number of payments	177.54
Payments saved	182.46
Dollars saved	$136,104.21
Less car loan cost	$20,603.52
Net benefit	$115,500.69

What is the current interest rate on your mortgage?

What is the prevailing, post-tax return on alternative investments such as money market funds, savings accounts or government securities?

What are the tax consequences if you rapidly repay your mortgage? Speak to a CPA or tax authority for more information.

Should you refinance or restructure or is your money better invested elsewhere? What about reducing credit card balances or paying off car loans?

What are the tax consequences of your prospective new financing?

FULL CURTAILMENTS:
HOW TO PAY OFF LOANS AT DISCOUNT

If that stock market hunch finally paid off or Uncle Jasper left you with a large chunk of cash, you may want to examine the idea of repaying your current mortgage with a single lump sum, a process known as a full or total *curtailment*.

A full curtailment differs from a restructuring program in two ways.

First, the loan is being paid off at one time.

Second, a full curtailment often involves a principal discount. Part of the loan debt is usually forgiven in exchange for the prepayment, particularly when the lender wants to close an unprofitable loan.

	Interest Rate	Yield
$25,000	6 percent	$1,500
$25,000	9 percent	$2,250
$16,666	9 percent	$1,500

Suppose you can get 9 percent interest from a simple savings account. Suppose also that you have a 6 percent mortgage with a remaining balance of $25,000 and 15 years left on it.

At 6 percent, $25,000 will earn $1,500 a year in simple interest. If you can get 9 percent, a savings account with $16,666.67 will yield the same $1,500. If you had $25,000 in the account you can earn $2,250.

Clearly you would do better to leave your money in the savings account rather than pay off the remaining loan balance. But what would happen if the lender said, "Look, give us the $16,666 and we'll consider the loan fully paid." Would you take an $8,334 cash discount—a one-third savings in this case?

While the lender obviously prefers to get the entire $25,000, a curtailment is a better deal than another 15 years of low-interest payments. For the lender, getting back almost $17,000 means getting rid of your old loan and putting more cash in the vault, money that can be re-loaned as new, higher-rate financing with up-front points and fees.

Loan curtailments are possible at any time but discounts are unlikely when your home is on the market. If the lender is aware that you are selling property, he is also aware that your loan is likely to be repaid in full at settlement—particularly if the loan value is a small portion of the total sales price. For this reason borrowers looking for a curtailment should approach lenders well before placing their homes for sale.

However, if you have a buyer who can finance the property with or without the loan, you again will be in a position to seek a discount.

One word of caution: The value of a mortgage discount, that is, the difference between the remaining principal balance and the cash used to repay the loan, may be regarded as regular income for tax purposes. Thus a discount may raise your taxable income, so when calculating the value of a discount, attention must be paid to the possible tax costs involved, taxes which will reduce the benefit of any discount you obtain.

Note that a discount on a principal balance is treated differently than a loan structured to pay less interest. Less interest is merely a "saving" and therefore not taxable.

For current information about curtailment tax angles speak to a tax attorney or CPA.

Questions to Ask:

What is the interest rate on your current financing?

What is the rate of return on alternative conservative investments such as savings accounts or money market funds?

How much cash do you have available for a curtailment?

What deal can you make with a lender?

If you pay off an FHA mortgage where the insurance premium was prepaid, how much of the premium will be refunded? When can you expect a refund? Speak to your lender or whoever services the mortgage for details.

What are the tax consequences of a curtailment?

CASH-OUT REFINANCING

One of the great benefits of falling interest rates is that budgets go further. While $500 a month at 10 percent interest is enough to cover principal and interest costs for a loan worth $56,975, the same amount of money can be used to borrow $62,141 at 9 percent, and $68,142 at 8 percent.

While a calculator can quickly tell you how lower interest rates will boost your borrowing power, there is an institutional problem to consider: lenders have traditionally shied away from so-called "cash-out" refinancing, deals where you walk away from the closing table with a fat check.

The problem is that lenders have long been convinced that if vast numbers of people refinance and have cash, suddenly such borrowers will head to Rio while leaving massive unpaid debts behind. The historic view, however, has begun to change, especially as lenders look for additional business, fees, and income.

Cash-out refinancing can occur in two situations. In one case you replace a current loan with a bigger mortgage and walk away with the difference, or you keep the old loan and use your property to secure additional financing.

To make a cash-out work you need an excellent credit history, solid real estate equity, and a local real estate market where values are at least rising at the rate of inflation. Given such circumstances, some lenders (though not all) will provide financing for as much as 75 percent of a home's value. (For investor properties, think in terms of cash-out loan-to-value ratios of 65 percent.)

To see how this works, consider the Kemp property. The Kemps bought 20 years ago for $35,000. Their property today is worth $175,000. They refinanced ten years ago and their current mortgage balance is $40,000.

How much can the Kemps borrow? Seventy-five percent of $175,000 is $131,250. That amount, less $40,000, means they can borrow $91,250 in the usual case.

To get either a full or a partial cash-out refinancing will require a complete loan application, closing, and the usual array of costs and charges. In addition, the lender will be keenly interested in why you want cash-out refinancing.

Desirable reasons—at least from the lender's perspective—include a plan to fix up your property, to expand, or to otherwise add value. Such improvements increase the property's worth and thus reduce the lender's risk. Other reasons for cash-out refinancing that will attract lender interest include paying off debt (this reduces the lender's risk because the borrower's financial security is improved), buying a business (or expanding one), or using the money to underwrite a college education.

Another trick associated with cash-out refinancing is the willingness of some lenders to make cash-out loans based on planned improvements. In other words, if your home is now worth $150,000 and $10,000 in cash-out financing can raise its value to $175,000, some lenders will make a loan based on the $175,000 value. The obvious requirement in such situations is that the money is actually used as intended.

Questions to Ask:

Do you have equity that can be used to obtain cash-out financing?

Are real estate prices in your community generally rising at the rate of inflation or above?

Do local lenders make cash-out loans? If so, what loan to value ratios do they use for prime residences? For investment property?

Are there local lenders who will make cash-out loans based on the value of your property after improvements have been made?

What rate of interest do lenders seek for cash-out refinancing? How many points? What are the rates and terms for investment properties?

REFINANCING IN A DOWN MARKET

Since at least the 1970s it has been very difficult to lose money on real estate. But in the 1990s we face a new world with borderless economics, jobs that flow overseas, massive debt at the federal and state levels, huge corporations that are downsizing, and the very discomforting feeling that earning a dollar is going to be a lot tougher than in the past.

The trends and conditions seen in the 1990s have a clear impact on real estate. If you live in a community with a declining job base, fewer government projects, and less commerce you can expect that the price of real estate will remain steady relative to inflation or possibly drop. In the latter case, in particular, there can be big problems.

One matter, obviously, is that as prices fall homes have less equity. Less equity means fewer dollars when you sell and a reduced ability to borrow. If you have a home equity loan, be aware that declining values can allow lenders to curb withdrawals from home equity lines of credit, a huge problem if you need that money at this particular time.

If you bought many years ago—say before 1980—you should have few practical problems. Yes your home is worth less than it may have been worth at the top of the market in 1989, but it may also be worth two or three times what you paid in 1980. To date, there is no place in the country where real estate values have dropped to the point where the equity of long-term owners is threatened.

If you bought in the past few years, however, it is entirely possible that your home is actually worth less than what you paid and—if you bought with little down—it may also be worth less than your outstanding mortgage. If you bought for $150,000, put down $7,500, borrowed $142,500 and your home is now worth $135,000, you and maybe your lender will have a loss.

This means that if you sell at this moment you will have to pay marketing costs, taxes, closing expenses, and moving bills. You will also have to pay off your mortgage debt and it is entirely possible that you will owe several thousand dollars—and perhaps much more for a larger property—money the lender will want in cash.

Is there a way to resolve this problem?

One choice is to not to sell, but that may not be possible if a new job awaits far away.

A second strategy is to declare bankruptcy. This is a choice that will scar your credit record for years.

A third choice is to rent the property. The catch to renting is that in a down market many properties are likely to be available which will mean depressed rents. Other rental-related problems include tenant selection, repairs, and management (especially if you are moving out of an area).

A fourth choice is to negotiate with the lender, a so-called "work out." The lender doesn't want to foreclose because that looks bad to regulators (it should) and also because foreclosure is unlikely to result in full repayment. If partial repayment is clearly in the cards, it may be possible to bargain with the lender so that the lender simply closes the loan with something less than full payment. As you can imagine, this is not a choice that thrills lenders, but it may be better than bankruptcy and foreclosure.

A fifth alternative is painful but perhaps the most practical solution when cash is not otherwise available. If you have a retirement account you may have the funds necessary to pay off the lender at closing. Pulling money out of a retirement fund means you are likely to pay income tax as well as a 10 percent penalty on the money withdrawn, but not always. Some retirement programs have hardship provisions and impending bankruptcy may qualify for special treatment. See a CPA, tax attorney, and your asset manager for specific advice.

Two other choices in the "must move" category should also be mentioned. There are cases where auctions have created enough demand so that even properties in distressed areas sell for good prices; good enough to at least pay off the lender.

A final alternative if you must move is to hold a contest. You'll need to outline your program with local district attorneys and lawyers to assure that what you are doing is entirely lawful and not, for example, regarded as gambling.

The best case I have seen is the Maine couple who organized an essay contest judged by local English teachers. Contestants had to write in 250 words or less why they wanted the beach-front Maine property and each entry cost $99. The winner would get the house and there was also a $5,000 scholarship for second place. Entry money was held in escrow so that if not enough entries were received, all funds would be returned.

While selling in a down market is clearly a problem, refinancing is plausible under certain conditions.

First, the property has sufficient equity to support a new loan.

Second, you have excellent credit.

Third, you are not looking for a cash-out refinancing.

Fourth, you do not want a bigger loan.

Fifth, you are not borrowing to improve a home. Such thinking is likely to be regarded with great caution by most lenders because in a soft market additional investments may simply represent more equity to lose.

Given the five benchmark conditions above it should be possible to refinance if your goal is lower rates and reduced monthly costs. In addition, lenders will certainly be interested if you are willing to make a cash infusion into the property; that is, if you can come up with an extra $5,000 or whatever to reduce the amount being borrowed.

Questions to Ask:

What is your house worth after selling costs, closing expenses, etc?

If the value of your house is less than the current mortgage balance, how will you pay off the lender?

Do you have other assets such as stock, bonds, pension funds, etc. that can be used to satisfy the debt?

Can you rent your property? If so, for how much?

If you rent, what about tenant selection, maintenance, management, etc?

Will the lender discuss a work-out?

Is there any level of loss which is acceptable?

Given the alternatives, what is the least damaging course if you must sell?

Do you have enough equity to refinance for lower rates and terms?

Are local lenders refinancing old loans?

Do you now have a line-of-credit home equity mortgage? If so, would it make sense to withdraw money merely to assure that funds are available? If so, at what cost?

To make refinancing easier, can you make a capital contribution to reduce the loan amount now outstanding?

DON'T FORGET HIDDEN REFINANCING COSTS

When considering either a partial or complete refinancing borrowers should be concerned with more than interest rates.

Because of the many add-on charges involved, the full cost of refinancing is often concealed in a maze of charges, fees, and accounting concepts that can easily distort the advantages of lower rates.

Suppose Mr. Grayson has a 30-year, $95,000 mortgage at 11 percent interest. The monthly payments for principal and interest are $904.71. With 9 percent money, the monthly cost drops to $764.39, a difference of more than $1,650 per year.

Although the new rate is certainly attractive, one must consider the one-time, up-front expenses required to get the better financing. If you expect to sell your property within a few years, these costs may wipe out the benefits of lower interest rates. Here are some of the charges to anticipate, items that alone may seem small but when added together seriously affect the true cost of borrowing.

- Points (loan discount fees): A point is equal to 1 percent of the value of a mortgage. Unlike a sales situation where buyer and seller may split the cost of financing, with a refinancing situation there is no one with whom the fee can be divided. Cost: 1 percent or more of the mortgage. For Mr. Grayson at least $950.
- Loan Origination Fee: Essentially a charge by the lender to grant the loan. Cost: 1 percent of the loan, or $950 in this example.
- Appraisal: An appraisal will be required by the lender to establish the property's value. Cost: $200 and up.
- Credit Report: A lender will examine your finances and charge a credit report fee. Cost: $25 to $50.
- Application Fee: A payment to the lender for processing the loan. Cost: varies and may be waived when refinancing with the lender who holds the current mortgage.
- Prepayment Penalty: A charge established in the original mortgage to discourage early repayment. Such charges are limited in many jurisdictions and in some cases may be waived by lenders. Cost: from zero to a fixed percentage of the remaining mortgage balance or the value of interest for a certain period, perhaps six months.

- Survey: In some cases, a lender may require a survey, particularly for detached property. Cost: varies considerably.
- Termite Inspection: May be required by lenders. Cost: $35 to $75.
- Taxes: Local jurisdictions charge recording fees to place documents in public files, others actually tax new financing. Cost: varies considerably.
- Title Insurance: Lenders will commonly require title insurance up to the value of their loan. In the event the title is faulty, "lenders" title insurance assures that the party making the mortgage will be repaid. Cost: varies by jurisdiction and according to the size of the new mortgage. Suggestion: see if you qualify for a "re-issue" rate. In cases where there has been a title search in the past five to ten years, many insurers offer a discounted rate and you may save 10 to 20 percent.
- Legal: New financing requires a new title search, document preparation, and other legal and paralegal services. Cost: expect to pay for specific services according to local regulations and the requirements of the lender.

Borrowers often ask if it is better to refinance in whole or in part. While there is no absolute answer that is correct in all cases, it should be said that partial refinancing is frequently advantageous for two reasons. First, with partial refinancing such as second trusts and wrap-around loans, original mortgages with low interest rates can often be retained. Second, non-interest costs are generally cheaper with partial refinancing because the overall loan size is smaller.

Time is also important when refinancing. If you expect to hold property for a relatively short period it may actually pay to keep current, high interest loans. The reason: the benefit of low interest financing may be offset by high non-interest expenses. To make the best decision, check with local lenders to see whether interest and non-interest-costs make refinancing worthwhile in your situation.

14
Cheap Refinancing

Few matters in life are more enjoyable for real estate owners than the vision of plummeting interest rates. As rates fall the result is lower monthly costs for owner-occupants and reduced expenses for investors.

Unfortunately it's not always easy or cheap to obtain those good-looking lower rates. Stories abound regarding owners who refinance once, twice, and even three times in the span of a year or two, each time paying points, closing costs, and taxes to reach the promised land of lower rates.

But refinancing is not the only path to lower rates. Rather than a formal refinancing ordeal with points and heavy closing costs, many borrowers obtain lower rates by simply *modifying* current loan terms.

To see how this is done, imagine that Mr. Graves borrows $100,000. The initial interest rate is 4 percent, but the rate can change by as much as 2 percent annually. In addition, the loan has a cap which prohibits monthly payment costs from going up or down more than 7.5 percent.

The ARM obtained by Mr. Graves permits "negative amortization," a phrase which means that if loan costs rise faster than monthly payments, the difference is added to the loan amount. Because of negative amortization, it is possible that the $100,000 originally borrowed by Graves could actually rise to $103,000, $105,000 or such amount as circumstances might direct. In addition, the Graves ARM allows the mortgage term to be extended from 30 years to as much as 40 years if the loan amount increases because of negative amortization.

What makes the Graves loan interesting is that while monthly payments, interest rates, and the amount owed may all go up or down, there has been only one settlement. In effect, Graves and his lender have a loan which is automatically modified over time.

But where is the rule which says loan modifications are restricted to ARMs? Is it not possible to modify a loan *after* closing and thus avoid the expense and irritation of additional settlements?

You bet.

As an example of how loan modifications work consider this experience: I have, or had, a three-year, $65,000 balloon note at 10.5 percent interest on an investment property—not the type of mortgage most consumers should consider because the failure to repay could result in foreclosure.

Several months before the loan was due I went to the lender (a private pension in this case) and made a proposal: since all payments have been in full and on time, since the value of the property greatly surpasses the loan amount, and since a full repayment of the loan will only mean that lender funds will have to be re-invested somewhere else, would you consider a five-year loan extension at 8.5 percent?

At the time, 8.5 percent was a somewhat higher rate then residential borrowers were paying, but then this was financing for an investment property and no points were involved. More importantly, 8.5 percent was substantially more interest then the pension could obtain from low-risk alternative investments such as top-grade bonds. The lender liked my proposal.

The next step was to change the loan agreement. We had recorded the original loan, conducted a title search, and obtained title insurance to protect the lender. I called my attorney and asked how the loan could be changed.

One choice would be to pay off the old loan and have settlement on a new one, an option that made little financial sense. A second alternative, said my attorney, was a simple letter to the lender outlining the new terms. By signing and dating the letter, the lender could accept the loan modifications and the matter would be finished.

I wrote a basic letter to the lender (a trustee for the pension, in this case) which described the old loan terms and suggested new ones. The letter also stated that other than changes in the interest rate, monthly payment, and loan term, all other conditions would remain in effect.

I faxed a copy to my attorney for review, and then mailed a copy to the lender along with a copy of the original note and an amortization statement showing payments to date. A few days later my letter—appropriately countersigned—was returned and my note was fully refinanced. The cost to refinance a $65,000 mortgage: $35 in legal fees and 29¢ in postage.

The alternative to my loan modification was a full or partial refinancing, a process that would have required application forms, paperwork, fees, appraisals, title searches, title insurance, points, origination fees, taxes, and a vast amount of bother, aggravation, and cash—perhaps several thousand dollars in the case of my $65,000 loan.

Modification Approaches

While lenders understand the concept of modifying an ARM, they are appropriately reserved when it comes to changing the rate and terms of a fixed-rate loan—especially when "changing" means lowering, reducing, and consumer savings.

Why would a lender modify a loan?

If you have been a good borrower—someone who makes complete and timely payments over a period of years—a lender knows that holding your mortgage is a mechanical process with few problems. The lender would like to keep your business and it thus becomes possible to speak to the lender in these terms:

"I'd really like to stay with you folks, but I can get a 7 percent loan anywhere. It would be much more interesting for everyone if we took the loan we now have and simply modified the rate.

"Suppose, for example, we agreed to modify the loan on this basis: Instead of 7 percent I'll pay 7.25 percent (or whatever number). Or, I'm willing to pay 1 point on the outstanding balance (not the original amount) if the loan can be modified

"As a lender, a loan modification is quick, easy, devoid of most paperwork, and continues your servicing income. Without a modification, I'll be forced to go elsewhere and you'll have to get another borrower and have all the expenses and headaches associated with a new loan."

If a loan officer cannot help, speak with the manager of the loan department. If the manager cannot help, ask for the name of his or her boss and continue up the corporate ladder. This may take some time, but considering the values involved it can be a worthwhile effort.

A more complex situation involves the institutions we view as "lenders." For instance, if Michaels sends a mortgage check each month to Smith Mortgage & Finance, Michaels is likely to believe that Smith is his lender. But Smith may have obtained the loan for Michaels and they may collect a monthly check, but they may also have sold the loan to an investor. Whoever holds the loan is the lender, while Smith is merely the servicing agent. Thus Smith does not have the right to change the loan terms, even if it wanted to change them.

But many investors—the people and institutions who actually own home mortgages—will go along with loan modifications under certain conditions.

Disasters.   When hurricanes, floods, tornadoes and other natural disasters hit, lender protection plummets. Having a $100,000 mortgage secured by a property which is currently underwater does little good for anyone. Compelling owners to make mortgage payments when their homes and jobs are entirely disrupted is a great way to earn long-term public enmity.

Thus, when disaster strikes, major lenders routinely modify mortgage terms, *but only on a case-by-case basis.* Typical approaches include:

- Allowing Late Payments. If the mortgage payment is due on the 10th, a lender might allow a later payment, say the 20th or 25th, for a period of one to several months. This is also known as a "temporary indulgence."
- Waiver Of Late Payment Fees. In disaster situations it is likely that local lender facilities are closed and that postal operations are curtailed, thus it makes sense to waive late payment fees.
- Credit Report Waivers. Because a disaster will delay payments, lenders commonly do not report late or missed payments to credit reporting agencies, the theory being that late and unpaid mortgage bills are not deliberate in such circumstances.
- Payment Deferrals. Lenders who offer deferrals allow borrowers to suspend monthly payments for two or three months. The

unmet payments are then paid back with somewhat larger future payments, say a payment-and-a-quarter or a payment-and-a-half until the lost payments are made up.

In extreme cases, lenders may use payment deferrals to re-organize the loan—for example, allowing a borrower to skip three payments now, but then adding three payments to the end of the mortgage

Temporary payment deferrals are also known within the industry as "special forbearance."

- New Terms. It is sometimes possible to adjust mortgage terms in a way that everyone benefits. For instance, suppose you have an ARM and rates have been dropping steadily. Payments, however, have only decreased 7.5 percent a year, and the result is overly large monthly principal reductions. In this situation, a lender might accept lower monthly payments because such payments will be more tolerable to the borrower and because interest is being earned on all outstanding principal.
- Foreclosure Freeze. For those facing foreclosure a disaster can bring relief of sorts. Lenders commonly halt foreclosure actions because foreclosures may be impossible to schedule and properties may be impossible to sell. Lenders want to avoid foreclosures in a disaster area—especially if a large number of properties are foreclosed—because mass sales will depress land values at the very time lenders are trying to recapture their money and local property values are already questionable.
- Reduced Monthly Payments. In this situation the borrower has income and can make monthly payments, but not all monthly charges. A lender might allow the borrower to make smaller payments for several months, say $500 a month rather than $750, with the difference paid out on top of future payments (say an extra $100 a month) or added to the mortgage balance.
- Refinancing. Rather than continue with a current loan, lenders may encourage refinancing to reduce monthly costs. Refinancing, however, may be enormously difficult if the value of the underlying security—the home—is greatly diminished.

For example, suppose a property was once worth $200,000 and financed with a $150,000 loan. A hurricane reduces the home to rubble and now the owners still owe $150,000, plus they need money to rebuild. If the property has sufficient value to underwrite a $120,000 mortgage, the owners will still have to come up with $30,000 to pay off the old debt—not an easy task for most owners, and certainly not a welcome thought in the midst of a disaster.

Operation of Law.   Mortgages are contracts and as a matter of public interest government may regulate the formation of agreements. The classic case involves the state of Iowa which declared a one-year foreclosure moratorium for farmers in 1985.

Widespread Loss of Income.   In cases where entire communities face severe economic conditions, lenders may agree to loan modifications. For instance, a town depends on the local wicker furniture plant for 60 percent of all jobs. The plant burns down and the owners cannot reopen. Suddenly unemployment is rampant, the town cannot collect taxes, merchants have no markets, and the entire community is in deep financial trouble. In such instances, lenders may modify loans by offering to replace contract mortgage rates with current interest levels, if lower.

Pre-Foreclosure Sale.   It sometimes happens that people have both general misfortunes and a property with some economic worth. If the situation persists, the owners are likely to go bankrupt and the property will probably be foreclosed. In this situation a lender may agree to reduce or suspend monthly mortgage payments providing the property has value and is actively marketed. The attraction of this scenario is that with reduced monthly costs the owners may be able to solve some of their financial problems. For lenders, forbearance can be attractive if it means avoiding a lengthy bankruptcy proceeding and the cost of a foreclosure. All missed payments will be recaptured when the property is sold.

Hardship.   On a case-by-case basis, some lenders (but not all) will modify loan terms in hardship situations such as a major accident or medical disability. In hardship cases, owners will be asked to provide extensive and compelling documentation to justify a loan modification.

Two-Way Street

A mortgage is a contract and as a contract it can only be modified with the agreement of both lender and borrower. While loan modifications sound wonderful when rates are falling, imagine the hue and cry if *lenders* sought to modify interest levels when rates were rising.

In fairness to lenders, it must be said that loan modifications are not always attractive. Suppose you're a lender with a 9 percent loan in a 7-percent market and a borrower asks you to modify the loan. From the borrower's perspective a lower rate is certainly a great idea, but perhaps as a lender you can get 7.5 percent elsewhere. Thus as a lender you might offer to modify the loan to 7.5 percent (or more), or you might simply ask the borrower to refinance and pay off the debt.

Moreover, it should be said that a large proportion of all mortgage debt is obtained in the open market through the sale of Ginnie Mae, Fannie Mae, and Freddie Mac financial paper. Those who invest in such securities expect a given rate of return and a given level of risk. If pro-borrower loan modification clauses are included in fixed-rate mortgages, then investors may want more interest, or they may simply invest in other market instruments. If enough investors leave the mortgage arena, mortgage rates will rise because the supply of investment funds will dwindle.

The point is that loan modifications should not be seen as a one-way street. As long as a loan is in place, lenders have a right to receive the contractual interest rate and all other benefits to which they are entitled as part of the original bargain.

Then again, if you ask a lender to modify a loan, they can always say "no." Asking—in and of itself—hurts no one and from time-to-time can lead to significant financing benefits.

Modification Versus Refinancing

So far we have seen that loan modifications are quick, cheap, and easy when compared to refinancing, facts which raise a question: if loan modifications are such a good idea, how come we don't see them more often?

One answer is that circumstances are not always right for a loan modification. It takes the agreement of both borrower and lender to modify a mortgage, and such agreement is not always present.

A second problem is that because loan modifications are quick, cheap, and easy they can reduce the income enjoyed by many players in the real estate financing game. Thus, if you were in the lending business or the closing industry you would have little incentive to suggest loan modifications.

But while two problems stand out, the case for loan modifications is compelling in certain situations.

If you are a lender and borrower Hansen is about to refinance a 9 percent mortgage for 7 percent, he will either refinance with you or refinance elsewhere. If he refinances with you, your stream of income declines because of the lower interest level but you get the benefit of additional fees and charges. If Hansen refinances elsewhere, you still get a lower stream of income because you'll loan the money to someone else and in today's 7 percent market, that's all that is available.

The bottom line is that whether Hansen refinances with his current lender or goes elsewhere, the result for the lender is largely the same.

But suppose we had a lender with a different perspective. Suppose we had a lender who thought like this:

"It's in my interest to originate as many loans and service as many mortgages as possible. If I say to people that the only way to obtain a lower rate is to refinance, some will go elsewhere. I can replace those folks with new borrowers, but my share of the marketplace may not hold steady or increase.

"As an alternative where possible—and knowing that it will not be possible in all cases—what about this idea: a loan modification instead of full refinance.

"The great advantage for me, the lender, is that it will allow me to keep current borrowers. I can still charge points and fees, but since the borrower will not have to pay for a new title search (the old loan is still in place) or a new closing (there is nothing to close), the borrower can save thousands of dollars."

In addition to marketplace advantages, loan modifications offer another benefit as well.

Suppose the Grafton house is financed with two loans, a $150,000 first trust and a $20,000 second trust. When the Grafton's refinance the first trust, they pay $150,000 to the old lender to settle that debt, and they then place a new loan on the property for $150,000.

The moment the original first trust is paid off, the former second trust—the $20,000 loan—becomes the new first trust. The new $150,000 mortgage becomes a huge second trust.

Why is the new loan a second trust? Because it was placed on the public record, recorded, after the $20,000 note. Is it important to be a first trust or first mortgage? You bet.

If there is a foreclosure the first lien holder must be paid in full before a dime is paid to second trust lenders. Thus a second trust has more risk than a first trust, and more risk means more interest. Because of the risks involved, it is very important for lenders to keep their place in line as creditors.

With a loan modification the original loan stays in place and that means the lender's position in the event of default is as safe as possible.

How Things Are Today

Whatever the merits of loan modifications, as a practical matter they are enormously difficult to obtain. Here, in capsule form, is how modifications are handled by major players in the lending game.

Fannie Mae—which holds one loan in four nationwide—will consider mortgage modifications *on a case-by-case basis* when there is a hardship situation such as a disaster, financial hardship (perhaps the loss of income from the death of a working borrower), or decreasing income for reasons beyond your control (after 30 years the plant closes and your job ends).

Fannie Mae has a massive loan portfolio which is why it can, in limited instances, modify mortgages. One possible approach through Fannie Mae is a rate reduction in those cases where the borrower's mortgage interest level is higher than currently-available rates. For example, if you have a 9 percent loan in a 7 percent market, it may be possible to obtain a lower rate. Since no points are being paid in a hardship loan modification, the "current rate" will not be 7 percent plus 2 points, it will be the interest rate without points, perhaps 7.25 percent.

Freddie Mac. No modifications are allowed by Freddie Mac. The logic is that mortgages are used as security for the bonds sold by Freddie Mac to investors. If interest rates were lowered, there would be less economic value for bond holders and thus less security.

FHA. FHA regulations do not permit rate-and-term loan modifications. In the event of disaster, FHA may be able to offer a limited measure of forbearance, say the postponement of monthly payments for two or three months.

VA. The VA—which has exhaustive regulations for just about everything—has no rules or guidelines regarding loan modifications. Given this scenario, it would seem that lenders are not prohibited from modifying VA loans, but in no case are they required to do so.

Portfolio Lenders. Portfolio lenders are institutions and organizations that make and hold loans. In those cases where mortgages are held, it may be possible to modify loan terms on a case-by-case basis. However, lenders—being rational—are reluctant to modify loan terms unless it is in their interest to make such changes.

Private Lenders. Individuals, pensions, and organizations not directly in the mortgage business that hold loans may be willing to modify terms, particularly for borrowers with an excellent payment history.

Questions to Ask:

What is your current interest rate?

What is today's interest rate?

Do you have a loan modification program?

Is my loan held by an investor such as Fannie Mae or Freddie Mac? If not, who or what actually holds my loan at this time?

If a modification program is available, what are the costs and conditions required to modify my loan?

Do I need to enter the loan modification agreement in local property records?

What closing costs, if any, can I expect with a loan modification?

STREAMLINE REFINANCING

Loan modification programs are the cheapest refinancing deals available, but a second form of refinancing—so-called "streamline" plans—also deserve consideration when loan modifications are not possible.

Streamline deals are quicker and less costly than new loans, especially if you work with your current lender. In many cases, a streamline refinance will offer these benefits:

- New financing without a new appraisal.
- No income, asset, or debt qualifications under some programs.
- A shorter loan term. For example, if you have 25 years remaining on your current mortgage, then under a streamline refinance a new loan can also be 25 years in length. This is a good deal for borrowers because excess interest costs are reduced.
- An easy way to move from an ARM to fixed-rate financing if you do not have a conversion clause.
- The ability to go from a fixed-rate loan to an ARM, but only if the new rate is 2 percent less than the old mortgage and the loan is for an owner-occupied property.
- No face-to-face interview.
- New borrowers may be added to the loan.
- "No cost" refinances—plans under which the lender pays some or all of the borrower's closing costs in exchange for a marginally-higher interest rate.

A variety of streamline refinancing programs are available today, including programs offered by the nation's largest lenders and loan programs.

Fannie Mae.   Under Section 103 of the Fannie Mae guidelines, streamline refinancing that does not pay cash to the borrower is available for both prime residences (up to 90 percent of the property's value) and second homes (up to 70 percent of the property's value).

Speak to your lender to obtain a streamline refinance for a loan held by Fannie Mae. The general requirements are that the lender must obtain a loan application, credit report, a pay statement from those who are employed, or the most recent tax return for a self-employed borrower. An appraisal may not be required if the refinancing is done through the original lender.

The lender must review the credit report to assure that general bills are being paid in a timely manner and that no mortgage payments were more than 30 days late during the past year. The lender must also assure Fannie Mae that the property has sufficient value to justify a new loan, a requirement which means that in communities where values are steady or falling lenders are likely to ask for a new appraisal.

With a Fannie Mae streamline refinance, monthly mortgage costs may rise by as much as 15 percent, a situation that could arise if someone went from 30-year to 15-year financing.

Freddie Mac.   Under the Freddie Mac program borrowers need a solid repayment history to qualify for a streamline refinance: no defaults, no payments more than 30 days late, and no pattern of late charges. Income must be steady or increasing, and the new mortgage payment cannot be 15 percent greater than the old cost for principal and interest.

The money available under the Freddie Mac streamline program can be used to pay off a first mortgage, junior liens that are at least a year old, and closing costs.

To start the streamline process, a borrower will need a new property appraisal, credit report, a payroll stub if employed, or a complete tax return if self-employed.

For a prime residence, as much as 90 percent of a property's value can be financed with a no cash-out loan, but only 75 percent if the deal involves more than 1 percent of the loan amount going to the borrower.

FHA.   FHA allows streamline refinances without an appraisal for rate-and-term refinancing, in other words where the size of the mortgage is not being increased to take cash out of the property. Streamline refinancing is available for second homes and investment properties, however the new loan documents must conform to FHA's present policies which mean the new loan cannot be assumed by an investor or someone who intends to use the property as a second home.

Under FHA rules, streamline refinancing is available with an appraisal, in which case there is *no* requirement to complete application questions concerning income, assets, or debts.

Borrowers may refinance 30-year loans under the streamline program to a shorter term, say 20 years or 15 years, providing that monthly payments do not rise by more than $50.

VA. The VA offers an aggressive streamline program, the theory being that as monthly costs decline the agency has less risk.

No property appraisal or credit underwriting is required for a VA streamline refinance, but there are certain baseline conditions which must be met. For instance, the new loan must be secured by the same property as the old financing, the vet must own the property, and in all cases the new loan must have a lower interest rate than the original mortgage.

No cash can be paid to a vet through a VA streamline refinance, nor can other liens on the property be repaid. The streamline loan amount is limited to the outstanding balance of the old loan plus allowable closing costs.

In the case of assumptions, loans can be refinanced under the streamline program, but only if a vet substitutes his or her entitlement for the entitlement of the original vet borrower.

One unusual concept adopted by the VA concerns death and spouses. VA rules provide that if a vet dies, his or her spouse is regarded as a vet for purposes of the streamline refinance program. The surviving spouse must own the property being refinanced.

In addition to the formal programs mentioned above, a growing number of lenders offer streamline refinancing for their portfolio loans, mortgages they keep and service as opposed to loans they make and then sell to outside investors. The rules for streamline deals vary among streamline lenders, but the basic point is that borrowers with solid payment histories can obtain lower rates with less time and trouble then a new loan might require.

Questions to Ask:

Do you offer a streamline refinance program? If so, what steps must I take to refinance and what will it cost? (Note: always ask your current lender about streamline refinancing before you contact other loan sources.)

Do you require a new appraisal?

Must I re-qualify for financing by showing my income, assets and debts?

Can I move from an ARM to fixed-rate financing under your streamline program?

Can I move from a fixed-rate loan to an ARM under your streamline program?

Do you have a no-cash program that will pay all of my closing costs? If so, what is your current rate?

Must I pay escrow fees for insurance and taxes at closing? (If you have a streamline refinance with the lender who holds your current loan, then escrow money is already in hand and additional funds should not be required. If you are refinancing with a new lender, however, you may need to pay escrow charges at closing. Money from your current escrow account will be returned by your present lender after closing and the old loan is paid off.)

What paperwork do you require for a streamline refinance?

ARM CONVERSIONS

ARMs have always represented more risk for borrowers than fixed-rate financing. While ARM rates can drop, and while ARM rates have largely fallen during the past decade and thus represented a good financing choice, it is equally possible for ARM rates to rise.

Many borrowers dislike ARMs, so to overcome public apprehension lenders have tried to make ARMs more appealing through the use of low start rates, liberal qualification rates, caps on payment hikes and interest rates, as well as the use of loan conversion clauses.

In a typical situation, an ARM can be converted to fixed rate financing within the first five years after origination. The fixed rate is determined by a pre-arranged formula, for instance: the current required net yield for the Federal Home Loan Mortgage Corporation plus 5/8ths of a percent rounded to the next highest quarter. Converting into English, this means if the base rate is 7 percent then the lender adds .625 percent for a total of 7.625 percent. The combined figure is then rounded to the next highest quarter, 7.75 percent in this example.

The cost for an ARM conversion is generally cheap, say $250 to $500 for loans of $500,000 or less. There are usually no appraisals involved, *no additional closing costs*, and no qualification headaches. Paperwork requirements may amount to one or two forms in most cases.

By any standard ARM conversion options are quick, easy, and simple, but conversions may be unavailable if not made within the contractual time frame, say five years after the loan was first originated.

For complete information, review mortgage documents with care and speak with your lender for details.

Questions to Ask:

> Do you have an ARM conversion option?
> How is a fixed-rate computed?
> What is the conversion cost?
> Must the conversion occur within a given timeframe? If so, when will your conversion option end?

SKIP-A-PAYMENT FINANCING

The usual relationship between borrowers and lenders is best described as "adversarial," an expression which also works nicely when picturing two countries locked in combat.

Borrowers and lenders—to judge from much of human history—are at odds over just about everything. Lenders want more interest, borrowers want less. Lenders want more paperwork, borrowers believe entire forests could be saved if only loan applications were less complex. Lenders believe that borrowers should pay their debts in a timely manner, while borrowers—like Einstein—feel that time is a relative concept.

But despite the vast gulf which separates their interests, borrowers and lenders are tied together by mutual need. Borrowers want cash, lenders have cash, and so with a little bartering back and forth everyone's wants can be satisfied.

All of which brings us to the world's strangest letter, a missive from one of my lenders which said, in so many words, that if at some point during the next several months I didn't feel like making a mortgage payment, forget it. No problem. We'll just up the loan balance by the interest not paid. *In effect, a loan modification proposed by a lender!*

The mortgage in question is an ARM secured by an investment property. Skipping a payment would add about $700 to the loan balance. Since the loan rate was roughly 7 percent at the time of the lender's offer, skipping a payment would increase future mortgage costs by roughly $4.75 per month if loan rates remain stable.

In looking at the skip-a-payment proposal one must admire its simplicity and elegance. Rarely can one find a deal that better serves both borrowers and lenders at the same time.

From the borrower's perspective the ability to defer a payment means that debt can be shifted from high-cost, short-term obligations to long-term, low-interest debt. For example, in the case above the payment is equal to the monthly interest cost ($700 in this case), plus the monthly amortization, say about $135. In total, $835 not paid to a mortgage lender can be used by the borrower for whatever purpose makes sense.

Let's say that the borrower elects to pay off a credit card bill with a nominal interest rate of 18 percent. Skipping a payment and adding $835 to the mortgage creates additional debt at 7 percent interest, a full 11 percent less than the credit card company charges. In terms of cash costs, the additional mortgage payment will total about $4.75 instead of credit card payments of $25 to $42 monthly, depending on individual repayment schedules.

A savvy borrower will take the skip-a-payment deal, pay-off or reduce credit card debt, and then apply the monthly cash savings to the mortgage. Adding $20 to $40 a month to a mortgage payment may not seem significant, but the savings can be impressive. For instance, going from $835 a month to $855 monthly for a $125,500 mortgage at 7 percent interest will reduce the number of payments from 360 to 333.50. That's a potential interest saving of $22,127, assuming a borrower starts higher payments as soon as the loan is established. If the payment increases to $875 a month, interest worth as much as $40,497 can be saved over the loan term.

It may seem surprising that lenders would favor a program that offers the possibility of substantially lower interest costs, but the skip-a-payment concept also generates a host of lender benefits.

To create business, lenders must advertise, fund offices, pay loan officers, etc. With the skip-a-payment program lenders can forget such expenses and instead invest in postage and printing.

Suppose a lender sends out 250,000 skip-a-payment letters. In a typical direct mailing, a 1 to 2 percent response is often regarded as successful, but here we have a letter from a known party (the lender) about a matter which most borrowers would find enticing (not making a mortgage payment). It's just speculation, but it's hard to imagine that a lender could get less than a 10 percent response.

If the average outstanding loan balance is worth $80,000 and a typical payment is $597 at 8 percent interest, then an everyday monthly interest bill is $533. If 25,000 people elect to skip-a-payment, then the lender has increased its loan volume by $13.3 million for the price of a mailing and a little paper shuffling.

No less important for both lender and borrower, the skip-a-payment program was done without a title search (the loan is already in place), closing costs (the loan is already closed), or massive paperwork (my loan required a half-page form). In effect, the skip-a-payment concept is nothing more than a shrewd mortgage modification plan, one with obvious advantages for everyone.

There is some expectation that skip-a-payment programs may become more common. One can easily imagine a shrewd lender offering loans with an automatic skip-a-payment feature. A loan could be structured so that after an initial period, say two years without a late or missed payment, a borrower would have an automatic right to skip one payment a year as long as all payments are timely.

To use the skip-a-payment feature, the borrower would notify the lender on or before the payment due date. Notices received after the due date would be regarded as late and subject to a penalty. The "due date" would be defined not as the contractual date when a payment is due, but the end of the grace period which follows the contractual payment date.

Skip-a-payment loans have an undeniable popularity, and for those with the willingness and discipline to save, a skip-a-payment feature offers great value from time to time.

Questions to Ask:

If you now have financing, does your lender offer a skip-a-payment program?

If you are looking for financing, do lenders have loans that include a skip-a-loan feature?

Does it make sense for you to skip a payment? That is, if you do not pay the lender how will the unspent mortgage payment be used?

15

Saving Money with Short-Term Strategies

Despite all the attention and emphasis adjustable-rate loans have received, there has always been an interest in fixed-rate financing— loans without gimmicks, indexes or the possibility of rising monthly payments. But if conventional 30-year loans have proved so costly in today's high-interest world, what is the alternative?

An increasing number of borrowers, particularly those who are refinancing or purchasing homes for the second time, are turning to 15-year mortgages. Such loans offer all the advantages of conventional financing but without enormous interest costs.

In addition, bi-weekly loans have been introduced around the country as an alternative to adjustable-rate financing. While such loans have received extensive publicity, they as yet represent a wrinkle in the marketplace rather than a trend.

THE 15-YEAR MORTGAGE

If there is a single word to describe the mortgage world of the 1990s, it is "complexity." We have GPARMs, GEMs and RAMs, loans with variable interest rates and mortgages with which you can wind up owing more than you borrow. But instead of all this confusion, what about something simple? Why not a self-amortizing loan with level monthly payments, one interest rate (preferably something low) and sensible overall interest costs?

At first it might seem that cutting a loan term in half will double monthly payments, but this is not the case. For a $90,000 mortgage paid out over 30 years at 9 percent interest, the monthly cost will be $724.16. If the loan term is only 15 years, the monthly payment will rise to $912.84, a difference of $188.68 per month.

The very fact that a loan has a term of 15 years rather than 30 years means monthly payments must be higher because there are fewer of them. However, because the loan term is shorter, less principal is outstanding over time and so interest costs are greatly reduced. The potential interest bill for the 30-year loan is $170,697.73, while the greatest possible cost for the 15-year mortgage is only $74,311.19—a savings of $96,386.54.

So now we have an example where the loan term is cut in half, monthly payments rise by $188.68, and we can save $96,000. Sounds okay, but there is one slight problem: this example is wholly unrealistic.

The reason this illustration does not work goes back to the concept of risk. The longer the loan term, the greater the risk to the lender. Conversely, the shorter the loan term, the smaller the risk. Less risk, in turn, means lenders can accept lower interest rates.

In our example we compared two loans with identical interest rates. Although some lenders will gladly charge equal rates, smart borrowers should be able to do better. How much better depends on local market conditions, but interest savings of one-quarter to one-half percent should be readily available.

If we cut the interest rate on the 15-year loan to 8.5 percent, we will have monthly payments of just $886.27, an increase of $162.11 per month. Total potential interest costs will drop to $69,527.81, and so we

15-Year versus 30-Year Financing			
Loan amount	$90,000	$90,000	$90,000
Loan term	30 years	15 years	15 years
Interest rate	9 percent	9 percent	8.5 percent
Monthly payment	$724.16	$912.84	$886.27
Additional monthly cost	None	$188.68	$162.11
Potential interest	$170,697.73	$74,311.19	$69,527.81
Potential savings	None	$96,386.54	$101,169.92

save as much as $101,169.92 when compared to our model 30-year mortgage at 9 percent interest.

The use of 15-year financing clearly results in significant interest savings. It is also clear that such mortgages are becoming increasingly common. But is a 15-year mortgage appropriate for everyone? Should it be the new "conventional" mortgage, the loan by which other mortgage formats are measured?

Even though 15-year loans have obvious economic benefits, the marketplace reality is that many people will not be able to select such financing. With the loan above, an additional $162.11 may not be feasible for first-time home buyers, purchasers with limited means or those buying on the brink of affordability. Fifteen-year mortgages can be extremely attractive, however, and they seem to make the most sense for three groups of borrowers:

- Second-time buyers who have accumulated cash from the sale of house number one. Such individuals typically can make larger down payments than first-time buyers and have larger incomes to support monthly payments.
- Those seeking an enforced savings program—people with additional money to spend each month but who will otherwise fritter the money away if not obligated to spend it for mortgage payments.
- Borrowers who look at potential interest costs and recognize that huge savings are possible with minimal additional payments.

Another growing use for 15-year mortgages is in the area of refinancing. Suppose Mr. Castle bought property and obtained a 30-year conventional mortgage for $85,000 at 13 percent interest. His monthly payment was $940.27. Later, Mr. Castle has another opportunity to refinance his property with a 15-year loan at 9.5 percent. His new monthly payment will be $887.59—a monthly saving of $52.68.

Not only will monthly costs decline, but Mr. Castle will also cut his overall interest bill. With the 30-year mortgage he faced a potential interest cost of $253,497. With his new mortgage his interest bill is limited to $74,766. Total potential savings: $178,731.

Mr. Castle, however, must ask a question: How much will it cost to refinance the property? If his cost is $3,000, then he must remain on the property for 57 months ($3,000 divided by $52.68) if he is to recover his refinancing costs from monthly savings alone. In addition, of course, he is paying off his debt faster and accumulating equity more quickly than with a 30-year mortgage.

A Look at Mr. Castle's Refinancing		
	Old Loan	New Loan
Loan amount	$85,000	$85,000
Loan term	30 years	15 years
Interest rate	13 percent	9.5 percent
Monthly payment	$940.27	$887.59
Additional monthly cost	$52.68	None
Potential interest	$253,497.20	$74,766.20
Potential savings	None	$178,731.00

Still another use of the 15-year mortgage is to raise additional capital in a refinancing situation. If Mr. Lawrence, like Mr. Castle, has a 30-year mortgage at 13 percent, he too is paying $940.27 a month. But what if he needs additional money? If he refinanced for 15 years at 9.5 percent and elected to still pay $940.27 per month, he can get a $90,045 loan. His potential interest cost will equal $79,203.60. Thus Mr. Lawrence can maintain his monthly payments, refinance, pull in an additional $5,045 in cash and still cut his potential interest bill by $179,493.45. Although some of his new-found money will undoubtedly go for up-front refinancing expenses, Mr. Lawrence is still ahead. (See table, p. 292.)

Whatever the economics of 15-year mortgages, these loans at least have the advantage of being understandable to consumers. With a 15-year mortgage no one worries about obscure indexes or negative amortization—the loan and its terms are clear. Lenders also like the 15-year concept because it offers less risk and fewer administrative problems than long-term mortgages or loans with changing payments and interest levels.

As for the interest "lost" by lenders under a 15-year repayment schedule, don't worry. The faster a loan is paid off, the faster lenders

How Mr. Lawrence Raised Additional Capital		
	Old Loan	New Loan
Loan amount	$85,000	$90,045
Loan term	30 years	15 years
Interest rate	13 percent	9.5 percent
Monthly payment	$940.27	$940.27
Additional monthly cost	None	None
Additional cash	None	$5,045
Potential interest	$253,497.05	$79,203.60
Potential savings	None	$174,293.45

can turn around and issue new loans that generate not only interest but also additional fees, charges and points. All together, not a bad deal for everyone.

BACK-DOOR 15-YEAR LOANS

As attractive as 15-year loans may appear, many buyers will not qualify for such financing because monthly costs are higher than monthly payments for 30-year loans. The solution to this dilemma is to create a back-door 15-year mortgage. It works this way:

- Find a 30-year loan, either a fixed-rate or adjustable product.
- Make certain the loan documents state that the mortgage can be prepaid in whole or in part, at any time, and without penalty.

Borrowers now need only to qualify for a 30-year loan. As income grows over time, larger monthly payments can be made voluntarily. If monthly payments grow enough, the loan can be repaid in 25, 20 or 15 years, as the borrower elects.

A major advantage to back-door 15-year loans is that borrowers do not have a contractual obligation to make large monthly payments. If a period arises when money is tight, just send in the smaller amount required for a 30-year pay-off. That's all the lender can expect.

Questions to Ask:

What is the interest rate for conventional financing?

What is the best local interest rate for a 15-year mortgage?

What is the cost per month for conventional financing?

What is the cost per month for a 15-year loan?

What is the additional monthly cost for 15-year financing?

What is the total potential interest cost for a 30-year mortgage?

What is the total potential interest cost for a 15-year mortgage?

What are the potential savings from the use of a 15-year mortgage?

What is the difference in terms of interest and monthly payments between your current mortgage and a 15-year loan?

How much will it cost to refinance your property?

If you refinance your property, based on monthly savings alone, how long should you remain in the house to recapture refinancing costs?

If you continued to make your present monthly payments but switched to 15-year financing, how much additional capital can you raise?

THE BI-WEEKLY MORTGAGE

In the eternal search for better mortgages, lenders and borrowers have tried every possible financial concoction. Today we have a tremendous number of loan alternatives, including what may be the most publicized and least-used home financing idea in recent history, the bi-weekly mortgage.

The bi-weekly mortgage is distinguished by the fact that instead of 12 mortgage payments per year, borrowers make 26 payments to lenders. Each payment, however, is only half the size of regular monthly payments, and so the results are lower costs per payment, higher costs per year, faster loan amortization, shorter loan terms and reduced interest costs.

If we borrow $60,000 on a conventional 30-year basis at 9 percent interest, we will have monthly payments of $482.77. The interest bill over 30 years will total $113,798.49.

Here's what happens if we borrow $60,000 at the same interest rate but on a bi-weekly basis:

First, we just about divide the conventional payment in half, paying out in this case $259.11 every two weeks.

Second, we make 26 bi-weekly payments per year.

Third, the loan is paid off in 18 years.

Fourth, the interest bill totals just $61,265.52, a savings of $52,532.97 over the conventional loan.

So we have a loan that does indeed result in a huge interest saving. But although the bi-weekly loan produces significant interest economies, it does so in a needlessly complex manner.

The basic question about the bi-weekly loan is this: Why bother? There are other ways to accomplish the same goal with far less hassle. For instance, why not just make monthly payments of $561.87? The loan will be repaid in the same 18 years and the potential interest bill will total $61,363.25—again a huge savings when compared with conventional financing.

Just as important, the annual cost of mortgage payments will remain essentially equal, going from $6,737 with the bi-monthly program to $6,742 when monthly payments are simply increased—a difference of about $5 a year.

From the lender's point of view, the bi-weekly mortgage poses new administrative headaches. There are 26 payments to record each year and 26 chances to enter the wrong information on a computer. At a time when lenders have their hands full trying to account for ARM variables, why would any lender joyously suggest a loan that is difficult and costly to administer?

One answer is probably related to lender competition rather than the economics of the bi-weekly loan. Lenders vigorously compete for business, and lenders who can get an extra bit of notice are likely to

The Bi-weekly Mortgage Compared			
Amount borrowed	$60,000	$60,000	$60,000
Interest rate	9 percent	9 percent	9 percent
Loan term	30 years	18 years	18 years
Number of payments per year	12	26	12
Payment size	$482.77	$259.11	$561.87
Annual cash cost	$5,793.24	$6,736.86	$6,742.44
Additional cost per year	None	$943.62	$949.20
Potential interest cost	$113,798	$61,266	$61,363
Potential savings	None	$52,532	$52,435

attract more borrowers than those lenders who are virtually anonymous. The bi-weekly mortgage is something to talk about, it draws publicity. Whether it makes sense as a practical mortgage option for either lenders or consumers can be debated.

Another possible attraction of bi-weekly financing is that payments can be tied to automatic deposit plans, which means borrowers must maintain accounts with the lender. Rather than sending in a check every two weeks, payments are deducted directly from an account with the lender. The lender benefits by opening additional accounts (which he hopes will allow him to generate extra loans and interest) and by the possibility of offering additional services to the borrower, such as auto loans and checking accounts.

Not only are bi-weekly mortgages needlessly complex and undistinguished in terms of the benefits they offer consumers, they have also spawned a mini-industry of advisers, helpers, and consultants who will gladly take your money in exchange for their assistance.

In essence, for $400 or so, a consultant will collect your money for you on a bi-weekly basis and then assure that your lender receives full and timely payments. Why anyone needs such a "service" is beyond comprehension, since lenders can calculate bi-weekly payments, you can send in payments by yourself, and if you otherwise feel compelled to spend $400 the money can be donated to a worthy cause such as a community group or your retirement account.

Bi-weekly consultants appear to be largely or totally unregulated. How do you know that the payments sent to a third-party will actually be delivered to your lender? Some bi-weekly programs mention that they are "insured" and "bonded" but they do not say how much insurance is available, the size of their bond, or whether such protections will cover all potential claims.

Worse yet, it is not clear that all bi-weekly programs offer true bi-weekly benefits.

To see how this works imagine that you send $500 to a bi-weekly agency every two weeks. Imagine as well that your regular mortgage payment is $1,000. In this situation you would normally pay $12,000 a year to the mortgage lender, but the bi-weekly collection agency is receiving $13,000 (26 × $500).

If the bi-weekly agency makes a $1,000 payment to your lender for

11 months and then a single $2,000 payment, your loan will be prepaid because an extra $1,000 has been deposited with your lender. The catch is that by not making payments every two weeks, the bi-weekly intermediary pockets the interest on the money not immediately paid to the lender and you do not get the full benefit of bi-weekly deposits.

Although one expects lower interest rates as loan terms become shorter, this is not necessarily true with bi-weekly mortgages. Even though there is a shorter pay-back period, which should mean less risk and therefore lower interest rates, the high administrative costs associated with bi-weekly financing may limit or disallow interest discounts. Until lenders can accurately assess administrative costs for such loans over several years—and until default patterns become clear—bi-weekly loans are not likely sources of discount financing.

Are bi-weekly mortgages a plausible financial option? They certainly save money when compared with 30-year loans, but one has to compare such programs with simple 15-year or 18-year financing as well as other mortgage options to make a valid decision.

Questions to Ask:

What is the interest rate for conventional financing?
What is the interest rate for bi-weekly financing?
What is the monthly payment for a conventional loan?
What is the payment cost for each bi-weekly installment?
What is the total annual cost of a bi-weekly mortgage?
Can you repay the loan whole or in part without penalty?
If you obtain a 15-year or 18-year loan with monthly payments, how much will you pay per month? How much will you pay per year?
If you have a bi-weekly mortgage, must you open a savings or checking account with the lender? If so, what interest will your funds earn?

16
Additional Information

The Common-Sense Mortgage is part of a series of real estate books designed to raise ideas, provide information, and suggest strategies that can have value for consumers nationwide.

In addition, you may want to consider other ways to gain real estate information.

First, speak to as many lenders, brokers, and agents as possible. Many will have financing ideas and suggestions that have value.

Second, consider taking a basic, low-cost licensure class. Such classes—which can be available from colleges, universities, real estate organizations, and private schools—will show you how the real estate marketing system works in your jurisdiction and qualify you to take an agent's licensure test.

Third, read local newspapers. Many real estate sections offer solid advice and information, so clip and save the items most interesting to you.

Fourth, visit real estate expositions, particularly those sponsored by local newspapers, real estate organizations, and builder groups. Such expos often have a variety of booths, little or no selling pressure, plus a goodly amount of information.

Fifth, check out personal finance publications such as **Money**, **Consumer's Digest**, **Worth**, and **Kiplinger's Personal Finance** that often carry extensive, timely articles of value to real estate consumers.

Sixth, if this guide has been helpful, then consider the other books in this series: **Successful Real Estate Negotiation** (with Douglas M. Bregman, Esq.), **Successful Real Estate Investing**, and **Buy Your**

First Home Now. These books, published by HarperCollins, are available from booksellers nationwide. An additional guide in the Harper real estate series, **How to Sell Your Home In Any Market (With or Without a Broker)** will be published in mid-1994.

Seventh, go electronic. Millions of people have a computer, modem, and mouse—all you need to be a part of the network nation. Local electronic bulletin boards may have real estate information, while a national service such the real estate forum I host on America Online has an MLS open to brokers and non-brokers, current mortgage rates, real estate software, online questions and answers, and much more. For additional information, call 800-827-6364. *Be certain to mention extension 5764 for such free software, online time, and introductory pricing as may be available when you call.*

Lastly, if you do well financing and refinancing, pass on what you've learned and make the marketplace easier for the next person.

Appendix A:
Loan Release Tips

Borrowers with financing who wish to get a release of liability will need the approval of both the lender who issued the loan and the organization which provided the guarantee, if any.

Veteran borrowers can be released from all VA liability, according to that agency, "by having the purchaser assume all of the veteran's liabilities in connection with the loan and having VA approve the assumption agreement and specifically release the veteran from all further liabilities to VA."

Being released from liability is a process distinct from the possible restoration of a VA entitlement. Again quoting VA materials, borrowers may have their entitlements restored when (A) "the loan has been paid in full, or the VA otherwise has been relieved of the obligation under the guaranty and the home has been disposed of" or (B) a VA-qualified buyer has "agreed to assume the outstanding balance of the loan, has consented to substitute his or her entitlement for that of the original veteran-borrower" and meets all other current VA requirements. For more information, contact the nearest VA office and ask for Pamphlet 26-5 and the "ROL/SOE Package."

The release procedure through the FHA varies somewhat from the VA format. With FHA loans, lenders submit an application for release (FHA Form 22-10) and a credit report (Form 2900) on the new borrower. If the FHA is satisfied with the credit-worthiness of the new borrower it will inform the lender.

Note that there is no requirement for the lender to release original borrowers even if they are released by the FHA. Also, FHA procedures, unlike those of the VA, envision communication between a lender and the agency rather than the agency and an individual borrower.

In the case of loans generally, as well as those backed by private mortgage insurers, be certain to contact your lender for complete release and assumption information. Ask for a list of all charges, if any.

For loans held or backed by the VA, FHA, Freddie Mac, Fannie Mae, private mortgage insurers or Ginnie Mae there may be restrictions on the extent to which lenders can charge release or assumptions fees. Write or call these organizations for more information if you have questions not answered to your satisfaction by a local lender.

Appendix B:
Specialized FHA
Loan Programs

While a variety of FHA-backed loan plans are described in detail throughout the book, there are additional FHA programs which may be of interest to limited numbers of single-family home buyers.

Sec. 203(h). This FHA program is directed toward individuals who live in major disaster areas. It provides up to the full value of Sec. 203(b) financing for home replacement or reconstruction.

Sec. 203(i). If you have an interest in acquiring a farm home with at least 2.5 acres this program will provide mortgage insurance. The maximum loans available under this section, however, are limited to 75 percent of the maximums permitted under 203(b). If the 203(b) maximum for a single-family home in a given area is, say, $102,929, then the maximum 203(i) loan would be $77,197.

Sec. 203(n). One of the most interesting, and least used, FHA programs, this section is designed to provide financing for co-op housing. Under this section, the FHA can provide loans for entire projects as well as individual units, but the use of this section to finance individual units is rare if not non-existent. The reason according to one school of thought: if Smith buys a co-op and finances the deal under Sec. 203(n), she can later sell the property to anyone, even an "anyone" whom the co-op board regards as undesirable. Since co-op boards do not want their authority limited, and since they want to control who moves into a project, they will effectively prohibit sales to buyers such as Smith who want to use 203(n) financing. Prohibiting sales to individuals because they elect to use a federal loan guarantee program can raise nasty problems, so co-op boards will reject Smith for other reasons.

Sec. 221(d)(2).   A program designed for individuals and families displaced by governmental action such as urban renewal or the construction of a new highway, Sec. 221(d)(2) provides mortgage insurance for up to $36,000 to individuals who need single-family, owner-occupied housing, more money for families of five or more or those who acquire two to four units.

Sec. 203(k).   This FHA program is designed to insure financing for the purchase and/or rehabilitation of housing. Initially such loans are viewed as construction financing and then, upon completion of the work, the loan is converted into permanent financing. The 203(k) program, unlike many other FHA-backed mortgages, is open to both investors and owner-occupants.

Sec. 223(e).   Not all properties meet FHA underwriting guidelines for 203(b) loans and in those cases where homes are unqualified because they are located in "declining" areas, financing may be available under Sec. 223(e). Down payment and maximum mortgage amounts available under Sec. 223(e) vary but such financing may represent a last-ditch financing choice since regular FHA lending standards are waived.

VA-Qualified Buyers, National Guard Personnel and Reservists.
Individuals who are VA qualified or who have served in the National Guard or a branch of the military reserve should be aware that FHA Sec. 203(b) contains a small, but significant, advantage for those looking for single-family, owner/occupied housing. Sec. 203(b) provides that a portion of the down payment normally required for FHA financing will be waived for qualified individuals. The FHA includes guardsmen and reservists with at least 90 days of continuous active duty service—including training periods—among those who qualify for this benefit.

Index